CONSTANCE
RING

CONSTANCE RING

By Amalie Skram
Translated by Judith Messick
with Katherine Hanson

Seal Press

Library of Congress Cataloging-in-Publication Data
Skram, Amalie, 1846-1905.
    Constance Ring.

    (Women in translation)
    I. Title.   II. Series.
PT8928.C613   1988   839.8'236
ISBN 0-931188-61-X
ISBN 0-931188-60-1 (pbk.)

The cover painting is a portrait of Amalie Skram by Leis Schjelderup, 1882. Our thanks to Universitetsforlaget, the publishers of *Kvinner ved staffeliet,* from which the painting is taken.

The cover design is by Deborah Brown.

Printed in the United States of America.
10 9 8 7 6 5 4 3 2 1
First edition, May 1988

Seal Press
P.O. Box 13
Seattle, Washington 98111

Acknowledgements

Over the years many friends and colleagues have answered my questions about *Constance Ring:* I particularly want to thank Linda Sørbø, Nan Skille, Randi Meyer, Kathy Bousman, Kjell Morland, Natasa Duravicova, and Hanna-Marie Nordby, among others. Elizabeth Aasen, brought *Constance Ring* to my attention in the first place, and sent me unfailingly thoughtful and encouraging replies to my numerous questions about the text. Torborg Lundell generously read my first version and encouraged me to go on with the project. Elizabeth Keyser gave me many helpful suggestions for revision. My greatest debt is to Katherine Hanson, without whose meticulous and creative collaboration, this translation of the novel would not have been published. I also want to express my gratitude to Barbara Wilson and Faith Conlon, their colleagues at The Seal Press, and the Norwegian Cultural Council for their commitment to introducing Scandinavian feminist writers to English readers. During the years I have struggled to render *Constance Ring* into intelligible English, my husband David has been an unfailing source of encouragement and support. From beginning to end, this translation has been a labor of love.

Judith Messick

Amalie Skram: Life and Work

1846   Born Berte Amalie Alver on August 22 in Bergen, Norway, where her father is a shopkeeper. The second of five children, she is the only daughter.

1863   Father's business speculations result in bankruptcy and he emigrates to America, leaving his family behind. Six months later, Amalie, a strikingly beautiful girl of seventeen, becomes engaged to a sea captain nine years her senior—Bernt Ulrik August Müller.

1864   Marries Müller on October 3. Joins her husband on a voyage to Mexico and the West Indes.

1865-69   Lives in Bergen. Gives birth to two sons, Jacob in 1866 and Ludvig August in 1868.

1869-71   The Müllers, with their two small sons, sail to ports all over the world. Amalie spends the long days at sea reading—novels as well as books on philosophy and religion—and teaching herself English, French, and German.

1871   The Müllers return to Bergen, where Amalie becomes part of a group of radical intellectuals who are associated with the city's newspaper, *Bergens Tidende*. During the next few years she continues to cultivate her literary interests.

1877   Her first published work, a review of J. P. Jacobsen's novel *Fru Marie Grubbe* appears anonymously in *Bergens Tidende*.
        The Müllers marital problems reach the crisis stage. Amalie's efforts to obtain a divorce meet with disapproval and objections from family members. She suffers a severe nervous breakdown and is admitted to Gaustad

mental hospital in Kristiania (present-day Oslo) on December 22.

1878   Released from Gaustad on March 16. Separation from Müller is granted and Amalie and her sons go to live with her brother in Fredrikshald. She earns some money translating, and writing articles and book reviews.

1881   Moves to Kristiania. Continues to write articles and book reviews which are now published in the liberal newspaper *Dagbladet*. Her circle of friends includes writers such as Bjørnstjerne Bjørnson and other radical men and women who support the new political Left.

1882   Her first story "Madame Höier's Tenants" ("Madame Höiers Lejefolk") is published in the new radical journal *Nyt Tidsskrift*. In the summer of 1882, Amalie meets the Danish writer and critic Eric Skram.

1884   Marries Skram and moves to Copenhagen.

1885   Her first novel, *Constance Ring* is published and causes a great stir. The novel is criticized for its sexual explicitness and its negative portrayal of marriage. Three later novels will also deal with the theme of women in destructive marriages: *Lucie* (1888), *Fru Inés* (1891) and *Forraadt* (1892). Two stories, "Karen's Christmas" ("Karens Jul") and "Prayer and Anxiety" ("Bøn og anfaegtelse"), appear in magazines.

1886   "Knut Tandberg." Story.

1887   *On Albertine* (*Om Albertine*). Pamphlet. Amalie Skram defends Christian Krohg's novel *Albertine,* which has been suppressed by the Norwegian government for indecency and immorality.

        Sjur Gabriel and *The Two Friends* (*To Venner*). First two novels in the four-volume cycle (1887-98) that will become her best known work: *The People of Hellemyr* (*Hellemyrsfolket*).

1888   *Lucie.* Novel.

1889   Daughter Johanne is born. *Mountain Folk* (*Fjaeldmennesker*) Dramatic comedy. Written with Eric Skram.

1890   "In Asiam profectus est." Story. *Children's Stories* (*Børnefortellinger*). Stories. *S.G. Myre.* Third volume in *The People of Hellemyr.*

1891   *Fru Inés.* Novel.

1892   *Betrayed* (*Forraadt*). Novel.

1893   *Agnete.* Play.

1894   Unable to reconcile the roles of writer, wife, and mother, Amalie Skram suffers another nervous breakdown and in mid-February is admitted to the psychiatric ward of the Copenhagen City Hospital. Less than three weeks later she is transferred, against her will, to St. Hans mental hospital. She finally succeeds in obtaining her release in April.

1895   *Professor Hieronimus* and *At St. Jorgen's* (*Paa St. Jørgen*). Autobiographical novels based on her recent experiences as a mental patient.

1898   *Offspring* (*Afkom*). Fourth volume in *The People of Hellemyr.*

1899   *Summer* (*Sommer*). Stories. Divorced from Eric Skram. Lives with her daughter Johanne in Copenhagen.

1900   *Christmas* (*Julehelg*). Novel.

1902-05   Her final, unfinished novel, *People* (*Mennesker*), is published in serial form.

1905   Amalie Skram dies on March 15, at the age of 58.

The bibliographic and biographical material above is indebted to Irene Engelstad's biography, *Amalie Skram om seg selv* (Oslo: Den Norsk Bokklubben, 1981), and *Amalie Skram og kvinnens problem* by Borghild Krane (Oslo: Gyldendal, 1951).

Katherine Hanson

CONSTANCE
RING

I

THE RINGS HAD BEEN married for two years. Since they did not have children, they still lived in the five-room apartment in Homansbyen where they had moved as newlyweds.

Their home was well furnished, the floors covered with Brussels carpets and the walls with paintings, some of which were good. The rooms were crowded with expensive knick-knacks and a multitude of small plump sofas and easy chairs of various styles. Flowers in season added to the air of luxury, and in the dim light of winter, when the splendid leafy plants behind the double curtains began to turn brown at the tips, they were quickly replaced with new ones from the flower shop in Oskarsgate.

The Rings' doors were always open. They did not give many parties, but they had a constant stream of visitors—men, for the most part, according to the maid—who came on their own or with Ring after work in the evening.

Mrs. Ring was twenty-one. As a young girl she had moved to Kristiania¹ from Molde,² where her father was a government official, and she had quickly become a favorite in her new circle. One admirer compared her to a rosebud moist with morning dew. An elderly gentleman of her aunt's acquaintance claimed she was like the first spring day to a mind numbed by winter. Her sweetness and gaiety warmed people's spirits, drawing wondering smiles from even the frostiest bachelors. There was a compelling charm in the simple candor and innocent frankness with which she embraced people, regardless of their social station, as if they were friends and allies. She went skipping and humming through the house, sometimes seizing the people she met and swinging them around and around until they begged for mercy. The lilting Molde dialect sounded enchanting in her mouth, and her laughter was irresistibly contagious.

Ring was sixteen years older than the young girl he made his wife. No one was quite sure why she had accepted him—unless she had been persuaded by her aunt, who had done everything in her power to establish the connection. Ring was a very good catch. He was wealthy; he sat on the boards of reputable companies; and he had reached a settled age, a great advantage from the aunt's point of view. He had been trained as a lawyer, gone into business, and now ran a large and prosperous brokerage firm. Moreover, he belonged to a respectable family and he was rather good looking, in spite of baldness and a tendency toward obesity.

After the wedding, however, there was a striking change in Mrs. Ring. She became quiet and timid and no longer seemed happy. Her eyes, once bright and full of life, were now red-rimmed and dull. In the morning while Ring drank his coffee in the dining room—he was always up early—she hid her face in her pillow and wept. When she heard his footsteps—he always came to kiss her before leaving for the office—she would leap up and begin to wash, plunging her face into the washbasin.

At dinner he found her pale and reticent, her face closed and unapproachable, an air of constraint in her movements. To raise her spirits he lavished her with affection, which she did not reciprocate but bore patiently.

He wanted her to enjoy herself, and she made no objection but let herself be led here and there, wherever he wanted. When summer came, he sent her off to a spa, and for her homecoming decorated the living room with two new paintings and a marble Venus de Milo on a granite pedestal. It was all to no avail. She was like an ailing plant that, in spite of every effort, would not thrive.

The Rings' apartment was on the second floor. French doors opened out onto a spacious balcony covered by a white awning edged in red. From the carefully groomed garden below, a grapevine wound its way up a lattice of steel wires that had been strung along the side of the balcony. The bedroom, facing in the opposite direction, offered an expansive view of the city and the nearby heights. On clear days, flashes of water could be seen glittering in the distance amid the lovely, undulating landscape of the Kristiania fjord.

Ring sometimes found his wife here—kneeling on a hassock by the window lost in thought, her elbows on the sill, head propped in her hands, a dreamy expression in her sad eyes.

She watched the delicately tinted shadows grow deep and long in the afternoon, until at last they wrapped the wooded hilltops in a violet mist. But it was the water especially that drew and held her.

She thought about the bracing sea of her childhood home. She knew it so well in all its guises: when it rose with a roar and hurled foaming black waves against the landing, spraying salt-spume up against the panes of her attic window, while the boats heaved below, yanking at their moorings as if they were terrified and desperate to get free. And there were the times when it was flat and blue, lapping gently in the distance on the white beach where she used to hunt for pretty shells to keep. And she remembered it lying in the sun, lazy and velvet-soft, winking conspiratorially, like an old nurse reminding her pet of the things they had shared in the old days.

Her thoughts always reverted to her childhood home, fled as if they had been let out of prison. She relived the delicious summer days of their holidays in the country, when she was constantly being scolded because she wouldn't stay away from the water and was always rowing out in the boat, regardless of the weather. She remembered boating with the little daughters of the Justice of the Peace and fishing trips with her brothers, when they stayed out very late at night and everybody helped drag the boat up on shore so as not to upset old Hans, the fisherman who had loaned the boat and gear. Sweet, cross old Hans, who always had the smell of summer about him. Did he still wear that crusty old yellow rain hat with the ties tangled up in his beard, and those dark grey mittens that were so stiff they could almost stand by themselves?

2

Ring was irritated that his wife did not behave like a happy housewife, and he went to her aunt with his complaints. She promised to speak to Constance, and did so at the first opportunity.

Mrs. Ring listened to her aunt's admonitions with a downcast face and an occasional monosyllabic reply: "Yes," "I know," "Yes," "Of course," and so on, until finally her aunt embraced her and gently asked her what was wrong.

Constance burst into tears and, with an effort, forced out the words, "I'm homesick."

The outcome of this conversation was later reported to Ring.

Homesick! A married woman and she was homesick. That was splendid! Her home was with her husband, dammit! Didn't she have everything she could possibly want, and more? Didn't he put her on a pedestal? Didn't he do everything in his power to please her?

What if he tried sending her home for a while, Aunt Wleügel ventured.

To hell with that! All the way to Molde! No thanks, he begged to decline. Hadn't she just returned from the spa? Hadn't he done without her for months? Even self-sacrifice had its limits!

If only there were little ones, Aunt Wleügel said.

Well if something like that were in the works, he wouldn't have said anything, dammit!

He stood, hand poised on the doorknob, while Aunt Wleügel murmured that everything was in the Lord's hands, and surely Constance's state of mind would improve.

But the winter passed, spring came, and everything went on as before. When she was at parties, or there were guests in the house, she might have a spell of her old liveliness, or even an occasional burst of real gaiety. But this was just a new source of irritation to Ring. She would laugh and flirt with these men who loafed around their house in the evening, whether he had invited them or not, but when she was alone with him, there was never a smile to be seen. If he wanted her to talk, he was forced, as he often said, to drag every word out of her—unless, of course, she was contradicting him or being disagreeable—then it was truly a marvel how well she could speak.

Ring was planning a trip to Stockholm and Copenhagen, partly for business and partly for pleasure, and he proposed that his wife come with him. For a moment she was enchanted; she had never travelled outside of Norway, and now, finally, she would get to see a bit of the world. But as quickly as her enthusiasm flared it subsided, for when she gave the idea some thought, she didn't find it particularly appealing. She could just imagine how it would be; they never wanted the same things and always had completely opposing ideas about what was pleasant and reasonable. The previous year they had taken a short trip to Mjøsa and Gudbrandsdalen, quarreling every step of the way: when she was hungry and wanted to eat, he was full; when she was tired and wanted to rest, he was in the mood to push on. Nevertheless, she didn't really consider not going with him until the subject of the trip came up one evening, and Ring pointed out how much more expensive it was going to be to take her with him; he hoped she would show her gratitude by being especially sweet and affectionate, both on the trip and afterwards.

"Thanks, but since you put it that way, I'd rather stay home," she burst out.

"Good God, you're touchy! You never can take the slightest joke. But have it your way—if you think I'm going to beg, you're mistaken."

"It wouldn't do any good. I'm not going, and that's final."

And so it went, developing into one of their frequent quarrels, ending, like all the rest, with crude words or violent acts by Ring: a newspaper ripped to shreds, the crumpled pieces tossed around the room; a book hurled to the floor, its binding smashed; Ring stalking out of the room in a huff, then sheepishly creeping back to ask her some inconsequential thing, the answer to which he knew beforehand.

In the days that followed, Ring tried to persuade his wife to change her mind. He was both surprised and impressed to find that she would not be moved.

And so he went alone. He threw himself into his bachelor life, visiting fashionable women, enjoying himself thoroughly, and feeling pangs of conscience every morning when he awoke. In such a state of mind, he wrote letters to his wife filled with love and longing, with assurances that life without her was meaningless to him. He knew very well that he wasn't worthy of her, etc., but he loved her so much—that was his only merit. When he was home again, she would see for herself how good things could be. The separation had taught him her true value; from now on he would be so thoughtful, so good, there could be no more discord between them, etc. The more he wrote, the more enthusiastic he became; he worked himself into such a fever that he thought impatiently about cutting the trip short and returning earlier than he had planned.

Meanwhile Constance was at home, bored by the city, eternally dissatisfied, longing for what she thought life should be but never was. The contentment that she had expected to feel in her husband's absence did not materialize. Never had she been so depressed and miserable. Though tormented by loneliness, she was not in a mood to see anyone. She rarely left the house, and pretended she was not at home when anybody came to the door.

Why hadn't she gone with him? She could not stop fretting about it. Why pay any mind to his talk—he went on and on about such ridiculous things, especially in the evenings, when he'd been drinking that hateful brandy and soda—still, he really didn't mean any harm by it. If only the time would pass and he would come back. In truth she actually wanted him home again. He couldn't help being what he was—anything was better than this consuming loneliness.

At night while she was answering his letters, she would drift into a mood of wistful melancholy, her mind filled with strange and tender images. She reconstructed things: she was a happy wife; her husband was her lover, burning to rush to her side and clasp her in his arms. The yearning made her sad and heartsick.

These fantasies slipped into her letters, adding a shimmer of tenderness to their style, a warmth and gentleness to her phrases. Ring read them with rapture.

But when he was suddenly standing before her, one week early, with his passion, his violent caresses, his gifts strewn over the tables and chairs, her heart sank. There he was, with his noisy, smug self-confidence filling the room from top to bottom, his maddening expansiveness that made the most insignificant thing into an earthshaking event. All the imaginary rubbish that had cast an artificial gleam of beauty over a couple of melancholy evening hours while he was gone was swept aside in an instant, and she saw more clearly than ever before that she felt nothing for her husband but contempt and indifference.

A few days later Ring ran into Aunt Wleügel in a streetcar. There were not many passengers, and the old woman seated herself beside him and asked about Constance's health and state of mind.

"Rotten," he said, frowning and shaking his head.

"I've been thinking, Ring," Aunt Wleügel said in a low confidential tone. "If her mother came down for a while, it might be a good influence."

"Do you really think so?" Ring answered, blinking his eyes doubtfully.

"It's worth trying, at least . . . one must do what's right. My sister is very wise and good—you hardly know her, of course —but a mother is always special."

Ring had arrived at his destination.

"I'll think about it," he said grudgingly, leaping off while the streetcar was still in motion.

9

"What do you say about inviting your mother down here for a visit, Constance?" Ring said abruptly that evening as he stood beside the stove filling his pipe.

Constance sat on the sofa crocheting. She lifted her head and answered in a surprised, somewhat guarded tone, "Isn't that odd, last night I dreamed she was here."

Ring lit his pipe and settled himself comfortably beside her.

"Would that please you, Constance?"

"It's a wonderful idea. . . . " She smiled reluctantly, as though unwilling to betray her pleasure.

Ring took a large swallow from the full glass in front of him.

"Write and ask her," he said, smacking his lips.

"Yes, all right," she replied in high spirits. Hurriedly she threw aside her work and stood up. Ring hadn't seen her like this since before they were married.

"But not right now," he said in a dissatisfied tone. "It's time for bed; surely you can wait until morning."

She sat down again immediately and began to crochet.

"So that's what the doctor ordered. Well, well, so that's what it takes to cheer her up." He gave her cheek a tweak.

"Ouch!" she said, pulling her head away like a child being teased. "You're hurting me."

"Being agreeable is so becoming to you, Constance. Quite a difference from that sullen face that's been coming between us lately."

"Just leave my face alone," she said with mock sulkiness.

"So then, you'll write to your mother tomorrow and invite her to come."

"Can she stay for a while?"

"As long as she likes, naturally."

"As long as she likes—yes. What gave you this idea?"

"I wanted to do something to please you."

"Well, you've been successful then," she laughed gaily.

"Now you have to give me a kiss and say you love me," he commanded.

Bending down, she gave him a quick peck on the cheek.

"Oh no, on the mouth, please."

As she was straightening up, he gave her an aggrieved look and jerked her back towards him.

She kissed him on the mouth.

"Now say I'm nice and you love me."

"Such a schoolmaster . . . " she said, feigning amusement. Like a child reciting her lessons she rattled it off: he was nice and she loved him.

He laughed and tried to pull her onto his lap.

"I need to water the plants, they're dry," she said pulling free.

He gave her a sour look and let her go.

"It's the old story, isn't it? Whenever I want you to pay a little attention to me you act like the world will come to an end if you don't do all your busywork." Flinging himself back in the chair, he jammed his hands in his pockets and fixed his angry and disappointed gaze on Raphael's madonna.

Constance had gone out to fetch the watering can. Now she puttered around the flowers, with the calm painstaking manner of someone with all the time in the world at her disposal. Tracking her with his eyes, Ring urged her crossly to hurry up. He was sleepy and wanted to go to bed.

He could go whenever he was ready, she told him. Everything was prepared for him in the bedroom.

Emptying his glass, he rose abruptly and walked stiffly out of the room, slamming the door to announce his displeasure.

When Constance had at last finished the flowers, she tidied up her sewing box, straightened the books and newspapers, and finally began rearranging the knickknacks on the etagere.

Then she settled herself among the flowerpots and plant stands by the bay window, where a couple of low chairs had been drawn up to a marble-topped table. She sat with her arms crossed, her lower lip caught in her teeth. The happiness she had felt about her mother's visit had evaporated, passed completely out of memory.

The door opened suddenly, startling Constance, who had not heard footsteps.

"What's keeping you, Constance?" he complained. "I can't sleep." He had gotten up out of bed to come find her.

She shivered and rose to her feet. There must have been a draft from the window.

"I'm coming now," she said with a slightly bewildered sense of having been caught at an embarrassing moment. She blew out the lamp and went in to him.

3

A TELEGRAM ARRIVED FROM Ring's father-in-law, Judge Blom, announcing that Constance's mother would arrive on the next steamship.

Constance counted the days, busying herself enthusiastically with redecorating the guest room and putting the house in perfect order so that her mother would be pleased with her housekeeping.

Ring had never seen his wife so lively and energetic. She actually looked happy as she bustled around the house.

The two of them went on board to welcome Mrs. Blom. All day Constance had been distracted and silent, darting repeatedly into the guest room with some trinket for the dressing table, making first one change and then another in her arrangements.

When suddenly she saw her mother on the deck, she burst into tears and clung to her.

Ring looked annoyed and muttered that a steamship was hardly the place for Constance to make a spectacle of herself.

Mrs. Blom quieted her with gentle words and affectionate caresses, and as the carriage moved toward home, directed casual questions to Ring about the name of a street or about a new church they were passing.

There were more than enough things to ask him about; she had not been in Kristiania for sixteen years.

When she thought Constance had recovered her composure, she began to talk about home—little things, for the most part— the doves and chickens; the beloved old horse that soon would have to be shot; the dining room they were painting; the old curtains she and Constance used to mend every

13

spring and that now, finally, were going to be thrown away. And there were all the people who had sent their greetings: her father and sisters, the boys and the coachman, the old servant Ane, friends and cousins, and numerous others.

But this chatter about things at home wrenched Constance's heart. As the memories came crowding irresistibly back, she struggled against tears.

"You certainly do look happy—fine way to show your appreciation," Ring said suddenly, clicking his tongue in displeasure.

"Why, Constance," Mrs. Blom reproached mildly when she saw the tears sliding down her daughter's cheeks. "What is the matter, child?"

"I can't help it, Mother," came the choked, imploring voice. She pressed a handkerchief to her eyes.

"Well, this certainly is uplifting for a man," Ring said, shifting his body angrily as if looking for a more comfortable position, then resuming exactly the same posture as before.

When the carriage arrived at their door shortly thereafter, they were all relieved that the ride was over.

Upstairs, Ring conducted his mother-in-law through the rooms. She had to see the whole apartment right away. He pointed out which things were gifts and which were not, confided what the paintings were worth and what he had paid for them, opened the door of the buffet so that she could see the silver and fine crystal, pulled her into the bedroom so that she could admire the fabric of the bed curtains. He pulled out his violin and played her a few bars, then seized by a sudden desire to show her the linen closet, dashed into the kitchen to get the key from Constance, who was preparing a salad. At last it occurred to him that Mrs. Blom might be tired and want to sit down. In an instant he had settled her in an armchair and was piling albums and illustrated books on the table in front of her, all the while talking in disconnected fragments about anything that popped into his mind. It all made Mrs. Blom's head swim.

At supper Ring was unusually loquacious. He described their homecoming on their wedding evening, the living room glittering with the vast array of presents. He told little stories about the first days of their marriage, laughing uproariously at his own witty delivery. To celebrate his mother-in-law's arrival, he drank three shots of aquavit with the cold dishes and a couple of glasses of sherry with the homemade apple cake.

Constance was silent and looked as if she were bored. He never seemed more disagreeable to her than when he was trying to be charming. Moreover, on occasions like these he had usually been drinking, and this was glaringly obvious, at least to Constance. She was thoroughly ashamed of him. Everything he said was distorted. To give a story a more impressive ring, he added things that were completely false. She, too, exaggerated sometimes, when she felt like it, but she didn't try to pass it off as something other than it was. Whereas he would get furious and stubborn if she protested and accuse her of being quarrelsome. Tonight, for example. Unable to stand it any longer, she had objected to something he said about the time they fired their first maid for stealing. He expressed his annoyance and Constance answered him back. Mrs. Blom put in a soothing word on Ring's behalf. Constance was taking him too literally—there was no point in quibbling about words. If someone was having a good time, he couldn't be expected to weigh every word so carefully— he wasn't under oath, after all. Constance answered her mother sharply. Why was she getting involved with something she knew nothing about? Regretting her words immediately, she held her tongue. Ring had the last word. He muttered something about how hard it was for a man when his wife always criticized him, no matter what he said or did. He shook his head and sighed deeply, with the look of someone accustomed to being misunderstood and determined to bear it patiently.

"You shouldn't contradict your husband so often, Constance," said Mrs. Blom. They had risen from the table and Ring had gone into the next room to smoke his pipe.

"Nonsense!" Constance said with a toss of her head.

"No, I'm serious. It isn't proper."

"Then I should just let him go on telling lies like that?"

"Lies. What an odd word."

15

"Yes, exactly. Lies. It's infuriating to have to listen to them."

"Come now, behave yourself. You simply must not treat your husband with such disrespect."

"You shouldn't humor him, mother. He can take care of himself, believe me, and if he sees that you're on his side, it will be impossible to be in the same room with him."

"'On his side,' 'humor him'—those aren't terms that belong in a proper marriage."

Constance stood drumming on the table with her fingertips, her nose in the air, the corners of her mouth pulled down in a frown.

"You certainly haven't had that kind of example at home. Your father and I have never been on that kind of footing."

"No, of course not—I know that," she said, her face and voice protesting the absurdity of the comparison. "Can you imagine father drinking and jabbering away in a slurred voice, making himself completely disagreeable?"

"So Ring has a drink or two with his dinner—it's nothing to make a fuss about."

"Oh nonsense, he drinks brandy after dinner, too."

"Well all right, if he doesn't overdo things. But going around with a sour expression on your face is the surest way to drive him to it."

The maid came in to clear the table and the two women went into the living room where Ring was smoking, a large glass of brandy and soda in front of him. He offered to bring them some cold punch, but they declined.

Ring had regained his good spirits. He went on blustering and gesticulating without a moment's pause and Mrs. Blom, the perfect audience, nodded agreement and laughed at the right places.

"Don't sit there like a sourpuss, Constance," he burst out in an excited tone. "Put that trashy newspaper down and come over here and be nice to me." He pulled her up from her chair and tried to draw her to him.

She resisted.

"Now sit down, Constance," admonished Mrs. Blom.

She went reluctantly, and Ring settled her on his knee. He

began to caress her and call her pet names. She wanted to sink through the floor. It was mortifying that her mother could watch this, that she could actually approve of it. The reek of tobacco and brandy sickened her; his lips and beard felt moist and disgusting against her burning face.

"Let me go—you're choking me!" she cried suddenly, wrenching herself free. She dashed out of the room, wiping her face with a handkerchief.

"Well, now you see what living with her is like," Ring said, getting to his feet in irritation. "I try as hard as I can to be nice and she's always like that." He paced restlessly back and forth across the room.

"She's just tired and nervous tonight," Mrs. Blom soothed.

"She's just exactly the way she always is." He sat down again in a determined manner. "I have to beg for the slightest crumb of affection—she acts as if she's doing me a favor."

"That doesn't sound like Constance," said Mrs. Blom, appearing to give the situation some thought.

"It's just some whim, of course. Some damned nonsense from those novels of hers—pardon me." He had hiccupped inadvertently.

"Do you really think so?" Mrs. Blom asked skeptically.

"Yes, of course I do! It's the only possible explanation. What else could it be, for God's sake?"

Mrs. Blom heaved a sigh and looked at her fingernails.

"If only I weren't so confounded crazy about her. If I could be cold and indifferent, she'd come around soon enough."

"Oh, Ring, don't do that. Constance will have to be won with love."

"L-love!" Ring said, leaning suddenly toward his mother-in-law. "I don't see how any man could be more loving."

"You have to be sensible about this, Ring. Most young wives are a little unsettled for the first couple of years."

"No, confound it, they act like they're in love—take Marie, for instance—now there's a wife for you—but Constance is so strange—I swear to you. . . . " He bent closer and spoke to her in a lower tone.

"Constance is still so young—I'm sure everything will

straighten out," Mrs. Blom said confidently.

"Well, no matter what, she's got to change if she's going to make me happy. I have high hopes for your visit—you've got to talk to her."

Constance entered the room and said that if her mother was tired, her bedroom was ready for her. Mrs Blom rose immediately and said goodnight. Her daughter went with her, lighting the lamps, aimlessly puttering around the room while Mrs. Blom prepared for bed.

When her mother was tucked under the covers, Constance perched on the edge of the bed beside her.

"It's so wonderful to have you here in this bed, to know you'll be here every single night for weeks." She laughed happily and kissed her, blissfully content.

"I just wish you were really at peace, Constance. . . . Tell me what's wrong."

"It's not something that can be forced, mother. Your new nightcaps are so pretty! Did you make them yourself?"

"Yes. You have a great deal to be happy about, Constance."

"I'll bet anything Helene did the embroidery."

"Yes, yes, of course. That's right, isn't it, Constance? You do have a great deal to be happy about?"

"Oh, yes, I recognize Helene's stitching. Her work is so beautiful."

"Surely you are happy with your husband—he's such a kind man!"

"Why do you suppose she chose that boring pattern—scallops are so much quicker and prettier."

"Please stop talking about the pattern and listen to me."

She hid her face against her mother.

"My sweet child, of course you love your husband—you do love him, don't you?"

"I don't know."

"What kind of talk is that? You don't know?"

She lifted her head and plucked at the ribbons of her mother's nightcap.

"I don't think I do," she said slowly.

"You frighten me, child. When you accepted his proposal,

wasn't it out of love?"

"God knows. Oh yes, I suppose it was, in a way. I've thought about it, believe me, but . . . but . . . " She broke off in obvious embarrassment.

"But . . . " repeated her mother, "go on . . . but what?"

"I don't like being married."

"What kind of foolish talk is that?" Mrs. Blom asked indignantly.

"Is it so foolish? Can't you understand at all? Isn't it often that way?"

"Well, if a husband is immoral, or cruel. . . . "

"And nothing else counts?"

"Nothing else *should* count."

"Does affection for a man always have to depend on how good or bad he is?"

"Really, Constance. There is no place in a marriage for talk like that. A wife has no right to think that way."

"I don't see why not."

"It's ridiculous, or childish at the very least, and it can destroy a marriage. Don't be a child, Constance, for heaven's sake."

"All right, let's not talk about it then. Listen to me, mother—now you mustn't say no—I'd like so much to sleep in here with you." She slid her hands under her mother's neck and lifted her head toward her.

"With me? Have you taken leave of your senses, child?"

"I'll make myself very small—don't you remember when we used to have guests in the country, and I would sleep with you," she coaxed.

"Well in those days, yes—you were just a little girl."

"Oh well, I've grown a few inches—that doesn't make any difference—and then I can imagine I'm home again and it's summer vacation and we can talk as much as we want. I'll run get my nightgown."

She was already at the door.

"It's out of the question, Constance. What would your husband say?" Mrs. Blom sat up in bed looking genuinely alarmed.

19

"He ought to allow me that much—since he's such a kind man."

"Come here, Constance," her mother said sternly. When her daughter was again sitting on the edge of the bed, Mrs. Blom spoke to her in an earnest, admonitory tone. She should not be moody or cold toward her husband. It was her duty to love him and to make him happy. She should think about how lucky she was—the daughter of a poor civil servant and so well situated now—really that was not something to look down upon; he was such a fine, kind husband, with such a sense of the comforts of home. She should really take care that he didn't get tired of her. There was always the risk that he would look for love somewhere else—that was just the way men were. Her words were mild and gentle and as she spoke she stroked the hand clasped in hers. If this were something she could not overcome by herself, she should turn to God and ask for His help. She should start by giving thanks for all His grace and goodness. If she would just turn to the Lord, everything would be blessed and good—and she would be her own dear Constance again, just as she had always been.

It was exactly what her aunt was always saying. Was her mother really going to give her the same depressing speech about how lucky she was—the same insistence that she spend her life on bended knees? They wanted to force her to be glad—to feel happiness. But what did she have to be happy about? She couldn't see it. True, she had plenty to eat and drink, but these were things she had always had. How could she help the emptiness she felt inside—this ever growing intolerance of her husband? If they would only leave her alone. She never complained or reproached anybody. If it really was so contemptible for her to feel the way she did, surely it was not her fault—she couldn't make herself into a different person. Sitting there on the edge of the bed listening to her mother's long speech, she felt bitter disappointment and a painful sense of abandonment. She had expected so much from her mother's visit. She had drifted along with the vague idea that when her mother came everything would be all right. But now they could not understand each other at all. Her mother was suddenly alien to her, in league with her accusers. A gap had opened between them—a huge room filled with things her mother walked past without seeing, without even knowing they existed. She suddenly felt self-conscious with her. If only they could avoid conversations like this. She would be affectionate and sweet to Ring. Then there would be no chance of it. And she would be sure to look happy, all right—it would just take a bit of pretending, that was all.

"Isn't that right, Constance, my dear—you will be a good sensible girl?" asked Mrs. Blom at last, after waiting a few moments for her daughter to reply.

"Yes, I will! I'll be very sensible—you'll see. Good night, Mother." She kissed her and got up and left the room.

4

THE LAWYER FOR the High Court, R.C. Hansen, made his home on Welhavensgate. His wife Marie, Constance's cousin, had spent her childhood in Bergen, one of eight daughters of an impoverished infantry captain named Foss. Every summer one of the little girls was invited up to Molde; they took turns, their fare paid both ways by their more prosperous Uncle Blom and his wife, Captain Foss's sister.

Ring and Hansen had been schoolboys together, and their friendship had continued through the years. Now that they were also related by marriage the two families were naturally on the closest terms.

Mrs. Blom could not be away from home for longer than a month. Her third daughter was going to be confirmed in October, and a number of things required her attention at home beforehand. Already September was far advanced and soon her vacation would be at an end.

She and her daughter had not returned to the topic of their first evening's conversation. Constance had lightly brushed aside all references to the subject, and Mrs. Blom thought it best not to bother her by talking too much about it. Besides, it was no longer necessary; she was pleased to see that her words had fallen on fertile soil and borne lovely fruit. Now Ring could see just how sweet and agreeable Constance really was. Simply calling the matter to her attention had been enough.

Indeed Ring did have to admit that his wife had become remarkably obliging. She laughed at his jokes and never neglected to kiss him after meals. Still, in his heart of hearts he felt mistrustful, for there appeared to be no end to her affection, except on the rare occasions when they were alone, and she suddenly looked like she wanted to hit him.

Meanwhile the days passed in a whirl. Their time was filled from morning to night with parties and visits, with shopping trips and entertaining guests—whatever the occasion, they were there.

Mrs. Blom was relieved that Ring and Constance were getting along so nicely. It was understandable, of course. They had everything in the world to make them happy. Ring's only fault . . . well, for heaven's sake, he took care of his business affairs, and he was never the least bit grouchy in the morning.

It was astonishing what a fuss people made about Constance. All Ring's friends waited on her hand and foot—but Ring did bring them home, after all, and Constance treated them all exactly the same—so there really wasn't any cause for gossip.

Yes, Mrs. Blom felt she had every reason for satisfaction.

In Mrs. Blom's honor Ring and the Hansens had arranged a day's excursion out to Sarabråten. The morning was beautiful and spirits were high as the party drove off in five carriages lavishly stocked with food and drink. On the climb up the narrow mountain footpath, Constance slipped and bruised her foot. At first it was not painful, but as the day wore on she began to limp, and finally she yielded to cousin Lorck's fervent pleas to assist her.

Lorck was a medical student. He had not yet taken the last part of his medical examination although he was now twenty-seven years old. His parents had been close friends of Ring's; their mothers were first cousins, and Niels Lorck, much younger than Ring, had called him Uncle Edvard since childhood. Years had passed during which they had scarcely met, but when Ring married Constance, Lorck immediately sought to renew the relationship. Ring had greeted him with open arms, entreating him to regard their house as his second home and to allow him to call Lorck "cousin."

As the travellers neared the city on their way home, someone in the front carriage called back a suggestion that they stop at Ingebret for supper. There was a chorus of approving voices; it would be pity to break up the party so early, everybody agreed. The difficulty was finding a place where they could have some privacy.

The Grand Hotel was mentioned, as well as Gravesons Cafe.

R.C. Hansen objected. He didn't like this business of going out to a public place. The others drowned him out, insisting that it would be fun. Marie fretted that the whole scheme would come to nothing.

"It might be fun to ask them to our house," she whispered to her husband, "if you aren't too tired, Rikard?"

"No, listen . . . let's just drop the whole thing. . . . "

Ring was strolling from carriage to carriage, pouring punch and apologizing profusely because they all had to drink from the same glass.

"Yes, of course—the thought just crossed my mind when they were talking about what a good host you are," she remarked casually.

"Who said that?" asked Hansen.

"Oh, just Lorck."

Leaning back in the carriage, Marie directed her seatmate's attention to the lovely view. She was quite ecstatic, in spite of the fact that it was nearly dark outside.

Hansen bit the side of his index finger.

"If that's what you want, Marie, well—all right, I'll go along with it," he said in a low, slightly grudging tone.

"What did you say, my dear?" she asked turning toward him, still chattering about the view.

"All right, you can invite them, if you want to."

"Ask who? Oh, tonight—no, absolutely not, my dear—it was a foolish impulse."

"No, really, I want you to."

"Well my goodness, if you really mean it . . . Oh Ring, while you're out there, won't you ask the others if they'll come have a bite with us—we'll just improvise—I don't know if I've got a thing in the house. Rikard, do you hear how pleased they are!"

It was a festive evening. Marie was the perfect hostess for such a gathering and R.C. Hansen always tried his best to be genial, without having any talent for it. His wife knew as well as everyone else that she was the one who made the house inviting.

While her guests took off their wraps and tidied themselves at the hall mirror and in the dressing room, Marie lit the lamps and moved the flowerpots away from the windows to more decorative spots. She placed them beneath the large palm and in front of the wide panelled mirror that reached from floor to ceiling, a narrow gilded railing around its base.

Everyone quickly settled themselves in comfortable chairs, and propped their legs up on soft footstools. Small tables covered with fringed, embroidered cloths were pulled forward for convenience and piled with trays of glasses, decanters, and ashtrays. Permission was given to smoke in all the rooms. They were all tired after their climb on the mountain, and their faces were sunburned from the long stay outdoors. All day they had been so cheerful and boisterous; now they felt relaxed and drowsy. They sat in pairs, talking idly, almost whispering.

"Oh Meier, won't you play for them a little—the table will be ready soon," Marie asked, hurrying through the room with a candelabra in each hand.

A rangy, broad-shouldered figure rose and sauntered to the piano. He had light curly hair and a head that would have been extremely handsome if it hadn't been so flat in the back. He struck a few chords as he stood there, then ran his fingers rapidly down the keyboard.

"What do you want me to play?" he asked indifferently, half turning his head toward the others.

"Something about the evening—about longing—love— Sarabråten," came the chorus of replies.

"And what did you say, Mrs. Ring?" He turned all the way around and looked at Constance, who was sitting on the sofa with Lorck.

"I didn't say anything," she said with a laugh.

He blushed and bit his lips, then with an irresolute shrug sat down on the piano stool.

"Play something about us, about all of us," cried Constance.

"All right, but one at a time—I'll start with you."

His head was tilted toward the ceiling as he spoke, so Constance could only see him from the side. She was struck by the beauty of his profile. He began to play snatches of melody—melting, tender and soft at the beginning; then cheerful and full of laughter, like the song of a bird; then an adagio, with the grave dignity of a Spanish fandango; and finally the yearning reproachful sound of a troubador's love song.

"Does he do it off the top of his head?" Constance whispered.

"He does it on a seat, can't you see?" Lorck retorted.

"Oh don't be silly. Is he really improvising?"

"Yes, for heaven's sake," he answered in an irritated tone. "Such a vulgar talent—I can't bear it."

"Isn't he planning to be a pianist?"

"He is one, of course!"

"Will you behave! I mean professionally."

Lorck shrugged.

"Stop blowing smoke in my eyes." She took the cigar out of his mouth and set it aside. "You can smoke it later."

"Oh for heaven's sake," Lorck remarked laconically.

"Have you ever heard anybody who could match him? It's a pity he can't make a career of it," remarked Lieutenant Fallesen, who had moved to a hassock next to Constance.

"Why can't he?" she asked.

"Well, it's his father—I think he wants him to study law—it's utterly preposterous."

"I heard the other day that the old cabinet minister had given in about it," said a sharp-featured little spinster with frizzy bangs and a lorgnette. "I believe he's going to study abroad," she nodded confidingly. "Doesn't he play beautifully, Mrs. Ring?"

"It runs in the family," said Fallesen. "His mother is a relative of Ole Bull."[3]

"How old is he now do you suppose?" asked Constance.

"Old enough to fall in love with you," whispered Lorck.

"In his early twenties, I expect."

"No Lieutenant, he's older than that, I'm quite sure of it,"

Miss Schwartz assured them.

"Twenty-three years, two months, minus four days," suggested Lorck.

Fallesen and Miss Schwartz laughed. Constance hushed them.

As Meier continued to play, his audience grew increasingly enraptured by the music. Finally the room became quite still: the men puffed their cigars more slowly and flicked their ashes carefully; Mrs. Wleügel leaned forward, her whole body intent upon the music; Mrs. Blom sat with her hands clasped in her lap, her head swaying; and Ring was so moved that he forgot to tend his cigar, and several times had to tiptoe over and light it from the candle behind the fan-shaped screen.

"Supper is ready, come to the table please!" Marie cried, throwing open the door to the dining room. Meier played the last bars at a faster tempo, ending with an ugly dissonant chord.

"You'll play some more after supper, I hope—if we ask you nicely?" Marie said as he was getting to his feet.

"Thank you," "Thanks very much," "Wonderful," "Splendid," "Marvelous!" The compliments buzzed around him.

Lorck offered Constance his arm; the others followed suit and led their partners to the table.

"Pull your lace higher, Constance," whispered Mrs. Wleügel, who was walking behind her with a student named Feyn. "Your neckline is too low; your bosom is showing."

"My bosom! That's impossible, Aunt."

"I saw him staring at you on the sofa. Fix it before your mother sees."

Staring! How could Lorck be so disgusting—and could he possibly have thought she had known it? Blushing hotly, she hurriedly yanked the white lace up as far as it would go.

"Now we can let down our hair," Marie said as the dishes were being passed around. "Drink wine, make toasts—what do you say?"

"What luck," sighed Lorck.

"Come on Marie, let's just be ordinary people."

"Please Rikard, for fun—it will be amusing."

27

"Oh, it's all right with me, but . . . " He helped himself to some tinned breast of grouse.

"The host has to go first," several voices called out.

Hansen filled his glass and urged the others to do the same.

"Well," he said, getting to his feet, "so I have been sentenced to give a speech. I say sentenced intentionally so you will all realize that I'm not doing this of my own free will, and you will be inclined—I repeat, inclined—toward lenience. . . . " "Hear! Hear!" came a cry from Ring's end of the table. "And so I shall be brief. We have had, I think we can all agree, an especially pleasant day, without a shadow of misfortune." "What about Constance's foot?" his wife interrupted. "Except Constance injuring her foot," he continued. "I lost my cane," put in Meier. "And Mr. Meier losing his cane," Hansen went on. "My dress is completely ruined," called out Miss Schwartz, who was sitting next to Ring. "Quiet now" was heard amid the general laughter. "And Miss Schwartz ruining her dress," Hansen went on with unruffled calm. "No shadow of misfortune—except those mentioned . . . " "So that's what you call brief," said Lorck with a look of mock desperation. Everybody burst into laughter. Marie clapped her hands and shouted "Bravo!" "Let the poor man finish, once and for all," said Constance.

"No shadow of misfortune, except those mentioned," prompted Marie.

"And there are quite a few of them," said Fallesen, also wanting to get a word in.

". . . has darkened the pleasure of the day," continued Hansen.

"What's this! Are we having an eclipse?" Ring called out, laughing so hard at his own joke that he didn't notice that no one else thought it funny.

"Therefore I believe," Hansen went on, "we are all in agreement, yes, in perfect accord, in our desire for an equally pleasant conclusion to the day." ("Hear! Hear!") "And therefore, my dear ladies and gentlemen, I welcome you to our table."

"Hip, hip hurrah!" Ring directed, waving his arms. "Hurrah, hurrah!" chimed in a couple of voices.

"Shh, shh," said Hansen, sitting down and letting out his breath. "We'll be evicted."

"How is your foot, Mrs. Ring?" asked Fallesen, seated at Constance's right.

"It's better, I think."

"I'm sorry to hear it," he said giving her a soulful look.

"Fill your glasses, gentlemen!" Hansen called out, tapping his glass, "Ring is going to propose a toast."

"We can still talk," Constance said in a low voice. "Just listen to the last few words so we know what it's about."

Fallesen was ecstatic that Constance seemed so willing to engage in private conversation with him.

"Good Lord, that's more than enough," he said laughing.

"Did you say 'sorry'?" Constance asked.

"Yes—I said 'sorry'—but never mind—whenever I talk to you I get all mixed up."

"Listen to Ring," Constance said with a laugh, "'the power of genius elevates the mind and ennobles the soul'—did you hear that, Lieutenant Fallesen?"

"No I didn't—how can you expect—I was going to say that if your foot were still sore, perhaps you would let me carry you home—I am very strong, I assure you—my arm muscles . . . "

"I'd prefer to ride," she answered, turning away.

As she glanced absently down the table her eyes met Meier's; he was gazing at her with a look of adoration.

A little shock went through her, and her heart beat faster. Meier did not take his eyes from hers. Confused, she looked away but could not resist a backward glance to see if he was still staring at her. This was repeated several times; she felt her face growing red and, half unwillingly, lifted her glass and nodded to him; he rose slightly in his chair, blushed to the roots of his hair, and with a radiant expression, bowed to her and emptied his glass.

"What kind of foolishness is that?" said Hansen, who had been whispering to his dinner partner and noticed Meier get up and sit down. "You're supposed to wait until he calls you by name."

Meier had heard nothing that he said; he was too overjoyed

at the silent greeting Constance had given him.

"Why are you making eyes at that infant?" Lorck whispered in an annoyed tone.

"What are you talking about?" Constance asked.

"Surely you see him staring at you—his eyes will be popping out of his head any minute. What do you want with him?"

"Shh—pay attention," answered Constance, turning her head toward Ring.

"My, my, I really think you are falling for that babyface over there," Lorck began again.

"Now stop it, Lorck."

"They say you can tell by a woman's eyes when she's in love. I wouldn't have believed you could have such poor taste—my God!" He emptied a large glass of Madeira.

"Taste! Oh come now, he's handsome enough, at least. Have you ever seen a mouth like that? Those teeth—and the way he holds his head—have you really looked at him I wonder?"

"No," Lorck answered curtly.

"And his eyes are so innocent and good. There is something pure about him."

"Hummph," said Lorck behind his napkin.

"You shouldn't speak ill of your friends, Mr. Lorck."

"Speak ill! My word, have I so much as opened my mouth?"

"No, but you laughed, and that's worse."

"Those are harsh terms, I must say. As a matter of fact I like him quite well—he's a fine fellow—but this talk about his innocence—well really, you'll have to forgive me. *Enfin*—if you want to destroy me right now, go on, fall in love with that boy over there—I'll never survive it."

There was something so amusingly mournful in Lorck's tone and expression that Constance couldn't help laughing.

"What nonsense you talk," she said.

"And therefore I urge each and every one of you to empty your glasses in honor of the talented young artist who plays the piano and harp so splendidly—" "Violin," whispered Miss Schwartz. "Piano and violin—Mr. Harold Meier," Ring concluded.

Meier popped up like a champagne cork. He had not suspected that the whole long-winded speech, of which he had heard scarcely a word, was in his honor. The toast was then drunk, amid smiles and nods and bows from all sides.

Next Ring proposed a toast to his mother-in-law, praising her so extravagantly that the poor woman was too mortified to raise her eyes. He was so moved by his own eloquence that tears came to his eyes. Voice trembling, he called her his guardian angel, his life's greatest blessing; he had no hesitation about saying this because she had brought his precious wife into the world and entrusted her to his care. And in that connection he also wanted to mention charming old Aunt Wleü-gel, whom he regarded as a second mother. A toast to Mrs. Wleügel and Mrs. Blom.

When desert was finished and the guests, having eaten their fill, had laid their napkins on the table, Ring rose for the third time and proposed a toast to womankind. Sighs and murmurs were heard around the room. Lorck muttered objections under his breath.

"Do you see what happens, Marie," said Hansen with a meaningful glance. "What a stupid idea! You might have known nothing could stop him."

Ring noticed nothing. Glass raised, voice high-pitched, he delivered his hymn in praise of womankind. He wanted to talk about the woman in the home, the woman God gave man to be his helpmate. He could speak of this woman with authority because for over three years now he had been a member of the happy ranks of married men. At first his words flowed unimpeded, but as he got further into his speech, he began to stop short, to stammer and grope for words. His uninhibited dinner partners made preposterous suggestions, which he adopted, then dropped abruptly when he noticed he was getting off the track. When he had repeated for the third time that a woman was a flower, a fragrance, a feeling, Constance laughingly called across the table, "All right, we'll drink to that."

Ring put his glass down on the table, crossed his arms on

his chest and asked Hansen resentfully if he thought his wife should act as critic?

There was a moment of embarrassed silence. Ring's fierce glance shifted from one face to another. Mrs. Blom signalled him to try to pass the incident off as a joke.

Suddenly Ring burst into laughter. "Damned if that wasn't a good one," he cried. "I took you all for a ride that time!"

They all laughed uproariously, some insisting they had known it all the time and played along with him, others asserting that nothing in the world could make them believe it.

"Well *I* certainly thought you meant it," said Constance.

"So let's lift our glasses to womankind," said Ring. Spirits were so high that, in spite of Hansen's protests, the toast got nine hurrahs.

All the guests shook hands with their hosts and thanked them for the meal. Hansen and Marie exchanged the obligatory after-dinner kiss. Ring went over to Constance and offered her his hand; she lifted her cheek for him to kiss instead.

"Well, like I said—you're a musical wonder—a—a—true genius," Ring said to Meier. "You must come see us—drop in any time, you know—any time you like—quite the custom—I've got a boat—you must come sailing with me. What a splendid fellow."

Meier bowed and thanked him and Ring went on pumping his hand as if he would never stop.

"What shall we do now, everybody?" asked Marie, turning to one of the chattering groups in the living room. "Oh Meier, play for us while we think of something."

He began a Strauss waltz.

Constance took Miss Schwartz by the waist and waltzed her around.

"Yes, dance, let's dance," they cried in unison.

"Your foot, Constance, remember your foot," her mother protested.

"The dining room will be cleared in a few minutes," said Marie, going out to hurry the maids.

"Now why did you start that?" Lorck asked Constance crossly.

"Don't you like to dance?" Constance inquired.

"Oh, the dancing at Klingenberg is all right."

"Then go down there—you can dance every night."

"No, I'm serious—we could be sitting over there in the shadows having such a pleasant talk."

"Dancing is more fun," she replied.

Just then Fallesen bowed before her and asked for a dance.

"Lorck asked me just now," she answered, giving his jacket a surreptitious tug.

"Well, the next one then?"

"We'll see."

"Does that mean no?"

"No, of course not—the next dance with you."

He bowed and retreated.

"Now you have to dance with me," Constance laughed, "I was just trying to get rid of him."

"Well thanks, that's perfectly obvious," Lorck replied with a bow.

"You mustn't dance, Constance—not with that foot!" said Mrs. Blom.

"Oh mother—I want to so much."

When the waltz was over someone requested a française.

"Let me relieve you, Meier," said Mrs. Blom. "I can't play like you do, of course, but for dancing it doesn't really matter."

Meier walked over to Constance and asked her to dance.

"Thank you, but I've promised someone else—I'm sorry," she answered.

Disconsolate, he turned away.

"But the next one—couldn't we dance the next one?" she called after him.

With a look of perplexity he thanked her and walked away.

"Why are you trying to put ideas in his head?" Lorck said. "Haven't you got enough on your conscience?"

"Why are you always sneering at me? You're really getting tedious."

Dancing the française, Ring performed a variety of antics, which his partner Miss Schwartz rewarded with bursts of laughter. He danced like a barber, then a tailor, and so on; when it was his turn to dance a figure, he would fling himself on one knee in front of the lady and still manage to get back to his place on time.

"What an intolerable brute!" Lorck said to Marie, who was dancing in the line of women.

"Actually, I think it suits him," she answered apologetically.

"Can't you dance like everybody else, dammit!" Lorck muttered to Ring, who for a moment was standing beside him.

"They enjoy it," Ring answered with a cheerful wink.

"You're driving me to desperation tonight," Fallesen whispered to Constance in an aggrieved tone.

"Stop carrying on like this," she answered grudgingly. "It's quite useless . . . "

He could not hear anything more because he had to step forward for the fourth figure.

"You haven't said a word to me tonight," he began again, "and you were so friendly during the trip today."

"Pay attention now, it's your turn to go out, Lieutenant,"

"He's flirting with my wife, the fool," Ring said to his partner.

"They all do, of course," she answered. "Doesn't it make you jealous?"

"Not in the slightest—I'm flattered to see . . . "

"Now pay attention, Ring—it's your turn!" Constance called with a gay laugh.

"Don't you have any explanation for me?" Fallesen asked, his eyes seeking hers imploringly.

"Really, Lieutenant Fallesen, you are starting to annoy me." Thank heavens for Lorck, she thought to herself—he never takes his flirtations seriously.

"Do you think my wife cares a fig for any of them? Not in the least; she's just having a bit of fun," Ring said when they were in their places again.

"When I listen to you, I can see why people want to be married—you're so tolerant."

"Well a man ought to be tolerant and easy to get along with. I'm easy to get along with, don't you think? If I had a brother, you could marry him."

"Why aren't you dancing?" Marie asked Meier, who had been looking on from the doorway the whole time.

"I can't find a partner."

"You poor thing! Always at your post. Oh, play us a galop, Aunt!" she called in to Mrs. Blom. "Will I do?" she asked turning to Meier.

"Thank you, but I'm engaged for this dance."

Involuntarily, his eyes sought Constance.

"Ah, I see. You sound like the knight in Ingemann+—it's her or no one." She had followed the direction of his glance.

When the galop started, Ring withdrew to Hansen's study where several of the men were smoking. The doors were open in all the rooms. As Ring sat drinking his toddies, his eyes followed Constance as she whirled away with Meier.

He was so proud of her—she was incomparable, head and shoulders above the other young women—and she belonged to him, Edvard Christensen Ring, to nobody else. And she was really so devoted to him—so willing lately to caress him. He was certainly a lucky man, he thought, pouring himself another drink.

"Look at all these truants," Marie said to the men as she came in. "Ooh, this awful smoke! Who's hiding in here? Please come in and dance, Rikard! And you, Lieutenant—imagine finding you in here!"

Fallesen excused himself, saying he had a headache.

"You've been moping around all night, Lieutenant. Come on, let's have a drink," Ring said.

Fallesen poured some cognac into a wine glass.

"That's what I like—the straight stuff—a toast to us."

Fallesen emptied the contents in one gulp.

"Look at Constance—a beautiful wife, by God—eh, Fallesen," and he nudged him in the side.

"She is, indeed, but how about Miss Schwartz? She's not bad either."

"Too flat," Ring sneered, "a stick—straight up and down."

"Her figure is pretty good."

"Padded," Ring laughed. "Look at those bony shoulders.

35

Believe me, Edvard Christensen Ring is not deceived."

They became deeply engrossed in their conversation about feminine beauty and its many arts; finally Ring proposed that they call each other "du"⁵ and drink to their new friendship.

"You're a fine fellow—damned if you're not—pity you don't come visit more often—come any night—doors are always open—d'you like to sail?—got a great boat, old boy—a sloop, steady as they come. Don't know why it is that I get along with young people best. Now take Hansen—we're good friends, but the chap bores me—just between us, you understand—youth is what counts."

Lorck came in to get some soda water.

"Ring and Fallesen are in there getting roaring drunk," he said to Hansen on the way back through the living room. Hansen peeked in and shook his head thoughtfully.

"What did you think of yourself?" Meier asked Constance during a pause in the galop.

"Myself? Ah, you mean the music! It was very beautiful."

"Did you recognize yourself?"

"Not at all—there were so many different things in it."

"If I knew you better—really knew you, I mean—I could do better, of course."

"Knew me! Well, how in heaven's name could you?"

"If you'd only let me talk to you, perhaps . . . "

"Nobody can really know another person. Talk! Do you really think that helps at all? One gets impressions, forms ideas—but never anything more than that—and then they're always completely off the mark."

"But surely it's possible to get to know someone else—if one doesn't purposely try to hide."

"But people do that all the time—not on purpose exactly—but they hide themselves. What do we let people see? What circumstances compel and allow. We're shaped by outside conditions, and I suppose by inner ones too. Haven't you noticed how much alike we all are?"

"You aren't like any other woman."

"Oh, yes. Life is a factory—we're all stamped from the same mold."

"But there is still something individual—something that makes a person walk and talk and understand things in a special way."

"Oh yes, of course, but the difference is hardly noticeable. Oh, I'm just talking nonsense. Come, it's our turn to dance."

"Why haven't you ever played at our house?" Constance asked when they had resumed their places once again.

"Nobody asked me."

"I had no idea! That time I came to the ball at your parent's house, were you playing then?"

"Like other little boys who plunk away at the piano."

"Lorck never mentioned anything about it—he was the one who brought you to our house last year, do you remember?"

"Yes, but your husband invited me. I had been playing ombre with him at Lorck's."

"You could have dropped in by yourself just as well. Everybody else does it and so should you—you will come, won't you?"

"There is nothing on earth I would rather do. Thank you for being so kind."

"There's nothing to sigh about," Constance said looking at him curiously.

"Oh yes, because this will be over soon."

"Are you going abroad?"

"That's the idea."

"Then you must make good use of the time and come often. I'm looking forward to hearing you play."

"And I to talking with you."

"Take care, people get bored with me quickly."

"Now you're joking."

"No, truly! Just ask Fallesen."

"That fool," said Meier.

They were both silent for a moment. Meier bit his lip and gave her a quick uncertain look.

Constance reached into her pocket and drew out a glove, which dropped to the floor. Meier slowly picked it up. She extended her hand.

"Would you allow me to keep it?" he asked with a timid

look.

"Yes, of course—if you really want to."

He pressed the glove to his lips and tucked it under his vest.

Mrs. Blom came over to ask if they shouldn't leave soon. Aunt Wleügel had left long ago.

Constance immediately rose to say goodnight, and the others promptly followed suit.

Hansen protested; Marie said that they must all be frightfully bored if they were leaving so early. In actual fact it was past one o'clock.

"Let's have a farewell waltz," a voice called out, whereupon Ring's figure appeared in the blue-grey haze of the smoking room door.

"Good idea! We'll end with a waltz," cried several voices.

"In that case, may I have this dance?" Bowing to Constance was a young man with a black mustache and hair combed smoothly across his forehead. He was Hansen's youngest brother, and like him, a lawyer.

"Pound away, mother-in-law!" Ring continued, leading Mrs. Blom to the piano.

"No, mother is tired—I'll do it instead," said Constance.

But Marie had already sat down and begun to play.

"Now, by damn, I'm going to dance with my wife," Ring boomed, pushing his way towards Constance and bowing elaborately.

"Too late, my dear!" she cried as she danced away with the lawyer.

"Your foot, remember your foot," admonished Mrs. Blom, sitting despondently in the corner of a sofa.

Ring stood looking after Constance, with a silly, somewhat irritated smile.

"Well go ahead and dance with her, the rest of you—as much as you want—just dance, dance, dance," he said waving an arm. "After all, there's only one Edvard Christensen Ring, and that's me."

"I beg your pardon," said a woman sitting in a nearby chair.

"I said, there's only one Edvard Christensen Ring, and that's me."

38

"Yes that's true," she answered with a laugh. "Does anybody deny it?"

"Well whether they do or they don't, I just want to say that there's only one, just one . . . "

Drifting on, he rather belligerently delivered the same speech to Lorck, who was standing by the piano, and after that to Meier, who politely asked him to repeat what he had said.

Ring sauntered off without replying and continued his speech.

Suddenly he encountered Constance being led to her seat by her escort.

"Isn't that right?" he began. "There's only one Edvard Christensen Ring, and that's me—isn't that right?"

"Of course it's right," she answered with a forced laugh.

"Then you'll d-dance with me, too." His tongue was sticking slightly. "If you'll permit me," he said, bowing to Hansen.

Constance instantly stood up and Ring began dancing her around the room like a man possessed. In vain Constance resisted and begged him to stop, but he just grew more excited; her feet scarcely touched the floor. If anybody thought he'd had too much to drink, he'd show them they were mistaken. But somehow or other he stepped on Constance's dress, stumbled, swayed for a moment, flailing his arms as he tried to regain his balance, and then went crashing to the floor, pulling Constance down with him. Before anyone had time to help her she was up again, straightening her bows and flounces, answering their questions about whether she was hurt with a smiling, "Not a bit."

Hansen got a grip on Ring and hauled him to his feet. Marie had stopped playing and hurried into the room when she heard him fall.

"Aren't you going to play anymore?" Ring asked, puffing like a whale. "We aren't finished."

Marie hesitated.

"No, no," could be heard on all sides. "Time to go—stop while we're ahead."

"If you deny me your company, you'll be committing a crime against yourself as well as me," Fallesen said in a husky voice as Constance was putting on her wraps in the hall.

She burst out laughing and moved away from him. He stared after her with steely eyes.

Ring walked home with Mrs. Blom on his arm. He enlarged upon the comfort he found in knowing that there was only one Edvard Christensen Ring; he was the man who was married to Constance, and he was no more jealous than that walking stick. Mrs. Blom agreed with everything, thinking she would be just as giddy as Ring if he went on much longer.

Constance followed with Lorck and Meier. After the fall, her foot had begun to hurt again; they walked very slowly, Constance supporting herself on Lorck's arm.

Lorck asked if she had started reading *Madame Bovary*, which he had loaned to her, and their talk turned to French literature.

"I'm so sick of all these immoral women," Constance said. "They really ought to find a new subject."

"Immoral! Now what do you mean by that?" Lorck asked argumentatively.

"Promiscuous—unprincipled, if you prefer."

"Those words are completely meaningless—they're biased, stupid categories."

"Oh, when you start like that it's impossible to talk to you, Lorck. Is everything equally good or bad—are there no immoral women, then?"

"Yes, the ones who submit to loveless relationships."

"You don't know what you are talking about," she said angrily. "We've talked about this before—it's as if duty and respectability don't exist in your scheme of things."

"Your narrow-mindedness is exasperating. You are completely blinded by the old ideas about virtue and the like."

"So nothing is immoral or corrupt?"

"Not in itself. Suppose I have an affair with my brother's wife, for example, or I kill my father—it isn't *necessarily* a crime."

"Oh stop that disgusting nonsense."

"The value of every action is determined by motives and feelings," Lorck continued.

"Ah, naturally—there can't be any rules of conduct—that's much too inconvenient."

"Yes, we should pursue what is reasonable and useful."

"But when no two people have the same idea about what is reasonable and useful?" Constance asked, jabbing the pavement with her parasol. "What kind of world would it be!"

"Calm down," Lorck admonished. "The world could hardly be in a worse state than it is—even if things didn't improve, it would be worth the attempt."

"He's a terrible man—," Constance said, turning to Meier. "Don't let him influence you or you'll be utterly corrupted."

Lorck laughed.

"Oh there's no danger of that—he's far worse than I am."

"Do you hear that, Meier?"

"I don't know what Niels Lorck means by being worse than he is, but I certainly think our present social system is all wrong."

"And he holds Christianity responsible for everything. A greater blasphemer was never born of woman—except Lord Satan, perhaps—but then they say he didn't have a mother."

"Why does Christianity offend you?" Constance asked in a tone indicating that she expected very little satisfaction from the answer.

"Among other things, because it has taught people to lie to themselves and to other people—or at the very least, to pretend things are different than they really are."

"What do you mean?"

"The teachings aren't suitable for anybody except a bunch of fanatics who don't have any earthly interests. 'My kingdom is not of this world' is the creed they live by. And they've turned this into a world religion, pretending there's no discrepancy between their teachings and papal authority, monarchies, empires, majority rule, female emancipation, and God knows what else."

"But that's hardly the fault of Christianity."

"But what use is it then, if it can't be applied to anything that ever has been or shall be, without becoming ridiculous or offensive—I think it has degraded humanity to such a degree that . . . "

"How can you talk like that, Meier?"

"Because it has set up impossible demands and given them divine authority. So poor wretches have to pretend they're able to live up to them—or they're striving to—and then there's the final insult, the dogma of human frailty. How demoralizing!"

He broke off with a wave of his arm.

"I don't understand what you mean at all," Constance said.

"Well, for example, this—you'll have to forgive me—this commandment of chastity. In old Jehovah's day only unchaste acts were forbidden, but then along came Christianity and said, 'Whosoever looks at a woman, and so on.' Have you ever heard anything to beat it?"

"Well, what about it?"

"So people just gave up and thought to themselves, 'Your sin is exactly the same whether you commit the act or not.' Well nobody can avoid lust, and you might as well be hung for a sheep as a lamb—and so things developed the way they did."

"But do you think things were better before?"

"Yes, I do. The Jews, for example, are more moral to this day, and as far as sexual matters are concerned, they're much more restrained than Christians."

"Sodom and Gomorrah belonged to the Jews," Lorck said with a laugh.

"But that was a long time ago," said Constance thoughtfully.

"And take the concept of chastity itself," Lorck began, "for God's sake, a commandment that has never done anything but give pangs of conscience to poor wretches with weak brains and bad stomachs."

"For shame, Lorck."

"And lead a bunch of warped women to lay their vitality and joy in life, like blood money, on an altar raised to something hideously unnatural."

"What a disgusting thing to say," Constance said in a trembling voice, letting go of his arm.

"The ideas are all backwards—that's what I find disgusting,"

42

Lorck burst out.

"And what's more, it's a lie! I refuse to believe it—that all men are—No, I won't believe they're that base—it's impossible."

"I don't know of a single man who would thank you for that opinion," said Lorck.

"Then I feel very sorry for the men you know," Constance answered indignantly.

"Hurry up, my friends," shouted Ring, who had ushered in Mrs. Blom and was now waiting beside the front door.

"But anyway, as I said, I don't believe it, not a bit of it."

"What don't you believe, Constance?" Ring asked in an unsteady voice.

"Oh, nothing," she answered curtly. "Goodnight Lorck, goodnight Meier." Hurrying up the stairs, she encountered her mother in the hall.

"Constance, did you hear Ring and Lieutenant Fallesen saying 'du' to each other? Were they on such friendly terms before?"

"No; so now they're saying 'du'—yes, I can believe it."

They said goodnight and went to their own rooms.

Ring seemed especially inclined to chat; he went on assuring Meier of his warm friendship, earnestly imploring him to come visit them again. Finally, he invited them both up for a drink, which they declined.

"Come on," Lorck said, tugging at Meier, who had tried several times in vain to extricate himself from Ring's grip on his shoulder.

"You really must go up now, Uncle Edvard! Goodnight!"

"He got a little drunk tonight," Meier laughed, after they had turned the corner.

"Who? Oh him—the brute always gets drunk."

"It must not be much fun for his wife," Meier said.

"Pah! You can get used to anything."

"Do you think their marriage is happy?"

Lorck stopped. "That's a damned insulting question!"

"To you perhaps," Meier said, giving him a sideways look.

"A happy marriage! In the first place, how can you even utter such a phrase—that idiot!—Constance? Please!"

"Still, there is something appealing about him," Meier insisted. "He's so good-natured and full of fun."

"A brilliant fellow for a drinking or sailing companion—but otherwise, impossible. He's such an awful windbag."

"Is he a Conservative?"

"Well, of course, and he's a believer," Lorck laughed.

"You don't say? She must find him so boring."

"You can bet on that."

"It's a shame she didn't marry someone more compatible."

"Why would you want that? Then she wouldn't be any fun."

"Cynic," Meier mumbled absently.

"Anyhow, if she had a different husband she would get bored with him, too—that's what happens to married people."

"You think you have all the answers, Lorck."

"A woman like that . . . "

"She's beautiful," cried Meier.

"She's beautiful, all right, and a brilliant coquette."

"That's a black lie," Meier burst out. "I've never known a woman who was less a coquette."

Lorck started to whistle.

"She is so sincere and open—just like she was as a young girl—I remember her perfectly; she has no idea what men are like."

"So you're as far gone as that—by God, she managed it fast enough; I've got to hand it to her."

"Go to hell!" said Meier.

"Dammit, what are you getting so excited about? If people know you're in love with her, no one will accuse you of bad taste, at least. I've been in love with her for ages."

Meier made no reply.

"Have you told her?" Lorck asked

"Told her—told her what?"

"That you love her."

"The way you talk about Mrs. Ring is inappropriate, to put it mildly, old fellow."

"How many relationships with women have you had, Meier? I don't mean sluts—ladies."

44

"None," he snapped.

"Then try Mrs. Ring—I give you permission to compete."

"I'm telling you to shut up—I won't let you talk that way about a woman I know and respect." Meier was shaking with anger.

"Oh come on Meier, don't be such a dolt. Not a coquette, you say—today when we were all playing hide and seek, she and I were standing over behind the shed—she was listening and peeking out to look, her finger to her lips, and she was so close to me that I could feel her body—but the instant I responded, she was away like a shot, just as if we'd done it by accident."

"For her it was, I'd bet my life on it. How gross you are."

"A woman who's been married three years? No, old fellow, she wants to lead you on, get you all stirred up, and finally let herself be taken—basically it's a rather amusing game if it doesn't go on too long."

Meier felt like smashing him in the face, but knew he would just look ridiculous if he let his anger show.

"She's much too good to associate with someone like you," he said as calmly as he could manage. "That's all I have to say."

"She enjoys it just as much as I do—now she actually wants me to teach her to play ombre so we can have a regular evening game—last year we played chess. Not a coquette! The passion she invests in everything we do—conversations and all the rest— it's pure coquetry. Not a crude form, naturally."

"That's her nature—she gives herself to the spirit of the moment. She can do it because her mind is pure and unashamed—go on, laugh. One time she was playing cards with my sisters—she was grown up by then—I was watching from the next room—the joy and fun that lit up her face—she was absorbed with her whole soul, just like she is now."

"That's something quite different," Lorck replied, beginning to hum a snatch of melody.

"Isn't her husband ever jealous?" Meier asked.

"Ring, that idiot! Sometimes when he gets a few too many toddies under his belt, he tells me his wife is as cold as ice—she loves him just the same, though, nobody else but him."

"Do you think she knows he talks like that?"

"Of course she does. Cold! She's pure fire—all feelings—a volcano covered with plush green grass. My God, when she erupts! But it galls me just the same that she's got to have everybody at her feet, with no exceptions. That idiot Fallesen—hasn't she been driving him wild?"

"Do you want to come up for a cigar?" Lorck had stopped outside his house.

Meier appeared to hesitate.

"No, on second thought—I forgot, dammit—what time is it?"

"Half past two," Meier said.

"She'll be in a lovely mood, I'm sure," Lorck muttered. "Goodnight."

"Goodnight," said Meier and took his leave.

He walked on thinking about Constance. When he was nineteen, he had been in love with her. It had begun the evening his father allowed him to lead off the first dance of the ball with her. She had been so friendly, talked to him so freely about life in Molde, singling him out several times to dance the figures with her. Dear God, how crazy about her he had been—lying awake in bed at night writing poetry, leaping up to jot down the verses, inventing the wildest strategems for getting near her. He only wanted to fling himself at her feet, to be allowed to kiss the hem of her dress—then he would immediately go away and kill himself. God, the days he'd spent walking the streets near her house, wearing his tobacco-colored gloves, a cigar clamped in his mouth. Once he had rung her front door bell and fled like a madman when he heard the chime. Far into the spring he had nursed this passion, nourished it by greeting her on the street, seeing her at the theater, once even walking her home from a women's party at his sister's house.

Then out of the blue, the announcement of her engagement to Ring had arrived. Like a clenched fist, it smashed down the finely woven cobweb of his dream; the unexpected blow had shaken him so severely that he ran off to Frognerseter. He had wandered through the forest on a piercingly cold spring night, thinking about how best to kill himself. Battered by the wind, nearly frozen, he dragged himself home the next morning, and sick and exhausted, spent more than a month in bed.

"Poor fellow, those were bad times," he muttered to himself, "and on top of everything else, you barely passed your examinations."

Surely this sickness wasn't going to break out again now—it would have been better not to have seen her, even though he was leaving soon—just as well that he was leaving—the sooner the better. But, oh God, how lovely she was—the way she listened with her head tilted slightly, her eyelids lowered, and then when she answered, and suddenly looked right at him. A hot current seemed to leap from those eyes—it was enough to drive him mad. And when she was sitting quietly by herself—serious, almost gloomy—and her glance suddenly brushed against a face gazing at hers—that smile—so gentle, fine, and calm—it positively glowed with goodness.

A coquette—her! That pig Lorck ought to be beaten. And Ring—what kind of husband was he for her! He was so utterly melancholy, so gloomy and brooding. Constance seemed so unprotected, so exposed to filthy attacks from every side—oh, if only she were his, he would carry her through life in his arms, pressed against his heart, cherished and guarded like a treasure, to the most beautiful spot on the earth.

"Constance, Constance Blom—why aren't you mine?" He felt a prickling sensation in his nose; it tingled and stung.

"God help me, here I am crying," he mumbled, taking a handkerchief out of his pocket. "What a fool I am."

5

Everyone slept late at the Rings' the next morning. It was nearly ten when Constance appeared in the dining room, where she found Mrs. Blom reading on the sofa.

"I'm so sleepy," Constance said with a yawn. "I thought I'd never get my eyes open today. Have you been up long, Mother?"

"Oh no, I stayed in bed until almost nine."

Shortly afterwards, Ring came in. His eyes were bloodshot and the pupils duller than usual. With an abashed look at each of them, he said good morning and sat down at the breakfast table, where a newspaper was waiting beside his plate.

"Your mother should go see *The Robbers*,"[6] he said with his mouth full of eggs and French bread. "A full house every night."

"Tivoli is a rather vulgar place, isn't it?" Mrs. Blom asked.

"Not the theater, mother."

"You see the best people in the city there, for that matter— really now, my dear Constance—how can you allow the cheese to be mutilated like that."

"It must have been Alette; we always slice it nicely in here, of course."

"Then you should speak to her about it—it's very unattractive."

"My goodness Ring, you've caught a cold," Mrs. Blom said sympathetically.

"It's nothing," he said, his eyes on the newspaper.

"He's often a little hoarse in the morning. It clears up during the day," said Constance.

"More fraud at the bank—those damned directors. . . . "

48

Ring went into the adjacent room to get his pipe.

"Shall I get tickets for this evening?"

"To *The Robbers*? Well, it's up to you, Mother."

"Shouldn't we just have a quiet evening tonight? We've been rushing around so much."

"All right, tomorrow then," Ring proposed, moving his coffee cup to the table beside the sofa and sitting down.

"We've been invited out, don't you remember?"

"And Friday we're going to the theater," said Mrs. Blom.

"What about Saturday?"

"We aren't going anywhere Saturday."

"So we'll say Saturday, then."

"Bring the tobacco box when you come, Constance," Ring asked, as Constance went to get the evening paper.

"Give me your pipe and I'll fill it," she said, taking it out of his hand. "I know how."

Ring stared after her in gratitude.

"Isn't Constance looking well these days? She's as radiant as the sun—and so beautiful! When we got married, she was nothing compared to now." He rubbed his hands together with satisfaction. "And she's so affectionate—it's astonishing."

"Yes, thank heavens," said Mrs. Blom.

"We're sitting here congratulating ourselves about you," he said when Constance returned. "Actually, we agreed you're just a shadow of your former self."

"Ah well," she said, handing him the filled pipe, "that's too bad for me."

"Thank you, my darling," he beamed, pulling her down on his knee. She placed one hand on his shoulder; he seized the other one and kissed it.

Constance stared dreamily in front of her.

This was what it meant to be a happy wife—or rather, this was how a happy wife behaved. And there was the happy wife's mother, rejoicing that her daughter was so adored. A quiet pleasure came over her, and she slipped into the fantasy that she was happy, that she was in love—but she felt so far away from it all—in another world. A buried childhood memory rose before her—a woman in a grey silk suit with an ostrich feather in her hat was sitting on the veranda at home, drinking raspberry juice and soda from a wine glass. Her accent was unfamiliar and she was talking about another woman, criticizing her. And then the words came that Constance remembered so distinctly, "So I wrote and told her: don't complain about being alone with the man who loves you more than anything in the world because that's paradise itself."

But what if she wasn't in love? Constance thought.

Ring's lips moved up her neck to her ear, her cheek, her mouth. She closed her eyes so that she could continue the dream of the happy wife, but a gnawing disgust gripped her. She would not let it show—it would be a pity when Ring was so happy—of course he would never understand—and there was her mother to consider.

"Aren't you going to the office today?" she asked, tweaking his ear.

"With a wife like you, who could think about going to the office?

"Here comes the itty-bitty mouse ... " he began, as if he were dandling a baby on his lap.

Constance swatted away his fingers.

"And what do you suppose your assistant is thinking?"

"My assistant can go to Hell—here comes an itty-bitty mouse mouse—we must remember to invite him over sometime—he'll appreciate that."

"What are my little girls going to do this morning?" he asked when he was finally standing with his hat and walking stick, preparing to leave.

"Little girls! Oh Ring, Ring," laughed Mrs. Blom.

"If only we don't have any company, we can read to each other," said Constance. "It's taking forever to get through 'The Woman from Tjele.'"[7]

"Well, well, be good girls now, and I'll bring you something nice when I come home." He threw them a kiss and left.

During the afternoon Constance lay on a sofa in her sitting room, a compress on her foot. Although it had been painful since morning, she had not wanted to admit it. Finally Mrs.

Blom told her she was limping and insisted that she would look at it herself. Upon examination the ankle appeared stiff and swollen.

All three took long naps on their sofas after dinner, and they had coffee in Constance's sitting room, as usual. Ring had gone back to his office, and darkness was beginning to fall.

Mrs. Blom sat in an armchair by the window, knitting.

"Would you like the lamps lit, Constance?" she asked.

There was no answer.

"Well my goodness, she's fallen asleep again," chuckled Mrs. Blom listening to her quiet breathing.

Putting down her knitting, she settled herself comfortably in the chair. She had dropped a stitch and could not see well enough to pick it up again.

In a moment the doorbell rang.

"Well who could that be?" she murmured.

"What did you say, mother?" Constance asked, instantly wide awake.

"Ah, to be able to sleep as soundly as you, child." Constance smiled. It was one of her mother's quirks to imagine that she suffered from insomnia.

"Yes, go right in, the mistress and Mrs. Blom are home," they heard Alette say as the door to the living room opened.

Mrs. Blom went out to greet the visitor.

"Oh it's you, Marie," she said cheerfully, patting her on the shoulder. Her initial greeting had been delivered in the formal tone used with strangers.

"Constance? An invalid, of course—just as I expected."

"Please come in here, I can't hear what you're saying," Constance called out.

Mrs. Blom lit the lamps in both rooms, and placed a large silver-plated lamp on a small table covered with bronze velvet next to Constance's chaise longue.

"Take off your coat and sit with us for awhile, Marie," said Constance.

"Frankly, I had planned to, but since you aren't well . . . "

"Please do, it doesn't matter if I'm lying in here instead of sitting in a chair."

"But Rikard is coming, too."

"Well let him—he's welcome, as long as he doesn't get cantankerous and insist I wait on him hand and foot."

"Oh you!" Marie laughed, taking off her wrap.

"My goodness, there's somebody else," said Mrs. Blom. They could hear Marie speaking to someone in the hall, where she had gone to hang up her wrap. In a moment she returned with Mrs. Wleügel.

"Good evening, Aunt, do take off your coat—you're planning to stay, I hope," Constance called in to her.

"So you had to give in today," said her aunt, shaking her head. "We were right, you see—it was foolish to dance. Has the doctor been here?"

"No Aunt, that's ridiculous! It's nothing at all. I assure you, the only reason I'm lying here is to please Mother. You're late coming in from the country."

"I took the noon train—I'll spend the night in town."

Mrs. Wleügel had scarcely seated herself when the bell rang again.

"We certainly are social tonight, aren't we?" Constance said, listening.

"Mr. Lorck is asking if anyone is home," whispered Alette, after closing the door carefully behind her.

"Of course we're home," Constance said, "just ask him to come in. What's wrong, Mother?" She turned toward Mrs. Blom who was vigorously shaking her head.

"Good evening," Lorck said and bowed to them. "What's this?—a sick room, with visitors and medicines and all the rest?"

"Oh it's just a little compress for my foot," Constance said.

"Is this really from your fall yesterday? It's not worse, is it?"

"Her whole ankle is swollen," said Mrs. Blom. "Of course—what else could we expect?"

"Let me take a look—you can't be sure that a compress is the right thing," Lorck said, approaching her.

Constance immediately agreed.

"It isn't necessary," Mrs. Blom said, stepping between them. "When there's no puncture a compress is fine. I'm doctor enough for her."

"Just as you wish—don't want to brag about my medical skills—but I am a medical student, after all, and that ought to count for something."

"Sit down Lorck," said Constance. "When Ring and Hansen get here you can all play ombre."

Lorck shook hands with Marie and thanked her for her hospitality the evening before. They all began reminiscing about the previous day, reliving a multitude of little things they had not had time to appreciate at the moment, but which now seemed all the more amusing.

"Shh—there's the bell," Constance said suddenly.

"Surely that must be Rikard," Marie said, looking at her watch.

"Be quiet so we can hear who it is," Constance said, putting her fingers to her mouth.

"Not a sound," Lorck whispered.

"No, I'm sure nobody rang," said Mrs. Blom.

"Shh, shh—you heard it this time, surely?" Constance said triumphantly when the bell rang immediately afterwards, loudly, as though someone were tired of waiting.

"Why doesn't Alette open it?"

"Maybe she's gone out to get something for supper," whispered Mrs. Blom, rising.

"No, let Lorck go, mother; his legs are younger than yours."

Lorck was already at the door.

"Are we home?" he asked in a low voice, coming a few steps back into the room.

"That depends on who it is," answered Constance. "Leave the door open and we'll signal if we want them to come in."

The others laughed softly.

"It's Meier," Marie called back into the sitting room. She was listening from the middle of the living room.

"Meier can come in," Constance called out, so they could hear her in the hall. "Free passage for Meier!"

"Free passage for Meier!" Marie repeated, laughing.

"Wait a minute while I change the compress," Mrs. Blom

said, bending over Constance's foot.

"There now—it's all right to come in," she added immediately afterward, smoothing the afghan over her.

"Did he make any trouble?" Constance asked with a glance at Lorck, when Meier had greeted everyone and taken a place in the semi-circle around the chaise longue.

"I can't deny it," Meier answered with a smile.

"I had to wait for the password," Lorck said.

"But Meier was with us yesterday, as you know very well. You wouldn't dare turn him away!"

"Oh, there, it's ringing again."

"This time, I'm sure it must be Rikard," Marie said, and in a moment it was clear that she was right.

"What did Alette ask you, Mother?"

"She wants to know how many places to set. Ring has arrived and he has somebody with him—she says they're out in the hall."

"See if you can hear who it is, Lorck," said Constance.

Lorck started to get up but Meier was on his feet before him.

"It's Fallesen—I'd swear to it," Lorck said.

"Oh no, don't swear," implored Mrs. Wleügel.

"You're quite right—I can hear it's the Lieutenant," Meier said as he returned.

At that moment the door opened and Ring and Fallesen walked in.

"Won't you please sit down again, Meier," Constance said impatiently, pointing to the chair closest to her, "otherwise Fallesen will sit there."

Like lightning, Meier slipped into the chair.

"Just what I like to see," Ring said after greeting his guests. "What a pleasant gathering! Why are you filling up on that punch—come in to my study and we'll have something else."

"But let's have tea first," Constance objected.

Ring set out cigars and ashtrays on the table in the study, then began rummaging through the buffet, placing brandy, soda, and glasses on a large tray.

At the supper table, Mrs. Blom poured the tea and fixed

some food for Constance; both Meier and Lorck wanted to carry it in to her, but Mrs. Blom assured them she could do it very well herself. They all went in the end, taking their own food with them.

"You forgot the salt," Constance cried, and instantly Fallesen appeared with it.

"If only somebody could tell me what they want, these radicals, this motley bunch of riffraff," Hansen said, continuing the argument from supper in Constance's sitting room.

"Yes, if only somebody could," Marie seconded.

"I've never been able to get anybody to tell me that," Hansen went on; he rocked back and forth on his heels, gripping the back of an armchair with both hands, making it move with him.

"I can well believe it," Lorck said ironically.

"Oh, why is that?" asked Marie.

"Your husband's terminology is so crude that it's impossible to argue with him," Lorck replied in an aggrieved tone.

Constance and Meier started to laugh.

"Well, what would you call people whose only interest in life is to break down respect for—well, for the status quo," Hansen said heatedly.

"That's exactly right," Ring said. "They do nothing but tear down the monarchy and every other kind of authority. The poor King wouldn't hurt a fly—it's a rotten business."

"By heaven, that's the truth," Fallesen said. "Well said, Ring!"

"And religion," Marie put in, "—that's the worst part of it."

"Yes, because that undermines everything," murmured Mrs. Wleügel.

"And corrupts both the soul and the body," added Mrs. Blom.

"Authority?" Lorck said. "How, may I ask, can you, a lawyer for the High Court, not regard the Storting[8] as the legal authority?"

"The Storting?" Hansen repeated uncertainly.

"And who is it who is working to undermine respect for that?" Lorck asked.

"The way the Storting is constituted now, it doesn't deserve respect," Hansen retorted.

"There is no authority except that ordained by God, according to the Bible," Meier interjected.

"Well in those days, they didn't have these kinds of institutions, dammit! Do you really suppose they thought about this egalitarian deviltry then?" Ring exclaimed. "That's a little far-fetched."

"They certainly didn't have a High Court either," cried Constance.

"Don't take their side," admonished Mrs. Blom.

"A loyal citizen can feel nothing but contempt for the Storting, the way it's constituted now," Hansen said forcefully, rocking back and forth in increasing excitement.

"Heavens no," said Marie.

"That's what the Conservatives think, and they behave accordingly," Lorck answered. "But then they shouldn't fault the Left when it acts according to its convictions."

"The Left!" Ring exclaimed. "No, there's a difference, dammit."

"Everything the Left wants is fundamentally destructive to society. My God—if they get power . . . " Hansen said, rolling his eyes toward the ceiling.

"What's destructive? Give me an example," asked Meier.

"Shut up, blockhead," muttered Lorck, "don't answer those idiots."

"Well take this business about the cabinet ministers, for example," Hansen lectured. "If they get that passed, it means the overthrow of the whole constitution, nothing more, nothing less."

"Well, then we can just make a new one," said Lorck, sitting down.

"Just put them to work on it—all those yokels down in the Storting—a fine mess they'd make of that," Hansen said angrily.

"God help us if it goes that far!" Ring burst out. "Oh no, they'll soon burn themselves out; the party has put its clubfoot forward too often—the country is frightened. Next time it will be the Conservatives all down the line, you'll see."

Lorck and Meier laughed.

"That's a rash prophecy," Lorck said.

"Which will come to pass, you'll see," Hansen assured them. "It will happen just the way that rabble-rouser said. When the farmers wake up, they'll wake up as reactionaries."

"That rabble-rouser?" Constance asked. "Who is he talking about?"

"Bjørnson,[9] of course."

"Oh him!" Mrs. Wleügel said with a grimace that was mirrored by Marie and Mrs. Blom.

"They are taking their time about it in any case," said Meier.

"About what? Oh, waking up—yes, it's a pity that these poor farmers are so easy to lead around by the nose, but once their eyes are opened. . . . " Hansen looked up at the ceiling again.

"Well you have to feel sorry for the farmers, but Sverdrup[10] and Jaabaek[11]—to think that the law can't punish those—those . . ." Ring paused, groping for the word.

"Those who *know* what they're doing—whose very purpose is to destroy this country," supplied Hansen. "If they aren't scoundrels, I don't know who is."

Lorck whistled softly and lit a cigar.

"How can you bring yourself to use such abusive terms about political opponents, Counselor?" Meier flared. "Educated people ought to have some conception of a man with honorable convictions."

"Don't give me that honorable convictions business," bellowed Ring. "We have justice and truth on our side—that's what it comes down to."

"And the testimony of history, the judgments of the courts, the institutions of law—everything that upholds our society," continued Hansen.

"And I must say," Ring said, having regained his breath, "that I didn't imagine even the most crackbrained left-winger was bold enough to deny that *Sverdrup*, at least, is a scoundrel."

Lorck burst out laughing.

Furious, Meier was going to respond, but just at that moment he met Constance's eyes; she hurriedly put a finger to her lips.

"And you might as well include all the rest of them," said Hansen. "Fellows like Bjørnson and Brun[12] and their cronies ought to be sent into exile, at the very least."

"They're the ones who get people all stirred up," Marie said.

"Yes, by heaven—and undermine things everywhere you turn," Hansen said eagerly.

"And that Bjørnson—that beggars' pope who even wants to take the people's faith away," Ring burst out, taking a quick turn around the table. "I ask you, what harm does faith do anyone?"

"He wrote *The King*,[13] after all—" Fallesen put in, "what else would you expect from a traitor like that?"

"But suppose what you believe is wrong?" Meier interrupted.

"Who says it's wrong?" Ring flared. "Even if some things aren't clear to us, a man can't expect to understand the supernatural, can he? The Bible says that our minds are in darkness. And where can we turn, I ask you, when things go wrong, if Our Lord doesn't exist? No, Meier, old fellow, we can't do away with God—you're young still, but just wait until you're older."

"Yes, heaven knows," sighed Mrs. Blom.

"There has to be something beyond human criticism," said Hansen with quiet dignity, "something that holds things together, so to speak, both what we see and what we can't see— and if a man starts digging around there—well, then everything gives way beneath our feet."

"And when we die," Ring continued in a lower voice, "I think it must be good to be able to lie down in Jesus' name and hope that something better is waiting for us beyond."

"Oh yes indeed," sighed Mrs. Wleügel.

"Not just that—" Marie said, "imagine going through life without the support of religion. I don't see how some people bear it. The poor, for instance... By heaven, I'm sure Bjørnson is one of the anti-Christs in the Bible."

"That's what makes me so furious," Ring said. "Let's hope the Lord takes him quickly."

"It's the Devil who's taken him," Hansen muttered.

Lorck got up suddenly and flicked the ash off his cigar.

"Well, as far as I'm concerned, he can be taken any time at all," he said.

"You don't mean it," Marie exclaimed.

"In my opinion, he's not radical enough."

"Well, I never," Mrs. Wleügel and Mrs. Blom said at the same time.

"Not one of them amounts to anything," Lorck continued. "What do they want—some paltry reforms that they hardly have the courage to put forward—when everything really has to be rebuilt from the ground up."

"Oh fine, and then what?—*dann hört alles auf*,"[14] Hansen said contemptuously.

"Do you want a revolution, then?" Marie asked.

"Yes, why not? That maneuvering down in number 22 isn't getting us anywhere."[15]

"You should go to Russia, Lorck," Hansen said. "You'll do better there."

"Become a nihilist," added Marie.

"Well, it's not a bad idea," Lorck replied laconically.

"Surely you're not going to defend the nihilists, too?" Marie asked in horror.

"Him!" Ring exclaimed with a laugh. "Do you think *he* balks at anything?"

"The nihilists—the greatest martyrs of the human race—the world's most noble martyrs," cried Lorck.

"The fellow has taken leave of his senses," Hansen said to no one in particular.

"I have nothing against the nihilists," remarked Meier, "but I haven't any real faith in the principle itself, since its source is the Bible."

"I think you're both possessed by the Devil," Ring said.

"If you don't mind, may I ask the grounds for that nonsense about a Biblical source?" Hansen asked with a contemptuous smile.

"What about the flood, for example, Counselor? Jehovah was history's first and most powerful nihilist, as far as I can tell."

A general cry of surprise and indignation stopped him.

"He found conditions on earth deplorable," Meier went on, "he wasn't satisfied with the way they were running things, and so he swept away the people and animals and everything else on earth. Isn't that nihilistic, I ask you?"

"Even though the Bible says that everything God made was very good," Lorck interrupted.

"Well, that was just irony, of course," Meier remarked.

"How can you raise such an issue!" cried Hansen. "The punishment that the Almighty was forced to send upon the earth because of man's depravity—see here, if this is a joke, it's in very poor taste—to put it mildly."

"My goodness, I won't let you quarrel any longer," Constance cried out suddenly, sitting upright. "What a disagreeable mood you're all getting into."

"Lorck started it," Marie said.

"Oh no, it was our counselor here," Meier objected.

"I think it was Ring," Fallesen said.

"Now everybody be quiet so we can hear what Constance is saying," Ring cried.

"You and Hansen play whist with Marie and Fallesen," Constance instructed. "Meier will play for us, and mother and Aunt Wleügel can fend for themselves."

"I have to go home soon," remarked Mrs. Wleügel.

"But Cousin Lorck, Constance, what are we going to do with him?" Ring asked.

"That wicked rascal? I'll keep an eye on him. If he gets in among the rest of you he'll just make mischief."

"Brilliant," said Ring. "Come on now, to the right, march!" he commanded.

"Ring has such a sense of humor," Mrs. Wleügel said to her sister as they sat in the living room knitting. "Always so good natured and cheerful."

"Yes, there's nobody like him," answered Mrs. Blom. "But I do wish he would forbid Lorck and Meier to engage in such unpleasant conversations. Constance shouldn't hear such things."

"Surely they don't mean anything by it—I think they're just showing off."

"Well heaven knows, young people are supposed to be such free thinkers," Mrs. Blom sighed.

"That's why I was so happy when Constance married Ring, you know. I saw right away that he was a man who respected religion. You remember, I wrote to you about it."

"Yes, Ring has kept his childlike faith."

"Well, thank heaven—both Constance and Marie have been lucky in that respect."

"It's especially good for Constance," Mrs Blom remarked in a worried tone. "She needs the support."

"Surely you don't mean she's been infected by these new-fangled ideas?"

"Heavens no! But sometimes she sounds so far to the Left—she sat here with Lorck the other day, making wisecracks about Job—they said Satan had made a bet with God for his soul, like Mephistopheles and Faust. Why, that's blasphemous."

"And she was so devout when she was confirmed," sighed Mrs. Wleügel.

"Well, that was too much of a good thing—lying in bed, praying and singing hymns to herself—I listened at the door—and once when I spoke to her about it, she fell into my arms and sobbed like a child, in despair, she said, because she didn't feel close to God. A child of sixteen—it was absolutely dreadful."

"But then it passed, of course, when she came down to stay with me. That was a lucky idea. Although such things usually don't last," said Mrs. Wleügel.

"No, thank heaven—what a dreadful time that was. Imagine, she was running to Bible readings and services, and even to the most ordinary prayer meetings. You can guess the state her father was in . . . "

"Hansen always says that people who go overboard with religion are hypocrites and scoundrels."

"Well, that's nonsense," interrupted Mrs. Blom.

"Exactly what I was going to say," Mrs. Wleügel said eagerly.

"But to get so overwrought—well, it was utter madness."

"Still, it's odd, isn't it," Mrs. Wleügel demurred, "that the Bible tells us to prepare for our salvation with eternal fear and trembling. It's a very important matter, you see."

"But the Bible also says to rejoice always," Mrs. Blom said with conviction. "Jesus himself went to weddings, and Luther took part in dancing and other things—so you see, Birgitte, there are many passages for us to follow."

"But it's not always so easy," answered Mrs. Wleügel. "As soon as we make the mistake of thinking for ourselves, we start going in circles—I do, at least."

"But then there are the words about making reason captive and obedient to faith, Birgitte."

"You have always been so pious, Emma. Dear me, we're just mortals after all—one must do what's right."

"Oh play some more!" Constance cried out when Meier showed signs of rising from the piano.

The piano was in the living room, diagonally across from the sitting room door. Constance could see the keyboard and the pianist's head and chest. Whenever she looked in that direction she encountered Meier's glance. At her request, he immediately began to play something else.

"Oh, Lorck," Constance asked, "change the lampshade, will you? Get the large red one from the buffet—this one is so short the light hurts my eyes."

"Little slam," Marie cried and came running into the sitting room. "Fallesen and I are having such good luck! What are you two doing?"

"Listening to the music, mainly," Constance said.

"And learning about spadille, manille, and ponto," Lorck added, a hand of cards spread out on the small table between Constance and himself.

"It's our turn now, Marie," Hansen called.

A few minutes later Mrs. Wleügel began making preparations to leave. "Now, you be careful with that foot, Constance.

I still have trouble with that ankle I sprained years ago. The doctor wants me to use a cane. Good-night, good-night."

"Go in and be the fifth, Mother," Constance said when her mother had seen her sister to the door. "You're so fond of whist. Ring! Mother will be the fifth."

"Well, Hansen says the party's over," he called back, then appeared at the door. "I can't get them to start a new rubber, the spoilsports."

Hansen and Marie said good night. Fallesen and Meier appeared to be following their example.

"What the Devil, there's no need to rush off," Ring said, pulling the Lieutenant back to the card table. "It's still early."

Mrs. Blom followed Marie out into the hall and helped her with her wraps.

"It was a good thing we played cards," Marie said. "I could see Ring was very upset. It's terrible the way Lorck talks."

"It just amazes me that men like him are accepted in society," Mrs. Blom answered.

"People are talking about all the time Ring lets Constance spend with him—let me tell you, his principles are as loose on the subject of love as everything else. And he writes in *Dagbladet*."[16]

"He's invited to your home as well, Marie," Mrs. Blom said somewhat stiffly.

"Very seldom, Aunt—just to really large parties—Ring and Constance brought him along yesterday."

"But he and Ring are related, you see."

"Oh pooh, it's not that! No, it's because he's amusing. All the women are ga-ga about him. It's disgraceful, really."

"They're talking about Constance, you say." Mrs. Blom looked thoughtful. "Actually it's Ring who always wants him around."

"Well, he wants everybody, Aunt."

"Constance doesn't really care whether he comes or not," Mrs. Blom went on.

"But people don't know that, you see. We know it, my goodness—but considering how much those two are together—well, it's nothing new that people will talk."

Hansen came in after going to get a cigar.

"Good night, Aunt."

"Good night, good night."

"Tonight was nothing," Mrs. Blom heard Constance saying as she came into the living room. "No, when Reverend Huhn is around, you can just imagine . . . "

"Really! Do you see a lot of him?" Lorck interrupted.

"Whenever they have really special dinners—he's the minister, after all. She quotes from the *Lutheran Weekly*—Hansen subscribes to all those things, of course. Then they cut loose on all the empty rhetoric of the day—the spread of free thought, people adrift in a sea of disbelief—Marie knows all the catchwords by heart."

"So they're as God fearing as all that down on Welhavensgate," Lorck said, "I didn't realize it."

"Oh yes, Hansen goes to church with Marie—every other Sunday in the winter . . . But this is the funniest part: whenever Marie is expecting, he gives fifty kroner to the poor," Constance said with a laugh.

Mrs. Blom stood up abruptly and went into the living room.

"Now we've made Mother angry. Good heavens, that's terrible," Constance said softly, with a look of utter bewilderment.

"What do you expect when you talk like that," Lorck asked in an equally subdued tone.

"You're the one! Wasn't it you? Meier, it was Lorck, wasn't it?"

"No, it was the business about Marie expecting that did it. I wouldn't dare talk like that, even around my father," Meier asserted.

Constance made a face at him.

Shortly afterwards, Lorck went in to Mrs. Blom; she was looking at an illustrated book.

"I expect you'll be glad to see us leave, Mrs. Blom," he said with an ingratiating smile.

"Oh don't hurry on my account," she answered without lifting her eyes. "But Constance is tired, I imagine."

64

"Pretty pictures. . . . " He began turning the pages for her.

"Just listen to Lorck," Constance whispered. "He's trying to wheedle his way into Mother's good graces again. She doesn't like him very much, by the way."

"But what about you?" Meier gave her a searching glance: she noticed it with a vague feeling of curiosity and astonishment.

"Oh yes, of course," she replied, "he amuses me."

"A lucky man. . . . "

"We'd better go, Meier. The sweet talk isn't working; Mrs. Blom is resolute," Lorck said from the doorway, looking like a submissive schoolboy.

Mrs. Blom had to laugh in spite of herself.

"Then please take Fallesen with you," Constance remarked, "or he'll never leave."

When the guests had all left, Mrs. Blom cleared away the glasses and cards.

"Is Lorck going to the Grimsgaards tomorrow?" she asked suddenly, glancing at Constance.

"I really don't know, Mother," was the indifferent reply.

"You ought to be a little more careful, Constance," Mrs. Blom said. "You're much too free in your conversations with these young pups. The way they look at you, the way they trot along after you—oh, I'd like to smack them."

Constance laughed.

"It's not funny, Constance. You're not behaving the way you should; you actually seem to enjoy it when they flirt with you."

"Oh, Mother, really!"

"That kind of thing can easily lead to trouble. There's always the risk they'll fall in love with you."

"Oh no, Mother, it's nothing like that. That's just how they are—for some reason they seem to think it's expected."

Mrs. Blom shook her head.

"You can't be too careful, Constance."

"It doesn't mean the slightest thing, I assure you. They behave exactly the same with all the women. It would be conceited and disgusting if I took it as anything more than a game. And I am married, after all, Mother," she added sleepily.

Mrs. Blom looked worried.

"Men have been known to fall in love with married women, you know."

"But not the kind of men I know. Love requires something a little more serious, Mother."

"If for no other reason than the gossip, you should be careful, Constance. People will talk about you."

"Well, that's my concern. Besides, I don't believe it—Ring is always with me."

"Ring?" There was suddenly a slight quaver in her voice. "He sits there with his tobacco and his whiskey and lets them swarm around you all they please. I don't understand him."

"There's absolutely no reason for him to be jealous," Constance said with a yawn.

"But take yesterday, Constance—he let you walk with Lorck and Meier, just as if you didn't have a husband to go with you. It doesn't look right."

"Lorck and Meier were going in the same direction, Mother," Constance yawned. "It was perfectly reasonable."

"The Meiers live out near Frogner Park, and Lorck's parents also live in the country," Mrs. Blom said vigorously.

"Well, at least this winter they go the same way," Constance yawned. "Besides, Lorck has a room in town. And you know Ring had all he could do to take care of himself."

"Well, you do let him drink too much," Mrs. Blom said crossly.

"Let him?"

"Yes, I'm sure you could stop him if you were just a little bit tactful."

"You told me I shouldn't go around sulking because he's had a few drinks," Constance said, sounding as if she wished the whole issue would go away. "That's the surest way to drive him off the deep end, you said. It was that first evening, do you remember?"

"I don't mean scold him. And as I said, I'm not worried at all about Ring—he's a man of principles, after all—but you could try to influence him, talk about it privately—lovingly."

Suddenly there was the sound of loud snoring.

Mrs. Blom jumped, but Constance laughed. "It's just Ring. He's fallen asleep. Listen to how soundly he's sleeping."

"I'm going in to wake him," Mrs. Blom said, getting up.

"Leave the man in peace."

"No! What if the maid came in and saw him—and it's bad for his health."

"Oh it doesn't hurt him—he's drunk again, of course," Constance said. She was tired and bored. They all made her sick: her mother, Lorck, Meier, Marie, Hansen, her aunt—every single person she knew—and the ombre, the party tomorrow, the paintings on the wall—everything—everything in the world.

Drawing her clenched hands to her breast, she sighed deeply.

Then something she had dreamed the night before popped into her mind. It was all so life-like and clear. There was an oak coffin in the dining room and she was lying inside it, dressed in her nightgown with the ruffled collar, a sheet pulled half-way up her breast. The lifeless hair stuck queerly to the sallow temples, and the eyebrows looked artificial—as if each hair were stuck in wax. The lips were blackish and behind them white teeth were faintly visible. The hands were so tiny, and blue-white; they stuck out horribly from the pleated, lace-trimmed sleeves. But the eyes were what she remembered most—they were not completely shut; the pupils stared into the room, rigid and lifeless. People she didn't know were standing around the coffin, crying. One of them said, "Look how peacefully she's lying there—like a child, asleep." And she had felt herself standing among them, watching, while at the same time she was lying there dead. She could come to life again if she really wanted to, but she did not—it was good to be dead.

"My goodness, Constance, is anything wrong? Are you ill?" Mrs. Blom was suddenly bending over her.

Constance threw her arms around her mother's neck and pressed her face against her.

"No Mother, I was just thinking . . . "

"But you are crying, child—what's come over you?"

"I had an odd dream last night—I'll tell you about it tomor-row."

6

THE DAY OF MRS. BLOM'S departure arrived at last. As Constance was helping her pack, she realized with a feeling of desolation that now she was going to be alone with Ring again.

Her mother's presence had filled the void—not her inner emptiness—but still, they had enjoyed themselves together, and the constant activity had been a distraction. She had been a daily stimulant for Constance. There were times when the superficial character their relationship had assumed pained her a little; it was depressing to feel that without this constant activity they would not find anything to say to each other. Occasionally at such moments her mother's presence had seemed a burden and Constance had almost wished she were gone.

But now that the time had come, she realized with horror how lonely she was going to be. She knew perfectly well that her mother had to leave, but she wept bitterly while they were saying good-bye and pleaded with her to stay just one more day.

She had seen her to the ship, and now, sitting at her old spot in the bedroom, gazed out over the fjord in the direction that her mother had gone.

She felt so bereft, so bitterly alone.

Her mother was travelling toward home, where life had been so safe and happy, where just being alive had seemed sufficient in itself, and nothing in the world had been dull or difficult.

It was this fatal marriage that had put her at odds with herself and everything else. Why in the world had she gotten married? What for? And to Ring, of all people—an unappealing man with whom she could never be in harmony.

She left the window and paced up and down the room, moaning softly and monotonously.

Was her life always going to be like this—until she was old, old, old—never free to be herself again? What if he died—oh, but he wasn't going to—there was nothing wrong with him— an accident, in the sailboat perhaps—oh, how could she think such a thing—where was her shame!

Worn out by pacing, she sat down on a settee and leaned back against the wall, her arms crossed on her breast. The moon was full, and the room was so light that every object could be seen distinctly.

If only her mother would come in through the door, just one more time—she would throw her arms around her neck and cry, cry until this frozen crust around her heart melted away. She would tell her she wasn't happy, that she never would be—no matter how much they tortured her—that she didn't feel, would never feel, it was her duty and her calling to make this fat, self-satisfied man happy, a man who never asked about her feelings, who treated her as if she didn't have a soul in her body—something to be wound up and played like a hurdy-gurdy.

Someone came into the hallway; it was Ring, she could tell by his footsteps. Now he would come in and pet her, and if she pulled away, get angry and shake his head as if she were a delinquent child. She could hear him walking through the rooms. Now he was in the dining room; now he was calling her—she couldn't stand his voice.

She jerked herself to her feet and took a few steps toward the door; her legs seemed to be fastened to the floor.

Suddenly, just as he was opening the door to look for her, she darted into the corner between the wardrobe and the wall. He retraced his steps and summoned Alette to ask her if the mistress had gone out. Mechanically, Constance slipped from her hiding place, smoothed her hair, and went in to her husband.

"Where the deuce have you been?" Ring asked in an injured tone. "I've been looking all over the house for you."

Without bothering to reply, she placed a shade over the lamp.

"Why don't you answer me?"

"Do I really have to give an account of myself to you?"

"Good God, Constance, are you going to be difficult again?"

"What a small vocabulary you have; everything is always 'difficult.'"

"Oh, that's just what I need, you're starting to act like this again."

She began leafing indifferently through a book.

"When it comes to being unpleasant, nobody can touch you," he said in exasperation. "But let Fallesen or anybody else from that crowd of yours come in, you put on a different face then."

"It's your crowd, not mine—I thought they were friends of yours."

"Like hell—they're friends who come to flirt and play up to you. And you certainly make yourself available—with a vengeance."

"You're so vulgar—I won't respond to that."

"Oh yes, certainly—I'm inarticulate, and vulgar, and stupid—just say it."

"You may well be right," she said coldly.

"But I am your husband just the same, and you would do well to remember that I won't tolerate impertinence." He stood there glowering at her.

Her contemptuous eyes slid down over his face and chest; she glanced towards the open book as she turned away.

"Do you hear me?" he asked, gripping her firmly by the chin and forcing her to look at him.

"How could I help it! I'm not deaf, as you know perfectly well. Let go of me," she said furiously, her eyes flashing as she tried to stand up.

"Sit still—I'll teach you." He took both of her wrists and squeezed them until they ached.

"Your fingers are stronger than your arguments," she said disdainfully, without making the slightest resistance.

He slung her hands away violently, and began to pace the room, hands jammed in his pockets, his face flaming.

"Ha!" he said after pacing a few moments. "What a woman! She could wring tears from a stone." He shot a glance at her as he spoke, as if expecting some response, but she made no reply.

"And that act you put on while your mother was here—she should see you now. But I knew how it was going to be when she left."

Ah yes, her mother had gone, and she was left behind with this disgusting, hateful man. What a bore he was!

A flush rose in her cheeks and tears trickled down them.

Ring saw that she was crying.

She's sorry, he thought, continuing to pace back and forth. Satisfied with this fortunate turn of events, he waved his arms and went on talking.

"An angel would lose patience—all my work and my dreams are devoted to her happiness, but it's water off a duck's back."

She had not wanted him to see her tears. Unable to prevent it, she hurriedly wiped her face with her handkerchief.

Ring seated himself directly in front of her. "If it were up to me, Constance," he spoke in a conciliatory tone, "there would never be a cross word between us. You could spare yourself those tears."

"I'm not crying," she said obstinately.

"Of course you are, and it hurts me to see it. Now tell me you're sorry and we'll forget all about it."

"Me!" she looked at him incredulously.

He leaned towards her.

"Listen Constance, let's be friends. Be a good girl and give me a kiss."

She jumped up as if she'd been stung and shook herself free.

"Go away!" she cried, "I can't stand you." She ran out of the room.

Ring was thunderstruck. He remained paralyzed for a few seconds, staring at the door.

"That bitch!" he growled. "By God, if she thinks she can sweet-talk herself out of this, she's got a few things to learn."

He stalked out into the hall and slammed the door violently behind him. A few minutes later he was striding down the street in the direction of Tivoli.

7

THE FOLLOWING WEEK Ring and Constance went to a large birthday party at Aunt Wleügel's country house. It was her custom to wait until her birthday had passed before moving back into town.

This year she was particularly fortunate in the weather. It was one of those glittering mild October days that are so glorious in Norway, a final taste of summer, with nature dressed in rich and vibrant colors.

They had eaten dinner at three and afterwards separated into several parties, the older women settling themselves with their knitting on the sun porch, the men retreating to the smoking room for cigars and liqueurs. A number of the young people went out on the lawn for a game of croquet; others played quoits. Later on they gathered for a game of widower seeks a wife, which they played on the wide grassy slope that dropped gently down to the fjord at the right of the house.

Meier and Constance stood together facing Fallesen, who was the widower.

When it was their turn to run out, she whispered in his ear that he mustn't let her be caught, then she dashed off at full speed down the hill. Fallesen tried his very best to catch her. At the last moment Constance disappeared behind the store house and Meier won the round.

Constance had been running so fast that Meier had to swing her around to keep her from falling; she was dizzy after the race and, almost involuntarily, rested her head for an instant on his shoulder. Just at that moment, he bent and kissed her ear. She jerked away and gave him a frightened, reproachful look.

"Forgive me," he said blushing, "I couldn't help myself." He looked so ashamed and miserable that Constance had to feel sorry for him.

"It's not the end of the world," she consoled him. "But don't ever do it again, Meier," she added seriously, an imploring expression in her eyes.

"Come on now, let's go back." She took his arm and they walked slowly up the hill and took their places again. For the rest of the evening Constance was as cheerful as usual, with no trace of a change in her behavior toward Meier. As they were leaving, she asked him if his departure date was set. When he replied that it would be sometime after the first of the year, she told him to be sure to pay them a visit soon.

When he left her he was more in love than ever. He was filled with a devotion he hadn't known one person could feel for another.

How innocent and honorable she was. The love she inspired purified him, made him good; he would not frighten her away by letting her see his passion, not even if it destroyed him. He would bear his misfortune like a man, consoling himself with his music and the bittersweet secret of his love.

As dusk was falling the next afternoon, Constance was sitting by herself at home. She had started a letter to her mother but, not in the mood for writing, had slipped it into her case to finish later. If only she knew what to do. This apathy towards everything in the world was a never-ending torment to her. If only she were sleepy, she could curl up on the sofa and take a nap—but no, not even that.

She paced up and down the room until her feet hurt, then went and stood by the window, hands clasped behind her back; but the street was empty.

Wasn't somebody going to come? Anybody at all?

Finally she lit the lamp and sat down to her embroidery.

Almost immediately the doorbell rang.

Her heart began to pound with curiosity. It was just the mailman, of course—but no, she heard somebody ask if she was home. That was Lorck's voice. In a moment he was seating himself in the armchair beside her. Pulling a book from his pocket, he offered to read her a new story by Kielland.[17]

Delighted, she told him that was a wonderful idea.

When he had finished reading, they began to talk about the story. The subject of love came up.

"Kielland doesn't seem to have much respect for the feeling," Constance said. "He's quite contemptuous. He could just as well have written something about a beautiful, true love."

"Well yes," Lorck remarked with a shrug, "but the idea of a beautiful, true love is outmoded, you know."

"I suppose," said Constance. "That must be why it isn't the main theme in books anymore, at least not in our . . . "

"Not in our lives either," said Lorck, turning his penknife in his fingers and watching her intently.

"Well, has it ever been, really?" Constance asked, then paused, her needle and a long length of red silk suspended in mid-air. "I wonder if it all hasn't been poetic nonsense."

"And you complain about Kielland! Why do you want him to write about something you don't believe in yourself?"

"We're used to finding it in books. But as far as that goes—complain—I certainly didn't mean to."

"At any rate, you're mistaken. People died of love in the old days."

"You mean, killed themselves if they couldn't get the person they wanted?"

"Yes, or just died of grief—consumption, or something like that."

"It must be wonderful," Constance exclaimed, suddenly serious.

"To die of love?" he asked, straightening up in his chair.

"I mean to be able to feel so intensely. But those days are gone forever, don't you think?"

"Lord yes—well, let's say that it hasn't been my fate to experience such a miracle."

"Nor mine," Constance said with a sigh.

"Although, Lord knows, somebody less well balanced could nurse an unrequited love for a lifetime," Lorck said, looking as though he had carefully considered the matter.

"Or one that's returned," Constance remarked.

"No that's something else. If it's returned, it isn't love any longer."

Constance let her embroidery drop.

"A love that's returned isn't love any longer?" She pronounced each word distinctly.

"Not according to common views of propriety—because there has to be marriage then, of course."

"Well, and what then . . . "

"Then it's over," he said, raising his eyebrows as if he very much regretted the fact.

"Do you really think it's always like that?" A strained expression appeared on her face, but quickly disappeared when she saw a triumphant smile on Lorck's lips.

Her mouth worked as if she wished she could take back her words.

"Yes, unless people are very simple, very naive—at any rate, without the capacity to develop."

"Now I really don't understand," said Constance, leaning back on the sofa, a needle in one hand and her embroidery in the other.

"Love fades, you see, especially between married couples—though they're in love when they marry, of course—it's worn away by time and habit, like everything else in the world. Besides, how can a man be expected to love the same person at forty, or even at thirty, as he does at twenty? The woman who thrilled me then might—would almost certainly—seem detestable when I was older and more mature."

"I suppose I can't argue with that," Constance sighed, starting to sew again.

"Unless I wasn't developing at all—was an idiot, in other words," Lorck continued.

"But according to that theory, no one should get married," Constance said, glancing up for a moment.

"No, marriage as we know it is a thoroughly objectionable institution," Lorck said with a smile.

"Well, at least not until the man and woman are a little older," Constance continued, "and completely mature."

"But you see," Lorck said with a shrug, "that has a bad side, too—especially for the women. The older they become, the harder it is to find a husband. And then children have to be considered."

"What difference does it make if fewer children are brought into the world?" Constance said with animation. "In a poor, small country like ours, how could it be anything but a blessing?"

"I wasn't thinking about that," Lorck said, "but the children of older parents don't turn out as well as they should."

"Well I guess things will just have to scrape along as they are," Constance said with a sigh of resignation.

"I suppose so," Lorck said. "In any event, the crucial thing is to keep an open mind."

"An open mind?—about what?" Constance asked, stopping her sewing for moment.

"About not letting ourselves be bound by chains we make ourselves—about following the heart's urge to love freely."

"But if love doesn't exist? You said yourself it was all rubbish, so something like that can't happen," Constance said indifferently.

"I was talking about outmoded ideas! Love not exist!" his voice suddenly dropped. "How could I, Niels Lorck, say such a thing, when for more than a year I've had to endure a love that, God help me, I think will end by driving me mad."

He seemed short of breath; his voice trembled, and his fingers fiddled nervously with the penknife. His behavior was markedly different from his usual calm self-possession.

Constance felt a nagging sense of alarm; she didn't dare look up.

Please don't let him be talking about me, she thought. What in the world could she say? How mortifying.

"Oh it will pass," she said, assuming a casual air.

"No, it isn't like that—it's gone much too far—it's become a passion that's consuming me."

His voice was so earnest; the sound bored into her ears.

You couldn't have said anything worse, she thought. She sewed intently, bending more deeply over her work. How on earth should she respond?

"And you've seen it, of course—you've known it as well as I have."

I'm lost! she thought with a sinking heart.

"Known—what—I—" she stammered.

"Of course you're the one I'm in love with, Constance . . . "

She had not seen him move, so she could not understand how he was suddenly on his knees in front of her. She wanted to speak, but her tongue would not obey.

"Constance," he whispered. "That's enough—don't resist any longer—you were made for love. I want you to taste the sweetness of giving yourself to a man who loves you without limits, as I do."

He took her hand, his face drew near. She felt his warm breath against her forehead.

"No, no, no!" she cried suddenly, springing across the room.

"Stop it, Lorck. Why are you doing this?" she said reproachfully.

"Are you refusing me?" He stood pale and menacing in front of her.

"Talking to me like that—it's horrid of you, Lorck," Constance complained, looking at him helplessly.

"I asked if you're refusing me?" He took a deliberate step toward her.

Constance jumped.

"Stop frightening me!" she said, shrinking away from him.

Lorck crossed his arms and looked at her steadily.

"I love you, Constance—it's serious—probably more so than I've known myself. I'm giving myself to you—my life, my soul—won't you take me?"

"No, oh no!" she cried, stepping back involuntarily.

"Why have you been playing games with me, woman?" he asked, taking a step closer to her.

"I liked talking to you—I never thought about anything else!" she said vehemently, her voice sounding close to tears.

"That's a lie," he said violently. "Who do you belong to? I want to know who you love—your husband perhaps?" He laughed scornfully.

"How can you insult me like this?" she asked, a mixture of outrage, fear, and pain in her eyes. "I've never meant to hurt you."

She walked over to the window.

He followed her, taking her by both wrists and forcing her to turn toward him.

"Coquette!" he snarled.

"Let me go," she cried angrily, snatching away her hands. "I am not a coquette, but you are a man; morally, you and I are a different breed—that's the reason for this."

She walked to the opposite side of the table and glared at him, her cheeks blazing.

A feeling that he had misjudged this woman rose in Lorck. He felt confused and humiliated, but with his habitual self-control, tried to retreat with dignity.

"Forgive me, I was too impetuous," he said with absolute composure. "I see I was wrong about you. This is a fateful hour for me—God knows what will come of it. I beg you not to hold this against me."

"I don't hold grudges," she said in a low voice.

"But will you be uncomfortable now when you see me?"

"I don't know—I can't think calmly about it right now."

"Do you want me to leave?" he asked in a low voice.

"Yes, I think you should," she said gravely.

"All right, whatever you want. But try to be sensible about it. You mustn't decide to banish me. I'll never bother you again the way I did tonight."

"It will be awkward for us to be together after this," she said.

"Very well, just as you command." He bowed and walked stiffly out of the room.

He strode down the street, swinging his cane, and walked straight into a friend he hadn't noticed until he felt a clap on his shoulder and a greeting shouted in his ear.

"Ah, it's you," he said absently, walking past without another word.

In the living room Constance was weeping, her face buried

in a velvet pillow.

So this was how they saw her—a bold coquette who laid snares for men. "Who did she belong to?" This was the respect he thought she deserved—this was how little he valued her! Asking if she loved her husband! Scorning her for that, too! But only her husband's love could honor her.

How rotten and filthy the world was—life was empty and worthless, its dregs poured down on her. That Lorck—that filthy, disgusting Lorck—she hated him.

She had not moved when she heard Ring come in. Instantly she stood up and went in to the tea urn. He was alone for a change, and after they had eaten he began to talk about a stag dinner he wanted to give for some Swedes who had sold him iron mines that should make him a very rich man. The date and menu were settled. He began enumerating the guests.

Lorck was one of them.

She interrupted, saying she wished he would not invite Lorck.

"Why not?" he asked in astonishment.

"I have my reasons," she said firmly.

"What's this! Have you gotten bored with him, too? Your good opinion is too unstable, Constance. Just the same, I insist we ask him this time. So—Storm, six, Lorck, seven . . . " he counted on his fingers.

"No, I'm serious," she said with irritation. "You mustn't ask Lorck—you can leave him out because I ask you to."

"Now don't be stubborn, Constance. The Swedes know Lorck—I've promised them he'll be here. So, Lorck, seven . . . "

"He's not coming," she burst out angrily. "He's an insolent, disgusting man. He's—well, it doesn't matter—just don't invite him."

"Did he get a little forward? You know Constance, I really think it's your own fault. It's always the woman who sets the tone."

"Oh be quiet," she cried, her hands to her ears.

Ring couldn't understand why she sounded so miserable, looked so beseeching. Constance was a mystery to him.

"Now you mustn't be so hard on Lorck, the poor fellow," Ring soothed. "He considers himself family, you see. You just need to set him straight one time and then be a little cool towards him."

"It doesn't bother you—what I've said? You're going to ask him anyway?"

"Yes of course I'm going to ask him! God help us, I can't let myself be governed by your whims when there are solid reasons for asking him. You are so full of wild ideas that . . . "

He stopped suddenly; the gaze she had fixed upon him made him forget what he was saying.

"What are you staring at?" he asked, grimacing as if there was something in his eye. "You look like you've seen a ghost."

"No, I'm just thinking about you," she said coldly. "All, right, ask Lorck," she continued, sitting down quietly again.

♦

For a time she wanted to isolate herself, to shut herself away from everything. People were unbearable, she told herself.

In the depths of this sad dark winter, when she would be sitting by herself in the evening, barricaded against the world—having given Alette strict orders not to let anyone come in—she would suddenly be seized by a longing for something to happen, something extraordinary, something terrible. Time would pass more and more slowly, as she tried to sew or read. She was dying of boredom, bit by bit. Every so often she would jump to her feet and pace the floor, wringing her hands and repeating to herself, "I'm going mad."

Ring was angry when she refused invitations that he wanted her to accept.

She was sorry, she was sick.

What was the matter with her?

She didn't know, she just wasn't well.

Why didn't she call the doctor?

That wouldn't help.

A couple of months passed. Then she reversed herself and told Ring she wanted to go to the theater. She had read an article about phobias that had frightened her.

When the Christmas parties began, she threw herself into them with greater enthusiasm than ever before.

Ring smiled and nodded in satisfaction. He had thought she would get tired of playing the recluse.

In the middle of January, Meier left for Leipzig. On his farewell visit to the Rings, he found Constance home alone.

It struck him that she had grown pale and somewhat thinner during her illness, but it was becoming; never had she seemed more beautiful to him. She was very serious, and though kindness itself, more reserved than before.

His heart felt hollow as he sat there struggling to talk about things that didn't matter to him. He kept up his pretense until the last moment, when his composure slipped, and he had to turn away. His farewell words were smothered when he kissed her hand; a moment later he was gone.

Constance often thought about his pale face and trembling lips as he walked out the door.

8

Constance generally was silent when religious issues were discussed at the Hansens. Nevertheless, a few remarks had escaped her, and Marie had noticed that something was not quite right about her faith. Eager to find out, she tried to bring up the subject, but Constance always evaded her.

"I'm worried about Constance, Rikard," Marie said to her husband one evening after their guests had left. "I'm sure she's been infected by this skepticism that's so fashionable—you heard her defending Bjørnson."

"No, did she really? Well, Constance has always seemed a bit eccentric to me, and eccentric women—well, I don't trust them."

"And Ring has absolutely no control over her. He really is spineless, you know. Of course, she's superior to him in intelligence and everything else, but it's cruel to let him see it just the same."

"You know, I've always been afraid it wouldn't be—well—a particularly happy marriage. They're incompatible. Ring is almost too good-natured, and she's just the reverse; he's head over heels in love with her and she just barely seems to tolerate him."

"But Ring really is awful when he's drinking and babbling nonsense. The conceit! He really guzzles them down, too, and strong ones—his glass is always dark brown. Was he always like this?"

"Well yes, I mean—he's never been what you would call a drinker—but it's something that was supposed to stop when he got married."

"If only he doesn't become a drunkard. Think how terrible

that would be for Constance." Marie had been straightening up after the party as they talked, and now she put out the lamps.

"In that case, she'll have only herself to thank; Ring is the kindest, most agreeable person in the world. You can make him do anything you want."

R.C. Hansen yawned and stood up.

"Well then, shall we go to bed?" He went in to see if his writing desk was locked.

At approximately the same time, Ring and Constance were arriving home. She had refused to take his arm when he offered it to her on the street; Ring was deeply offended and vented his feelings by repeating in a thick, unsteady voice, "You shoun' act like that Constance. Never mind, I jus' m—mention it." The last sentence was accompanied by a mysterious nod. His tongue failed him at last; a vague realization rose in him that it might be prudent to be quiet, so he continued the rest of the way in silence.

Constance was annoyed with him. She had been irritated all evening, but she was used to that by now. Before leaving the house she had asked him to be careful about his drinking. In an impatient, injured tone he had replied that of course he would, and immediately started talking about something else.

Scold him, exert her influence—it was easy for her mother to talk! How many mornings had she told him that she had been ashamed of him the night before? How could a man let himself be treated this way, let his wife beg and coax him not to drink himself insensible—how could he make promises right and left, then go straight off and do it anyway?

When they came up into the hall, Ring found it quite impossible to dispose of his hat properly.

He couldn't figure out how it happened, but every time he put it on the hook, it fell on the floor. Finally he gave up, muttering that it was possessed, and set it on the table.

Constance went into the living room to get the book she wanted to read in bed. Suddenly Ring was beside her, still wearing his coat and one of his gloves. "Have I offended you, Constance?" he snuffled, swaying back and forth slightly.

She continued to search for the book.

"I s-said—have I offended you?" he repeated.

She had found what she was looking for, and as she stalked past him, she gave him a quick appraising glance, then disappeared through the door.

Staring after her with sleepy, baffled eyes, Ring made a move to follow her, then quickly abandoned the idea. Shaking his head, he sighed deeply and began to examine his boots with great concentration.

He staggered around unsteadily for awhile, mumbling a few broken words, waving his arms, clenching his fists, giggling, grimacing as if he were on the verge of tears, and occasionally just standing quietly, lost in thought. Suddenly the idea of beer popped into his head. He took the little hand lamp Constance had left behind in the living room, and weaving unsteadily, made his way to the kitchen, where he tried the key to the pantry door. Unable to open it, he crossed to the maid's room and slipped in.

"Alette, pst! Alette!" he called softly, bending over the bed where the girl was fast asleep, a blanket pulled up to her chin.

"What! What's that!" Her words came in short, gruff bursts. Completely disoriented, Alette sat up in bed and stared at Ring with sleepy, frightened eyes. The blanket had slipped off and she was wearing only a shift; her arms and throat were bare.

Ring was stirred by her white shoulders and ample bosom, the rounded contours half exposed to view. His nostrils quivered slightly and his face grew pale. His hand fumbled toward her bosom as he pressed his moist lips against her shoulder. Alette twisted away from him, uttering little shrieks. Ring's fright nearly sobered him. "Shh! Shh!" he said, straightening up and waving a warning finger at her. "Why are you shrieking like that? Is anybody hurting you? Lie down again." He pushed her gently down on the pillow and pulled the blanket up over her.

"A luscious body, just luscious," he whispered. He couldn't stop himself, he had to touch her again.

"Uff, no! Won't you get out of here!" Alette complained,

wanting to push him away, but the gentle touch of his smooth hands exerted a paralyzing effect on her. Hiding her face in the pillow, she let him caress her.

Suddenly Ring thought he heard a door open and then close again immediately. He slipped out, silent as a cat, pulling the door softly shut behind him. He listened intently for a few minutes. All was still. He came out into the long narrow hall that ran between the kitchen and dining room, at the end of which was the bedroom door. Holding the lamp in front of him, he tiptoed up the hall and listened. Constance's boots were there. She had been putting them out when he heard the door. With a sigh of relief, he went into the dining room; he had remembered that there was usually beer in the embroidered wicker basket beside the stove. When he had emptied his stein and smoked part of a cigar, he went in to bed.

Alette had trouble getting back to sleep. Thoroughly awake, she still felt the touch of his soft hands on her body. The room was filled with the appealing smell of a fine gentleman. Tossing and turning in her bed, she stroked her bosom, her firm arms, and repeated to herself: a luscious body. She had worked for the Rings since the previous autumn, and she was quite happy in service. Ring was an especially kind master. On Christmas Eve, after she had already received pretty gifts from the mistress, Ring had slipped her a five kroner note, a finger to his lips. That was because of the mistress, of course; she wasn't supposed to know. But he was frisky, all right. He'd been after her before, though he'd never gone as far as tonight—but he'd been tipsy, of course—it happened now and then. And with a wife like that! Well, people had different tastes, and she, Alette, was beautiful, too. A luscious body—well, Ring was a man who should know.

9

OVER A YEAR had passed since Mrs. Blom's visit. It was a frosty afternoon in mid-December with crisp snow on the ground. Constance had been out shopping. She had met Lorck on Karl Johansgate, and he had walked by with a respectful greeting. Since the incident between them, his visits had ceased; he came only at Ring's particular invitation and treated Constance with perfect courtesy. His deference and restraint were strikingly different from his former free and playful tone. From time to time Constance told herself that she actually missed him, but when she remembered his words that night, her anger flared again.

As she neared the house, she noticed a dim light in the dining room and assumed that Alette must be lighting the stove. She was already halfway up the stairs when she remembered that the doorbell was out of order. Not having a key to the front door, she turned and went up the back way. Entering the kitchen, she found the lamp smoking furiously and the tea kettle boiling so violently that water was shooting out of the spout and across the floor. Without taking time to remove her coat, she went to the dining room to ask the maid to take care of the mess. The door was ajar, and when she pushed it open she saw Ring from behind, standing with something clasped in his arms, leaning so far forward that his body looked as if it didn't have a head. Without realizing what she was seeing, she entered the room, and at the same instant, two figures stepped apart. Ring turned abruptly and looked slowly from one woman to the other. The corners of his mouth twitched feebly into a foolish smile. Alette stood there, her face averted. She was flaming red and her hair was disheveled; her eyes darted wildly as she fumbled helplessly with her apron.

A strange dizziness seized Constance. She felt as if she were sinking, she and the room and everything mixed together, sinking without end. She wanted to walk out of the room, or at least to move from the place where she stood, but she was paralyzed from head to toe and could not do it.

Alette was the first to gather her wits, and she slipped quietly out of the room.

"Aren't you going to take off your coat?" His voice sounded so meek, so unlike his normal tone. She almost wondered if it was Ring who had spoken. But the sound roused her; she took a couple of steps and gripped the table to steady herself.

Ring began walking slowly back and forth, avoiding the spot where Constance stood. The second time he approached the door Alette had left open, he closed it quietly. Then he walked back to the buffet, moved a bottle and glass behind the tea urn, and stood there, not quite facing her, leaning on the palm of his hand.

"Constance—I beg you—ah . . . " he shifted his feet, "believe me—it was—wasn't as bad as—perhaps it looked."

She stood without moving, staring straight ahead.

"I can certainly see—well, that it must have looked—I mean, seemed peculiar to you." He paused slightly after every third or fourth word.

"But I assure you—if only you'll believe me—it was—well really, it was just a joke, a prank, you might say, just a boyish prank—something came over me—I don't understand it myself."

It was impossible to tell if she had heard him or not.

"I'm so sorry about it, I can't tell you how sorry. Frankly—I'm disgusted with myself."

Constance somewhat absently lifted her hand to her forehead and looked as if she were making an effort to collect her thoughts.

"I don't know what—well—what I wouldn't give—ah—to undo it," he went on in the same meek tone. "If I dared, I would get down on my knees and beg you to forgive me." He went up to her and touched the muff that she was still holding in the hand dangling limply at her side.

"Don't touch me!" she said jerking away. She walked out of the living room and quickly descended to the street. She was seized by a wild desire to fly up in the sky and not come down until she reached her home in Molde; then she would bury her head in her mother's lap and beg them to let her stay forever. She burst into violent sobs, holding the muff to her face as the tears streamed down her cheeks. She felt chastised, crushed by what had happened to her. What had she done that she should be punished like this—that she should experience disgrace for the first time in her life? She had often felt harassed and tormented before, but that was nothing compared to these searing lashes that whipped her around like a sapling in the wind. She felt so humiliated; she could have fallen on her knees and begged for forgiveness for being dissatisfied with her life when there had been no real cause.

She told herself that it was no concern of hers, he could kiss whomever he pleased—but no, no, no! He was married to *her*. Did he really think he could look at other women that way—and dare *behave* like that! How could he be so filthy and base!

Indignation boiled up in her and then the intolerable pain returned. Against her will, she began praying to the God she wasn't sure existed, reproaching herself for ingratitude and pride. She was being punished now, and she should bow her head under His admonishing hand. There was only one thing she would not put up with—to live with Ring after this; surely neither God nor man could ask that.

"Good evening, miss. Out for a walk in the fine weather?" someone said in her ear.

Under normal circumstances, she would have been extremely frightened by such a remark from a strange man on the street at night. Now she scarcely noticed; she walked on calmly without replying, and the fellow drifted away. She had walked as far as Welhavensgate and was approaching the Hansens' house.

Of course; she would go up and confide in Marie. Though there was little sympathy between them otherwise, on this point they would understand each other. She climbed the steps and rang the bell.

Yes, Mrs. Hansen was alone; she was shown in.

A shaded lamp glowed brightly in a corner of the large living room. Marie was sitting on a velvet sofa, embroidering a piece of red cloth with golden silk. There was a faint scent of hothouse flowers in the room; a beautiful screen embroidered with gold palettes and arabesques stood in front of the large white porcelain stove.

When Marie saw Constance enter the room, she laid aside her work and with a warm smile went to greet her.

"Constance, how nice—this is so good of you—you'll stay, of course—we can send for Ring, too." And she eagerly began to help Constance with her coat and hat.

Constance passively allowed her do it. Marie took the clothes out into the hall, continuing to talk through the open door.

When she came back she put her arm around Constance's waist to lead her to a chair. But suddenly her expression changed; she stared at her cousin's tear-stained face, the rigid features and distracted gaze. The moment their eyes met, Constance threw her arms around her and burst into passionate sobs.

"My God, Constance, what's the matter?" Easily moved, she began to cry, too.

Constance was so affected by this sign of sympathy that she clung to her more tightly.

"Oh Marie, you've got to help me. I'm so miserable," she finally said in broken tones.

"But what's happened? Come sit down and tell me about it."

"I won't live with Ring any longer—I can't." And she told her everything.

The frightened expression on Marie's face gradually gave way to grave concern.

"Of course, I understand very well how terribly hurt you are, but it's nothing to make such a fuss about." She paused for a moment. "A man steals a kiss from a housemaid—it doesn't mean so much."

Constance felt as if the ground were collapsing under her.

"A married man, in his own dining room—with his wife's housemaid?" she stammered.

"Well it's wrong, of course, and I wouldn't have believed Ring was like that. But Constance, are you quite sure you aren't to blame yourself?"

"What do you mean by that?" Constance asked.

"You are always so cold and disdainful toward him—both Rikard and I think so."

Constance felt her heart constrict. That Marie would turn the attack against her was something she had not considered. She stared at her helplessly.

"His behavior doesn't bother you at all?" she asked.

"Good heavens, Constance. Of course it does. But you have to remember that men are completely different than we are. They get accustomed to these affairs when they are young, and it's so easy for them to slip back if their wives don't—I'm afraid I have to say it—devote themselves body and soul to holding them fast. A wife *can* do that, especially when she has the physical attributes you do."

A choking resentment welled up in Constance.

"That's disgusting!" she said, wringing her hands distractedly.

"Come, come, Constance—you're going to have to view this in a different light. If you only knew how few men are faithful to their wives—there isn't one pure marriage in a hundred."

And she began to tell her, in copious detail, about the affairs married men were conducting while their wives turned their heads the other way. She mentioned several examples from their own circle, as well as others that they knew by name.

Listening to her, Constance felt sick at heart.

"But my God," she cried at last, "if this is true and everybody accepts it, why don't we get rid of this hypocritical institution? Why in the world don't we practice polygamy openly?"

"Like the Turks and the pagans. Yes, that would be lovely."

"At least it would be honest then, and we'd know what we

were getting into."

Marie refused to engage in such meaningless talk.

"Well, as I've told you, I'm convinced that the wife has a great deal to do with the way a marriage turns out. You could have such power over Ring, if you wanted to. He's so nice, so easily led, and he truly loves you—even if he kissed that girl a hundred times."

Constance laughed bitterly.

"It's just a game men play. You can still make an excellent husband out of him, and it's a wife's mission, I would almost say, to influence her husband for the good."

"But I have no desire for that kind of mission," Constance said contemptuously.

"Show how noble you are, Constance, and forgive him—you'll see the blessings that will come of it. An incident like this is often the way God brings our hearts closer together, if only we can use it wisely." Marie's voice quavered and her eyes were moist.

There was a pause.

Constance sat with her arms crossed, staring stiffly in front of her.

Marie thought this was a good opportunity to bring up something that had been troubling her for a long time.

"You know, Constance, I can think of something much worse—a husband with a weakness for drink."

"Oh yes, there's that as well. I suppose that's my fault, too," Constance answered, looking as if she were braced for anything.

"Well Constance, I can't help thinking, and Rikard agrees, that Ring is unhappy because you're so cold to him. He drinks to forget it."

"Poor man, he's going completely to the dogs because he's married me."

"And I must say, an unfaithful husband, you could accept that—though God knows it's horrible—but one who drinks . . . "

Again Constance felt the same wordless bitterness rise inside her.

"A man who drinks," Marie continued, "can't take care of his business or provide enough to maintain a home—he's ruined, for all practical purposes."

"Where did you put my things?" Constance said, getting up.

Marie went out in the hall. "Now I won't ask you to stay," she said, coming back. "Just go straight home and make up with Ring. Do it—oh, do it right away, Constance."

"Very well, I'll go home and beg his pardon for not taking care of him properly—I'll promise to reform. Isn't that what you want me to do?"

"You're bitter now, I can understand that, but when you give it some thought you'll see that I'm right. Do you want my maid to come with you?" she asked when Constance was ready.

"No! For heaven's sake, let me go! Good night."

"Good night, Constance."

At home, Ring was in a state of painful turmoil. When Alette heard Constance leave the house, she came back into the room and stood there sobbing, her apron pressed to her eyes. Now he had disgraced her and the mistress would throw her out. Why hadn't he let her be—she'd considered herself a decent girl before this, but now—Oh, sweet Jesus, how could a thing like this happen to her? Ring assured her that he wouldn't let her down; he told her to calm herself, to behave as if nothing had happened. He could smooth it over, and nothing more would come of it.

He wandered back and forth across the living room, stopping stock still to curse the fates that had put him in this dreadful predicament. He squirmed at the thought of what Constance would say to him. She would not be merciful, but it would all blow over in time, he consoled himself. At this point in his deliberations he decided that he needed a glass of brandy and soda to cheer him up. Why was Constance always like this—it was her fault everything was such a mess. Why couldn't they live together like two lovebirds?

Every few minutes he peeked out the window; periodically he went out in the hall to listen.

The longer he waited the worse he felt. His mouth was twisted into a dejected grimace, his eyebrows drawn together sharply, his forehead lined with deep furrows. He dreaded the moment when she would enter and at the same time agonized about her failure to appear.

Finally he heard someone at the door. He went to open it.

Constance walked calmly past him and began to take off her coat. Then she went into the living room, sat down on the sofa and picked up the evening paper. Ring slipped into a chair some distance away and leaned forward, his elbow on his knee, his hand shading his eyes. Occasionally he shot a glance at his wife, but he did not have the courage to address her.

At last he gathered his nerve and said, "Constance, can you forgive me?"

She put down her paper and looked at him as if she were going to say something, then she thought better of it and picked up the paper again.

"Today I'm going to turn over a new leaf," he began.

"Spare me the platitudes," she said dryly. "I can't bear to hear them."

"I know how terribly I've offended you," he stammered, "and I'll take whatever punishment you give . . . "

"I have very little to say," she interrupted with a movement of her hand, "since you seem to be having an affair with my housemaid."

"I'm not having an affair with anybody."

"Since you're having an affair with my housemaid, it goes without saying that I won't have anything to do with you. If you want to have her, then go ahead—but you'll have to leave me alone. I've agreed to be your wife—that's bad enough— but one of your mistresses, never." She got up and started out of the room.

Ring thought she had never seemed so lovely and desirable as she did at this moment. There was nobody like her. Pierced by the fear of losing her, he jumped up and blocked her way.

"Insult me, step on me, spit on me, kill me!" he cried out. "I'm despicable, a miserable fool who didn't recognize the treasure I had—I'm not worthy to tie your shoelaces, but I love you, Constance. No, let me speak. I love you, worship you—I'll lie in the dust and kiss your feet. I don't care about anyone in the world but you—despite what you think." He was holding his head in his hands, writhing as though in pain.

"Nonsense," she said with a grimace. "You bore me."

"Yes, I know it—I know it, and it's an everlasting torment. You've never loved me, not one bit. But once in awhile you've seemed—well—I've almost been able to imagine you cared for me—I've been so confused. Oh, Constance, if you had loved me, you could have made me a different man. If I hadn't been dying for your love—that's what caused this." His voice became choked with tears. Sinking to his knees, he buried his face in her skirt.

"Get up—you're drunk," she said grudgingly.

"I'm just as sober now as you are, Constance."

He looked at her with whipped, beseeching eyes. "I won't get up until you say you've forgiven me."

Constance felt a kind of compassion for him. It pained her to see him so humble. "But how can I believe you?" she said.

"No, you're right, Constance, you're so right. Ah, but do it anyhow, just this one time, and you'll be praised and rewarded for it. Someday you'll believe in me again, perhaps even feel some kindness toward me because I've been faithful and undemanding for so many years, never complaining once, and then you'll be glad to know you saved me. Don't push me away—without you I'm lost." He remained on his knees, clutching her skirt with both hands and kissing it.

His deep emotion was contagious. Constance bowed her head and began to cry.

"You know the old saying, it's better to give than receive," he went on in the same passionately imploring tone. "Look at me, Constance—here I am, begging you on my knees, and you are so far above me—my fate is in your hands. Don't be heartless. Let yourself be moved, Constance."

"I'm not trying to be cruel," she said in a tearful voice. "But what has happened can't just be wiped out of our life."

"Yes it *can*, it *can*, Constance. Oh, try—try. Take me on faith and let me prove myself."

Like a schoolgirl, she did as she was told. She sat down opposite him.

"Since you seem to be taking this with the seriousness it deserves. . . . " she said, smoothing out her handkerchief in her lap and folding it into tight little squares. "Can I trust you to answer truthfully?"

"You can depend on it, Constance."

"Tell me how far this has gone between you."

"Gone! It hasn't gone anywhere. What more could have happened than what you saw—that was bad enough."

If Constance had been more experienced, and if, in spite of Marie's warning, the truth had not seemed so incredible to her, she would have been alerted by his unsteady gaze and faltering replies.

"And is that all?" she asked, looking directly at his face.

"Yes, I assure you. Do you believe I—no, you have to be sure I'm telling the truth . . . "

"Was that the first time you did—did that with her?"

"I've told you, Constance. How can I reassure you? What's the use, if you won't believe me?"

"You look so peculiar," she said doubtfully.

"How do you expect a man to look when he's being stretched on the rack? Oh Constance, spare me—I'm so ashamed. Let that be enough."

She believed him. Not so much because she had any special confidence in the honesty of his character, but because she couldn't conceive of the possibility that the disaster that had befallen her was so enormous. Such things happened, of course, but not in her marriage, not under her very eyes—in such a banal way. Ring was an impulsive man, certainly, but that kind of depravity wasn't in him. "And you'll give me your word of honor that you will never do it again?" she asked almost beseechingly.

"I swear by eternal God! Oh Constance, believe me—I've learned my lesson—if for no other reason than to spare myself this pain, I'll know how to behave from now on."

Constance could understand this well enough; certain that he must be completely cured, she became more conciliatory.

"Well then, I'll try to forget it," she said, two large tears trickling down her cheeks.

"Thank you, oh, thank you, darling!" he cried, jumping up to embrace her.

"No, please, not yet," she said, turning away. "I need some time."

"Your hand—give me your hand, Constance." She extended her cold white hand to him and he greedily pressed it to his mouth.

"I'll tell Alette to leave by Easter."

"Of course, Constance. Wouldn't you prefer her to go right away?"

"Oh no, it's not worth making such a fuss. And now you've given me your word of honor."

IO

A COUPLE OF MONTHS after this occurrence, Ring and Hansen were walking together up Karl Johansgate. They had left their offices and were on their way home for dinner. When they passed the university, Hansen turned right.

"I can go this way just as well," Ring said, keeping him company, although he normally walked through the Slotts-park.

"You know—" Hansen said, with a sudden leap in his chain of thought, "you've really got to throw that girl out. For God's sake, anybody can see it now."

"Damnation!" Ring exclaimed in alarm, suddenly starting to bite the nail of his right index finger.

"Do you want to know what Marie told me after we left your house the other day?"

"Well, out with it, man!"

"The minute we were out the door she said, 'Did you notice Alette's appearance?'"

"Naturally, I assured her she was mistaken, but she just laughed and said I must be blind."

"Damn!" Ring said, his eyes narrowing as if he were walking through driving snow.

"Yes," Hansen went on, "and now she's going to tell Constance that she shouldn't let her stay in the house on any account."

"Oh damn," Ring mumbled. "You've got to stop her, Hansen."

"I can't, without letting it slip that ... "

"Does she suspect anything?

"Absolutely not. It's amazing, don't you think—imagine,

she knows and yet—well, our wives are incredibly trusting. It must be because they're so much better than we are."

Ring had again started biting his nails. He pondered about the best course of action, asking himself if Constance was as far from discovering the truth as Marie.

"By God, Rikard, you've got to be careful that your wife doesn't get wind of it," he said, emphasizing every word.

Hansen waved his hand. "As far as I'm concerned, it's a nasty business—Christ, so trite—why, it makes me feel sorry for your wife. Carrying on like that in your own house—there's something dirty about it."

"When an accident has happened," Ring said with a shrug, "there's not much point in moral lectures after the fact. Besides, it's easy enough for you to talk. But with a wife like Constance . . . "

"You were an incredible blockhead for not firing the girl right away."

"An idiot," Ring said, shaking his head disconsolately. "But who could have imagined—she only told me about it afterwards."

"Well, as I said, I can manage the money part of it for you, when it gets to that." Hansen stopped outside his house.

Ring sat a half hour later than usual over his afternoon coffee, hoping that Constance would go out, but luck wasn't with him. Contrary to custom, she didn't put aside her reading when the light began to fade, but immediately lit the lamps when it grew too dark for her to see; the book seemed fascinating.

Ring sat in his room by himself, smoking one cigar after another. As he watched Constance through an opening in the curtains of the door, he was struck by how thin and white her cheeks had become.

The poor thing, this business had hit her hard, but God willing, she would get over it. If he could just get things straightened out with Alette.

Constance had been so gentle and unassuming since it happened. Ring softened at the thought. Perhaps it had occurred to her that she wasn't free of blame herself. But nothing like this would ever happen again. He would be faithful to her—as good as gold. He loved her—why did he bother with girls he could have for a kind word or a few pieces of silver? Why hadn't he sent the girl away? What if this got out? He began to sweat; he prayed that God in His mercy would help him avert a disaster and spare his poor wife—for her sake not his; it was out of concern for her that he had hidden the truth when she questioned him; God understood that and had forgiven him— he was sure of it. Now if he could just make himself trust in His help and support.

Well he couldn't wait any longer. He wouldn't be able to talk to her today, but early in the morning, before he left for the office—he'd seize his opportunity then.

"Aren't you going out this afternoon, Constance?" he asked as he walked through the living room.

"No," she replied without looking up.

"I thought we might walk together." He had the vague idea that he could double back after he left her.

Constance shook her head.

"All right, then. Good-bye my dear." He patted her head affectionately. "My word, I really must hurry."

Out in the hall he opened the door a crack, hoping to signal Alette to go down the back stairs, but the kitchen was empty and he dared not call out. So he had to leave with his mission uncompleted.

Constance laid aside her book and leaned back on the sofa. She was thinking about her husband. He certainly seemed to have been affected by what had happened. A becoming gravity, almost approaching sadness, had come over him. He didn't drink as much, either, and lately there had been evenings when he voluntarily asked for tea.

When he behaved like this she felt that perhaps, in time, she could come to love him. He was her husband, after all, and he was entitled to her love.

Apparently she felt more affection for him than she had realized, or why else would she have been so hurt by the episode with Alette? For it was not just anger that she had felt. Perhaps it was true that if she tried in earnest to show him affection she could make him into a better man. It really seemed that way. When he came home tonight she would chat with him and let him know her feelings. The finest thing in life, when it came right down to it, was to mean something to someone else— besides, one should learn to be contented, reduce one's demands for happiness.

Her thoughts were interrupted by the doorbell, and a moment later Marie entered the room.

She wouldn't stay long, Marie said, taking off her coat; she would just sit for a few minutes.

"Then we'll have a cup of tea," Constance said, and she went out to tell Alette.

They began talking about one thing and another, but the conversation flagged.

Alette entered and set the tea tray and other paraphernalia on the small table Constance had put there for the purpose. Marie inspected the girl from head to toe. Alette turned beet-red and, in her confusion, tripped over a footstool and nearly fell. Marie's pitiless eyes followed her until she reached the door and almost crept through it. Constance had not looked at Alette; not since that evening had she looked at her, condescending to speak only when absolutely necessary. When she heard Alette stumble against the footstool, she glanced momentarily in that direction and caught a glimpse of the expression on Marie's face. Constance was annoyed. Really, it was vulgar to let the girl know she was in on this disgusting secret; couldn't Marie stay out of it—for her sake, at least?

"That girl is shameless!" Marie burst out, furiously stirring her cup of tea.

"She doesn't have much time left, now," Constance remarked indifferently.

"But Constance, surely you're not thinking about keeping her here the whole time. It simply won't do to let her flaunt herself in front of people—and of course it must be disgusting for you, too."

"Let her flaunt herself," Constance said in amazement. "What are you talking about, Marie?"

"Don't you see her condition?"

"Her condition?" Constance repeated mechanically.

"My God, Constance. Well, I'll be blunt then—she's expecting, of course."

Constance clasped her hands together.

"Haven't you got eyes, Constance?"

"Oh Marie, you must be mistaken!"

"Just look at her," Marie cried. "She's so far along that even the smallest child could see it."

"No, not Alette! Oh dear, what a dreadful business," Constance said with an expression of distaste.

"I'm not a bit surprised," said Marie. "It always happens to the ones you would least suspect—she has a sweetheart, I suppose?"

"I don't know," Constance said.

"Hasn't she had some young fellow calling on her? They all do, of course—it's always a brother leaving for America, you know—coming to say good-bye. Really, the housemaids these days!"

"Oh, what should I do?" Constance asked in bewilderment. "It will be so embarrassing to have to speak to her about it."

"Don't say a thing—just tell her to pack her bags immediately. Believe me, she'll leave without asking any questions."

Constance stared dejectedly into space.

"I'll find someone else for you in the meantime—I know an excellent girl who's available, and you can get her on a day's notice," Marie continued cheerfully.

"Well, thank you. That's fine, of course, but ... "

"You mustn't change your mind. Listen Constance—for decency's sake, if nothing else—imagine having guests here—men—you'd feel like sinking through the floor."

"Yes, you're right, of course," said Constance. "But oh, I dread it."

When Marie had gone, Constance paced back and forth, an odd mixture of eagerness and embarrassment in her face. She was nervous about the approaching interview, yet she wanted to deal with it at once; she did not want to sleep on it. What in the world was Ring going to say? It would be painful to see his embarrassment when she told him about Alette. On the other hand, it might do him good.

She walked over and rang the bell.

Alette came in and asked what she wanted.

Constance examined her carefully and saw immediately that Marie was right. It was amazing that she hadn't seen it before.

Alette realized that something unusual was about to happen. For the last couple of days she had sensed trouble brewing.

She tried to look proud and unconcerned. Boldly, almost defiantly, she met Constance's eyes, but she could not sustain it for more than a few seconds—her eyes wavered uncertainly down to Constance's dress, shifted to the leg of a chair, down to the rug, up to the legs of the table, and quickly down again. Finally she stared straight down in front of her.

"I've called you in to say that you have to leave here tomorrow," Constance said breathlessly.

"I've been expecting it," Alette replied in a muffled voice, her head hanging. "I said at the time it would be best for me to leave right away."

Constance didn't hear what she said and didn't bother to inquire about it.

"Well, you understand that you can't stay *here*—not after the way you've conducted yourself," Constance went on.

A sudden cry sliced through the stillness of the room, and in the next moment, Alette had fallen at her feet, sobbing harder than Constance had ever heard anyone cry before. She didn't know what to say or do, and wasn't far from tears herself.

"Mercy, mercy," she finally heard from below. The words were forced with difficulty out of a constricted throat. Alette clutched with both hands at a fold of Constance's dress; she was almost prostrate; the tears streamed down her face, her back and shoulders shuddered convulsively as if an electric current were running through her.

"I've cried so much," the girl went on, the violence of her weeping repeatedly forcing her to stop. "Oh, at night—I've often thought I should kill myself—yes, I have, I have—for your sake ma'am—my kind is bound to get in trouble—I told him that when he tempted me, God knows I did! Think of your wife, I said." Her voice faltered and she began to hiccup. "But he had to have his way. Mercy—have mercy on me! Oh, God help me—God, help and comfort me." She crept closer to Constance and tried to kiss her feet.

Like a light glimmering far away in the mist that grows gradually larger and clearer as one approaches it, the truth dawned on Constance. Clenching her fist, she bent over the crumpled figure, her arm raised to strike. For a second she could have ground this creature under the heel of her boot, but then, almost instantly, she was pierced by the misery and humiliation of this fellow human, lying there so wracked by storms of weeping, and an aching compassion filled her.

"Get up," she said calmly, almost gently. "There's no use in lying there."

Slowly, with great effort, the girl got to her feet. Covering her face with her apron, she stumbled toward the door.

"Does he know—Ring, I mean—about—about—your condition?" Constance asked.

"Yes," Alette whispered.

"And he admits that it's his child?"

"Yes, oh yes," Alette said with a wave of her hand.

"Has he continued the relationship since that evening—you remember . . . "

The maid's answer was so low that Constance had to ask her again.

"I tried to say no," she whispered.

"Good," Constance said, "go on now."

Alette fumbled for the doorknob and slipped out.

II

CONSTANCE SEETHED WITH HATRED for Ring. That lecherous, deceitful man—she had condescended to listen to his apologies and promises; she had felt sorry for him and started to believe in him again.

Of course the despicable wretch would beg her to forgive him again. He would fall on his knees and take God as his witness that he loved her, that the other thing meant nothing. Involuntarily she clenched her fists.

Dear God in heaven, what a fluke it was that she had learned the truth. She could have clasped Alette's hand in gratitude.

If only she knew how to go about getting a divorce. She stood with her hands folded, pondering. The minister would know, she was sure of it—she would hurry over to see him.

She put on her hat and coat in feverish haste. Trembling with dread that she might meet Ring on the stairs, she slipped out unhindered and walked rapidly down the street. The minister lived in a corner house on Holbergsplass. Soon she was at her destination, making her way up the gaslit stairway. His door was on the second floor. The shiny brass plate read: The Reverend F. B. Huhn, Visiting Hours 9-10 and 4-5. So he was probably not at home, or not receiving visitors, at any rate. Her knees were trembling and her heart was beating so violently that she could feel the pulse in her throat; she felt as if her soul were leaping out of her body with every breath she took.

She lifted her hand to ring the bell, but then let it drop again. What should she say? She tried to make a start, but her wits failed, her thoughts skittered away. Everything was whirling around in her head, whirling endlessly; that was why she couldn't find the words. If only this pounding in her left side would subside a bit—it was going to drown out the sound of her voice, or choke it off from inside. Finally, almost mechanically, she pressed the doorbell and then jumped back, startled by the noise. A dreadful fear seized her. Her pulse raced wildly and for a moment she thought of running. Gathering her skirts, she was starting down the stairs when she heard someone coming; she turned around quickly and stood her ground.

In a dry thin voice hardly recognizable as her own, she asked if Reverend Huhn was at home.

"No," came the uncertain reply.

Constance was relieved, and with relief came a grain of courage.

"He isn't receiving callers right now?"

The maid looked at her curiously.

"I'll speak to Mrs. Huhn," she said with some hesitation; she took a few steps and turned back.

"May I ask for your card?"

Again a sense of dread seized Constance, but in some way she felt that the maid had taken charge of her.

"I don't have one," she stammered. "Just say a lady—my name is Mrs. Ring."

The whisper of muffled voices reached her. She heard a distinct "yes, it seems important," then footsteps moving away and coming back again, then a brief answer, and the maid reappeared to say, "Come this way, please."

In a moment she was standing just inside the door of a small room jammed with large bookcases; there was a small pattern in the carpet, and all around the room were quantities of faded needlepoint on chairs, pillows, footstools and pipe racks. Over by the window on the left was a writing desk littered with journals and papers. The room was full of tobacco smoke, and the stove burned with a loud roaring sound.

Constance saw everything through a mist. The minister's voice reached her ears from an immense distance.

"Please sit down, madam," said the kindly old man, placing a chair directly in front of the rocker from which he had just risen.

A moment later Constance was astonished to hear someone say, "I'm sorry to bother you outside your visiting hours." She couldn't believe that the voice belonged to her.

"Not at all, not at all—I'm glad to be of service, but there are so many who come here on every kind of mission—I have to limit myself. One must have time for one's sermons, too."

Constance twitched nervously in her chair and did not answer; she looked very peculiar, the minister noted. "Do you have something particular on your mind?" he asked sympathetically. "Can I help or advise you in some way?"

The sincerity of his tone encouraged Constance; she held her handkerchief to her eyes for a second, collecting herself, then said firmly, "I've come to tell you that I want to divorce my husband."

The minister jumped as if he had been struck.

"Oh no, don't say that. Perhaps I didn't hear you correctly," he said almost imploringly.

"Yes, I've made up my mind." She looked directly at him. "Would you please tell me how to go about it?"

"First, I must hear your reasons, and after that, it's my duty as a counselor and fellow human being—and, of course, as a representative of the church—to advise you to give up your plan."

"But that would be quite useless, Reverend. No power on earth can make me do that," Constance said calmly.

"But what man cannot do, the Lord of Heaven and Earth may still accomplish. You don't want to oppose Him, do you, Mrs. Ring?"

"I want to be divorced from my husband," she continued more intensely, "no matter who or what opposes it." She was twisting her muff in her hands and it dropped to the floor.

"Remember the Scriptures—" he began.

"I don't care about the Scriptures," she interrupted, her forehead wrinkling as if she were going to cry.

"You don't mean that," the minister admonished.

"And besides, divorce isn't against God's commandments," she went on nervously, gripping the wooden arms of her chair.

"Oh yes," he interrupted mildly. "How can you get away from the words: 'What God hath joined together, let no man put asunder.'"

"But surely you wouldn't say that all married people have been joined by God," Constance exclaimed.

"You've been infected by the skepticism of the modern age, Mrs. Ring! God's ways are not our ways. Marriage is made by God—when the servant of the Lord stands at the holy altar and administers the sacrament to the bridal couple, the binding words of God are heard. The unworthiness of man does not detract one particle from the holiness of the institution—just as the sacrament of communion is still Christ's body and blood even when it is taken by the most unrepentant sinner. Because of the hardness of your heart, remember what Moses told the Jews."

"Moses and the Jews have nothing to do with this," she interrupted.

"Another sign of skepticism. As long as the Lord's church exists in the world, the laws of Moses will apply to us. But if you won't submit to Moses, perhaps the words of our Savior will find their way into your heart. Listen to what He says about marriage." He took the Bible, which was open on the table, flipped through it and then began to read Matthew, chapter 19, verses 5 through 10.

Constance had difficulty restraining herself enough to sit still while he read. Her temples were throbbing, her ears ringing. This irrelevant talk exasperated her. In her inmost soul she knew that what she wanted was right; she had not come here to ask him that. Trying to stop her was a shabby trick; he was making himself part of the filth she was trying to escape.

"There you are! It explicitly says that divorce is permitted," she said, as the minister laid the book aside; her eyes were flashing, her voice cracking with emotion.

"Yes, for adultery, but for that reason only," he replied, raising his hands.

"That's precisely why I want a divorce," she said.

Reverend Huhn bent forward with a sudden jerk of his head.

"What are you saying! Poor, poor woman—can it be possible, can it really be possible?"

The deep compassion in his tone struck a note in Constance's heart that could not be touched without an answering chord. She abruptly put her hands to her face and wept bitterly.

"Poor woman, go ahead and cry, cry it all out—it will ease your burden. How can such things happen in a congregation of the Lord? Ah, the sins of mankind have grown alarmingly among us."

"But are you certain your judgments aren't based on mere suspicion?" he asked when Constance had become calm again.

"You are making a terrible charge against your husband," he added quickly, when he saw her shake her head in impatience.

"And even if appearances were strongly against him," he continued, "they could still be wrong. Women have a tendency to be jealous, and being jealous is like being struck blind." The minister's voice had the exasperated ring of a man defending himself.

"Our housemaid is expecting a child, and it's—well—it's his," she blurted.

He flinched, then stared at her in speechless horror.

"Long-suffering God, are Your eyes to be spared nothing?" He sighed and folded his hands. "How sore Your paternal heart must be! And you are certain," he said, turning to Constance, "that there is no possibility of a mistake."

"She told me herself," came the response.

"What a calamity," the minister mumbled to himself, rubbing his fingers as if he were washing his hands.

"It's really not that unusual, I'm told," Constance said, staring emptily in front of her.

"No, no, you mustn't talk like that—it shows a moral deficiency in your thinking that is fundamentally unchristian."

"But what if it's the truth! To behave that way is surely more unchristian than to know or talk about it."

"You mustn't lose faith in goodness, Mrs. Ring. Keep thy heart with all diligence, the Scriptures tell us."

Reverend Huhn was lost in thought. Constance sat quietly

waiting for him to speak.

"This is a terrible chastisement," he began, after pausing for a moment. His voice was mildly admonitory. "Now it's a matter of turning it to the good of your eternal soul."

She squirmed uncomfortably in her chair.

"It's difficult for flesh and blood, to do what God demands of us," he went on, "but nothing else can bring peace to our souls."

Constance remained still; the minister regarded her attentively.

"Be merciful, just as our Father in Heaven is merciful."

"You mean that I should forgive him," she cried, her attitude suddenly defiant.

"Yes—no matter how strong your reasons, you should not destroy your marriage."

"I haven't destroyed it—he's taken care of that!"

"A Christian woman never abandons her husband. You would have cold justice on your side, of course, but not the love that forgives all, bears all, believes all, hopes all. Believe me, it is blessed to forgive."

"It's despicable, outrageous, and immoral," she burst out, trembling with indignation.

"Suppose our Lord answered us like that when we begged Him for mercy," Reverend Huhn said with a quiet smile. His tone indicated that he had found the right words at last. "What if in our final moments, when we cried out to Him for forgiveness for the sins of an entire lifetime, He treated us as we deserved?"

"But the two relationships are not the same at all," Constance said vehemently. "First, there is no marriage between God and man, and second, He is the One who made us as we are."

"You frighten me, Mrs. Ring. You are mocking God with your sinful talk." His voice was stern.

"Is it mocking God to speak the truth?" she said, standing up.

"The spirit of skepticism is speaking through you," he said, shaking his head dejectedly. "My warnings are obviously useless. Only God can help you. I've done my duty by begging you to show Christian gentleness and mercy. If you won't let yourself be guided by the Scriptures, I have nothing more to say."

"Tell me, Reverend Huhn," Constance said in a lower tone, "suppose it had been a man whose wife were going to have a child—by his office boy, for instance. Would you say the same thing then: that no Christian husband abandons his wife?" She looked at him almost belligerently.

"That's a different matter. When a woman falls into that path it is a sign of such degradation, such moral depravity, that we must view her presence in the home as a contamination."

"Yes that's what we always hear, but I no longer believe there's such a great difference," Constance said defiantly.

Reverend Huhn extended his hand and looked as if he expected her to leave.

"Will you tell me what I have to do?" she asked, picking up her muff.

"Just write a request, or get somebody to do it for you, and send it to me. I'll make a note that the required attempt at reconciliation has been fruitless, and then—well, I'll be willing to help you go ahead with it."

She thanked him and said goodby.

"The Lord be with you and make you humble and meek at heart, His will be done," the minister said with a troubled face.

"Good night!"

He saw her to the door and closed it after her.

12

W HEN CONSTANCE CAME DOWN to the street, she paused for a moment to think. Then she hurried away in the opposite direction of her house. When she reached Incognitogaten, she entered a large building with narrow pointed turrets and rang the doorbell of Aunt Wleügel's apartment.

Her aunt was at home. The maid who answered the door said she was in having tea.

Constance walked through the spacious paneled living room, past the heavy old-fashioned furniture that she knew so well. She had been sitting over there by the piano when her aunt had handed her Ring's letter of proposal, and this was where she had stood, gripping the back of the couch, when he came to visit the first time as her fiance. The memories made her shudder.

Over in the corner, a small lamp with a pink shade glowed in front of the semi-circular corner sofa. The large white porcelain stove emitted a gentle warmth, and the room was fragrant with the scent of potted flowers. The dining room door was ajar, and a shaft of bright golden light stretched toward the soft rosy glow of the lamp.

As Constance walked into the dining room, her aunt was rising from the tea table. Her hair had recently become quite white. She was wearing a ruffled cap, and covering her dress, a large scalloped shawl trimmed with silk fringe and ending in two long points. The pain in her foot had grown worse, and this winter she had begun to use a cane.

"My goodness, Constance, what are you doing out so late? I've just finished my tea. Shall I get you a cup?" she asked.

"No thanks, Aunt, nothing for me—I want to talk to you."

Mrs. Wleügel looked at her sharply. There was something disquieting in her niece's voice.

"Nothing has happened, has it?" she asked.

"Yes, Aunt. Come, I'll tell you about it." Hastily taking off her coat as she talked, Constance ended by saying: "So now I've come to stay with you until it's settled."

Her aunt had listened in silence, eyelids lowered, the corners of her mouth tightening.

"And then what will you do, Constance?" she asked, looking at her gravely.

"Go home," Constance answered, bursting into violent sobs.

"Your parents will never allow it." Mrs. Wleügel shook her head sadly. "One must do what's right."

"When they hear what Ring has done? No, Aunt, they couldn't be that cruel."

"My poor dear Constance—God knows I feel for you." The old woman's lips were trembling. "It breaks my heart—oh God, oh God, there's no end to what we women have to bear—but I never dreamed it could happen to you."

Her voice dwindled to a whimper and she brushed her hand across her eyes.

"Believe me, I know what you are feeling," she went on after a moment. "You see, the same thing happened to me."

"Was your husband like that too?" Constance cried, throwing herself on her knees in front of her.

Mrs. Wleügel took Constance's head in her hands and kissed her hair.

"Dear me yes, Constance, and he's not the only one. We always think we're the exception, but that's very far from the truth. It's such a problem with men—if they marry when they're young, they haven't sown their wild oats; if they wait until they're older, their habits have become too much for them."

"But Aunt, Aunt," cried Constance, "why didn't you say anything before? Why were you so eager for me to marry?"

"Constance, my dear, when you are as old as I am, you'll understand things better. One must do what's right! The world is arranged so that women must marry. We may be unhappy for a while, but an unmarried woman has far greater burdens to bear. We have to choose the lesser of two evils."

"Well, I know what I would have chosen if I had known," Constance exclaimed bitterly, rising to her feet.

"The one who wears the shoe knows where it pinches," her aunt said, rocking gently back and forth.

"Believe me, Constance, if you were an old maid, being unmarried would seem to be the one thing standing between you and happiness."

"All right, Aunt, let's not quarrel about this now, it doesn't do any good."

Unable to stay still, Constance prowled restlessly around the room.

"And you've been to the minister, you say. My God, my God—to the minister. And Ring—what does Ring have to say?"

She then discovered that Constance hadn't spoken to Ring, that he was unaware of her decision.

"Constance, you must stop and think, you must think very carefully before you decide about this." She lifted a hand in warning.

"There's nothing to think about, can't you understand that, Aunt?" Her tone was impatient. "Don't start picking on me now—I can't bear it!"

"Yes, but Constance, my dear, you must be sensible. Of all misfortunes, divorce is the worst. You simply must listen to what Ring . . . "

"If you want me to go back to him, it's no use," Constance burst out. "I won't do it. I won't do it." She was shifting from one foot to another, as if she were ready to bolt.

"You must take your time, Constance—don't do anything right now. The pain is so overwhelming at first. One must do what's right."

"No Aunt, it isn't pain, it's disgust, contempt—contempt and loathing. I can't stand the sight of him—the thought of him makes me frantic." She wrung her hands distractedly.

"Yes, yes, I know, of course," her aunt said with a wave of

her hand. "But that will pass. After a while, you'll feel better. It's useless to make such an uproar, Constance! What good would it do if you were divorced—surrounded by scandal and pain, looked down on by everybody. Go home, you say. If your mother were here she would beg you, implore you to go back to him. You couldn't cause your parents any greater sorrow, Constance—believe me, I'm telling you the truth."

With a muffled groan Constance fell to her knees in an armchair and buried her face in her hands.

Her aunt hobbled over to soothe her.

"Now go home nicely, Constance, be a good girl. I'll come with you. We'll take the carriage and I'll speak to Ring; he won't bother you. You can do whatever you want—come here every day. The days are getting longer now—before we know it summer will be here and you can go to Molde. It will be just as if Ring doesn't exist, until you've gotten over it—come on Constance...."

Constance lifted her head and looked at her. Her face was contorted with pain, her eyes filled with despair. Her lips were compressed with bitterness. With a violent jerk, she threw back her head and said forcefully, "If you send me away tonight, I'll kill myself—now do as you please."

Appalled, her aunt took a step backwards. She saw there was no use trying to persuade her.

"My dear Constance, you must know I am more than willing to shelter you," she said in a tearful voice. "I'm just trying to do what's right. If you're that desperate you can stay, in the name of God—in the name of God."

Constance let her head drop onto her hands, which were clenching the back of the chair.

Mrs. Wleügel hobbled over to the writing table and scribbled a few words to Ring.

"Constance is here, and she's not coming home tonight. She is completely distraught and insists on getting a divorce."

She sent the maid away with the letter.

Then she went over to Constance and with tender gestures and soothing words, persuaded her to sit down on the sofa.

"Now then, here's a stool for your feet—put the pillow behind your neck and the blanket on your lap—there, you'll be comfortable now."

Constance sat back limply, with her arms dangling, her eyes closed. Her face looked hollow, and around her mouth were deep lines of grief.

"I'll make you a nice cup of tea," Mrs. Wleügel chattered, "and then I'll get things ready for tonight—you can sleep on the sofa in my room, how about that, Constance?"

Constance nodded.

"Dear me, dear me, one must do what's right," the old lady mumbled to herself, walking out of the room with little mincing steps.

13

AFTER THE SCENE in the living room, Alette had thrown herself face down on the bed and cried until she couldn't cry any longer.

She thought about what her mother would say when she moved back home—her mother had been the housekeeper in so many fine homes, and now to suffer such disgrace. Not that she had been any better when she was young—Alette herself was the daughter of a gentleman, but that was a long time ago. When her brother got his hands on her he would beat her for sure, not that she didn't deserve it. And Hans Olai ... Whenever his name came into her mind, her sobs swelled to a wail that she could only contain by clamping her teeth on the bedclothes. Hans Olai, Hans Olai, who was due home on the ship Hope. He would be beside himself when he saw her—such a handsome, faithful boy. Oh if she could just sink down into the blackest ditch. At last her sobbing stopped; she felt as if she had no tears left, as if she were utterly wrung dry.

She stood up, fastened the bodice of her dress, and after tying on a clean apron, started to fix supper.

She had just finished when she heard Ring come in. A twinge went through her. Picking up the small hand lamp, she fled into her room and mechanically began to smooth the covers of the bed.

In a few minutes, Ring opened the kitchen door to ask her if she knew where Mrs. Ring had gone.

Alette poked her head out of the bedroom door, told him she didn't know, then withdrew.

Ring walked into the kitchen and closed the door behind him. He stopped in the doorway of the maid's room.

She was standing stiffly beside the washstand, gripping its sharp corner with one hand. Her hair was disheveled, her face swollen, her lips white and pinched. An occasional hiccup racked her body.

Touched by her apparent misery, Ring felt the first nagging stirrings of remorse.

"You do look a sight, child," he said, trying to strike a light tone.

Alette's eyes remained fixed on the squares in the wallpaper. Her lips opened so slightly that it was astonishing her words were audible, yet they came distinctly:

"After the terrible thing I've done, I suppose . . . "

"This won't do, dammit. You've got to leave, Alette—before it's too late. It's starting to show."

"Yes, that's what the mistress said," Alette said without moving.

"The mistress! Has she spoken to you?" Ring asked, gaping at her.

"Yes,"

"When?"

"Just a little while ago."

Ring went pale.

"Has somebody been here?"

"Mrs. Hansen was here."

"To hell with her! Damn that female chatter! You didn't let on, of course."

"Let on? You said yourself that it's starting to show."

"Did she ask whose it was?"

His manner was so threatening that Alette would have been frightened under other circumstances.

"It wasn't necessary. She caught us that time."

"And you admitted it—you gave me away!" His face was chalk white, his eyes distended. Swaying unsteadily on trembling knees, he raised his fist to her.

"What was the use of denying it," she said tonelessly.

"You scheming, malicious slut!" he hissed through clenched teeth. "You vindictive bitch. I'll show you what it means to ruin a man." His clenched fist struck her on the back of the neck and she pitched forward, hitting her face on the edge of the table. She clutched at the legs of the table, but the force of the fall sent her skidding with the table across the floor, where she landed in an awkward sprawl.

Blood was streaming from her nose as she rose laboriously to her feet and dried her mouth with a corner of her apron.

"Go on, hit me—kill me right now if you want to. You've ruined me, why not go on and finish it."

His fury evaporated suddenly.

"You don't know what you've done, Alette," he said in an altered tone, walking out of the room.

He was utterly beside himself, shivering with a terror that left him powerless.

Collapsing into one of the living room chairs, he slumped forward, his arms extended, his head dangling between his knees. A wave of dizziness swept over him; he felt as if everything inside him had been drained out, and nothing was left but a shell.

In a few minutes he got up again and went in to the buffet, where he poured himself a large brandy that he emptied in one gulp. It strengthened him, restored him to his senses. There would be a huge ruckus. Constance would want a divorce—he could see it now—and the minister and the relatives would all get mixed up in it. There would be hell to pay—gossip, scenes—pure hell. It wouldn't be easy to talk her out of it this time.

What should he say to her when she came in? The unpleasantness of the thought made him tear his hair.

He could not stay still. He stood up and then sat down, prowled restlessly around the room mumbling fragmented sentences under his breath—Yes, yes—good heavens—be all right—Constance's fault, too—oh darling, lovely Constance!

He began to weep and blow his nose noisily. If only she had been willing—oh, oh—what a life! But he'd be faithful to her from now on, he'd humble himself—beg, plead, cajole—oh yes, he'd calm her down. She'd have to be made of stone not to be moved by him, and she wasn't made of stone—no, not stone. His voice rose to a falsetto pitch and he wept again. It relieved him.

All of a sudden he began to wonder where she could be. It was so late—surely she would never—no, that was silly, he waved it away. Surely she would never—no, no, no—he stamped his foot—she would—he was shaking from head to foot. He would pray, oh so devoutly; he folded his hands— no, not standing up—he would kneel.

He was still on his knees when the doorbell rang.

Unsteadily he made his way to the door. It was the letter from Mrs. Wleügel.

He arrived at Incognitogaten before the maid. Mrs. Wleügel opened the door for him.

"Good evening," he stammered, stepping timidly over the threshold.

Mixed with her grief, Mrs. Wleügel felt a certain relish in being able to play such an important role in this distressing drama. She shook her head and raised one hand to indicate how terribly serious she found the matter.

"You must be very worried, of course," Ring said, anxiety in his face and voice. "This is an unfortunate turn of events."

"Heaven help that girl in there," sighed Mrs. Wleügel.

The last words were choked with emotion. Wrapping a bit of handkerchief around her index finger, she slowly dried her eyes, first one and then the other.

"Thank God she's turned to you," said Ring. "It was the only right thing to do. Ah, Aunt Wleügel, you see the state I'm in." He covered his eyes with his hand and tried to collect himself.

"Oh Ring, how could you do such a thing," the old woman said reproachfully.

"Don't talk about it," he said, lifting his hand as though warding off a blow, "I think I'm going out of my mind."

He turned toward the wall and wept.

"Come now," Mrs. Wleügel said, "hush—it's dreadful to see a man carrying on like this—you must stop crying, Ring."

"If only I could purge my soul by crying. God knows I would gladly give my life to spare Constance sorrow," he sniffled.

"One thinks too little about such things beforehand, Ring. Afterwards it's too late," Mrs. Wleügel sighed.

"Yes, that's where we humans err," Ring said, blowing his nose, "and then we have to pay for it."

"And what about the people we hurt—that's the worst part, Ring."

Ring shook his head as if too overwhelmed to reply. "Can't I speak to Constance?" he asked.

"It would be too upsetting for her. She is overwrought— you might almost say distracted."

"And she told you she wants a divorce?"

"She won't hear of anything else. There's no point talking about it tonight, Ring."

"Oh let me see her, just for a minute," he begged. "I'll leave at once if I see it's upsetting her—only a minute."

"I'll ask her."

"No, don't do that, Aunt Wleügel, she'll just say no," Ring said, restraining her. "Let me go in now—I'll be very quiet and careful. Where is she?"

"There." She pointed to the door of the living room.

Ring set his hat on the hall table, opened the door without a sound and stepped quietly into the room.

Constance was still sitting in the same position on the sofa. When her aunt had asked if she would please drink the tea she brought her, she had just shaken her head.

She felt so listless that it seemed an impossible effort to lift her head. Her mind felt strangely heavy and inert; fine streams of cold water seemed to be running continuously from the top of her head down the back of her neck.

She sat there in a daze with her eyes closed. It was so good not to have to think. But what was this warm, wet thing that was pressing itself against her hand? Someone appeared to be whispering, "Constance."

Something heavy was resting on her knee—what was it, anyhow? Very slowly she opened her eyes. A large brownish mass was in motion; it had a shiny white circle in the center and something wide and black stretching down to the floor. There was a sniffling sound.

It was not until the mass lifted and she was staring at a pair of reddened, bleary eyes that she came fully to herself.

Shrieking as if she had been bitten by a snake, she leaped off the sofa and dashed wildly around the room; seeing a door, she hurried through it, and on through the next one into a darkened room where she collided with something heavy and sharp. The violence of the blow knocked her cold, and she fell prostrate on the floor. Ring and her aunt ran into the room. Mrs. Wleügel was beside herself by the time she managed to light the lamp.

They both kneeled beside Constance. She had a large bump on her forehead, otherwise there was no mark visible. She seemed lifeless; they lifted her hands, which fell back limply.

"Go get the doctor, Ring. Be quick about it, for God's sake," said the aunt.

Ring rushed out.

With the help of the maid, who had returned in the meantime, Mrs. Wleügel managed to restore Constance to consciousness. They sprinkled her face with water, dabbed eau de cologne on her temples; and after slipping a pillow under her head, unhooked her dress and corset. By the time the doctor arrived, Constance had shown the first signs of life. He propped her upright in a chair and she quickly revived.

Opening her eyes, she saw Ring bending over her, and with a wail of anguish she buried her face in her aunt's breast and waved him away.

"Go into the living room, Ring," the aunt whispered.

The doctor waited while Constance was prepared for bed. After he had examined her, he declared that she was on the verge of serious illness, though he could not say anything further. He wrote a prescription, gave some instructions for the night, and after shaking hands with Ring and Mrs. Wleügel, promised to come back early the next morning.

Mrs. Wleügel made preparations to keep watch over Constance, who was lying quietly with her eyes shut, her breathing shallow and irregular. In the light of the green lampshade she had a deathly pallor; a wet cloth lay across her forehead. Now and then she started, as if in terror, and looked around dis-

123

tractedly, but she quickly grew calm again when her aunt assured her that she was at her house, and there would be no more talk about going home.

In the living room, Ring was pacing the floor, his chin sunk on his chest. From time to time he flung himself in a chair, buried his face in his hands and wept. Then getting to his feet, he would set off again. Sometimes he stopped and clasped his hands before him in fervent prayer. With a wave of his arms he uttered an impassioned cry: "She will be mine again—oh she will, she will—so help me God, amen."

14

CONSTANCE DEVELOPED A CONCUSSION of the brain.
For more than a week she lay in a sleepy daze, waking for brief
moments, but in her delirium unable to recognize either her
aunt or the nurse. Nevertheless, after a few days the doctor
declared that she was in no real danger, and that in all prob-
ability her illness would leave no permanent effect. When consciousness returned and the mental disturbance appeared to be
over, she slowly began to regain her strength. Scarcely had the
doctor pronounced her out of danger when, from every direction, hidden wheels were set in motion to make her give up
the thought of divorce.

Whenever she brought up the subject, they countered that
she was too weak to think about such things. She should be
patient and wait until she was stronger. She was staying with
her aunt, after all, and Ring wasn't making any trouble; surely,
for the time being, that was divorce enough.

Letters began to arrive from her mother, who was being
kept informed by Aunt Wleügel.

In response to the first letter, Constance wrote that she
would rather be burned alive than remain Ring's wife; she
would like to be spared a recital of the heartbroken vows and
promises he was sending up to Molde.

But gradually her mother's pleas began to make an impression. Mrs. Blom begged her in the name of God to spare them
the grief of this separation. If it didn't put them in their graves,
she said bluntly, it would be a sorrow that would consume
them daily.

From this quarter also, Constance heard that she was not
the only woman who had been deceived. Some dark hints in

one of the letters made Constance wonder if her own mother wasn't among the multitude of wives who had been betrayed. Gently her mother pointed out that she had perhaps not been as good and loving a wife as she might have been, that perhaps she wasn't entirely free of guilt herself.

Her father had also written a heartfelt appeal. He pointed out that the position of divorced women in society was questionable. The world, such as it was, looked askance at a woman who didn't follow the usual paths. His letter was loving in tone; he recalled many little things from her earliest childhood—dandling her on his knee, crawling around the floor playing cat and mouse. He had ended by assuring her that she was, and always had been, his dear little girl, so she must understand that he wanted what was best for her, the very best for all time.

Constance wept so long over this letter that the ink was washed away by her tears.

Reverend Huhn made frequent short visits to Mrs. Wleügel's home. The first few times, Constance had left the room when he arrived; but one day when her aunt begged her not to go, she yielded and remained in her seat. He talked quietly, but amusingly, about everyday things. Constance couldn't help liking him. One day he made her laugh at an anecdote about a dinner party where he had been seated next to a woman who had responded very oddly to everything he said. Finally he discreetly asked the man beside him if he thought his dinner partner was all there; he had discovered then that she was deaf.

One day, finding Constance alone, he led the conversation to her marital situation. He did so with delicacy and tact. She should not be anxious; he wouldn't press her for anything in the world; he just wanted to say that the deep despair Ring had shown when he, Huhn, visited him was different from anything he had ever encountered in his work as a minister. It was more than just sorrow at the prospect of losing a wife. This was genuine remorse, a kind of spiritual agony and contrition, which by psychological necessity, must bring about a new life. He had no right to censure her if she stood firm in her intention, no right at all, but he would say this much: if she did return to Ring, he would take off his hat to her—good deeds of that magnitude could not be measured by human eyes.

Sometimes they talked about religious subjects. Huhn said it interested him to hear all the petty rationalizations that man in his benighted understanding inevitably raised against the revealed word of God, but that faith, praise God, would triumph, would trample them underfoot just as surely as the seed of woman crushed the serpent's head. Once, shaking her hand as he was leaving, he said that he prayed constantly that God would give her the illumination of faith; he couldn't help himself, even if it did make her smile, and he had a premonition in his heart that his prayers would be answered. When Constance shook her head dubiously, he continued, "You see, you aren't the kind of unbeliever who sins against the Holy Ghost—you simply have honest doubts."

One day when Marie was sitting with her, she mentioned that Meier had been home for a visit and had now gone back to his conservatory.

"He asked about you, Constance, and he wanted me to send his regards."

"Do you think he will get anywhere with his music?" asked Mrs. Wleügel.

"The newspapers are raving about some songs he sent home. They were sung in a concert the other night. One is especially lovely—and very melancholy."

"I'd really like to buy them," Constance said. "Are they difficult?"

"No, you could play them easily. 'When I see your eyes shining . . . '" Marie sang. "Oh, I don't know the music by heart. They cost a krone—I bought them, too. He's working on something longer now, I believe."

The thought of Meier saddened Constance. She remembered their conversations, his playing—all the pleasant times they had spent together. It struck her that she had actually been happy when she was with him. She suddenly recalled the expression in his eyes as they rested on her, and she saw his pale face, overcome with emotion, when he had said good-bye. She was disappointed that he had been in the city and not come to see her; it seemed so dreary and sad that he was gone now, and she might never see him again.

The sound of a name roused her.

"Did you say Lorck?" her aunt inquired, pushing her glasses up on her forehead. She was embroidering.

"Yes, what do you think about that! It's so ridiculous," said Marie.

"What about Lorck?" asked Constance.

"Well, would you believe that people are saying you're getting the divorce because of Lorck? Really, I ask you . . . "

"Because of him?" Constance said, letting her work fall to her lap.

"They've made up an entire history," Marie went on. "He'd been making advances to you for heaven knows how long, and finally you gave in and told Ring you wanted to divorce him and marry Lorck. Ring went into a rage, you flew off to Aunt Wleügel and fell ill out of sheer terror. As you see, they're at no loss for ideas."

"What impertinent rubbish!" her aunt said furiously.

"So poor Ring is trying to get some ready money for the settlement," Marie went on, "and that's the reason he's selling his bank bonds."

"*Is* he selling his bank bonds?" interrupted Mrs. Wleügel.

"He sold one because of the Swedish iron mines," Marie replied. "Imagine Rikard having to listen to that nonsense when he knows the truth."

"So people are busy with me and my affairs?" asked Constance.

"Well you know it doesn't take very much to make people talk. You aren't taking this seriously, Constance?" Marie said, with a look of concern.

"Not at all!" Constance answered. "Let them talk."

"But you're so pale, Constance." Leaning on her cane, Mrs. Wleügel clumped over to her. "Nobody is safe from gossip—especially a wife who wants a divorce—that's something you have to prepare yourself for. It's not something to take lightly, believe me."

"That's why I really wish you would drop this, Constance," Marie said earnestly. "Lord knows you have grounds enough, and Ring has certainly deserved it. But it will be so awful for you—people will talk behind your back, suspect you—I'm really just thinking about you."

"What Marie says is true," said Mrs. Wleügel, picking a bit of lint off Constance's sleeve. "A divorced woman is like a garden with no fence—anybody who pleases can tramp all over it. I either read that or heard somebody say it, I don't remember, but I think there's a lot of truth in it."

"Or if they don't tramp all over you, they give you pitying looks—that's not so pleasant either," Marie said.

Constance turned her chair toward the window, propped her chin in her hand and stared out through the pane.

Mrs. Wleügel signaled Marie not to say anything more.

Shortly afterwards, Marie rose and said good-bye.

"Actually, they say he's very much changed," she told her aunt out in the hall.

"Who? Oh, Lorck—don't mention his name," Mrs. Wleügel replied with distaste. "Imagine a story like that!"

"But it's not his fault, Aunt. The other day I saw him at a party and he asked about Constance in such an earnest, charming way. I was struck by how different he seems."

Hobbling back into the living room, Mrs. Wleügel went over to the sewing table by the center window. Constance was still in the same position. Mrs. Wleügel gave her a quick glance, then went over and touched her head. Constance pulled away, and cupping her face in her hands, put her head on the window sill and started to cry.

"Now Constance, my dear Constance—what is it now, child?"

Constance lifted her face enough to move her lips.

"Why can't you leave me alone! You never give me any peace." The words came with difficulty through her tears; she put her face down again and continued to cry.

Her aunt shook her head sadly and went into the dining room to feed the canary.

Constance stood up suddenly and picked up the letter that had come from Ring that morning. She had read only the first few lines; now she ripped it to shreds, tossed the pieces on the floor, and ground them underfoot.

She hated him, she wanted harm to come to him, she wanted to smack his bold face—the wretch—how dare he ask her to forgive him, to swear he would be faithful, imagining how things would be if she would—oh, she wouldn't even let herself think about it.

And all the rest of them—always trying to talk her into going back to him, so willing to hand her over—what spineless, contemptible people. They were the worst! No indignation, no rage at what he had done. How could she expect anything else from a man like him when they were all on his side.

Was the world really just one huge mire? Was a person supposed to be happy if she could just keep from sinking all the way to the bottom?

15

On the advice of her doctor, Constance agreed to go to Modum. Her aunt had succeeded in persuading her to put off preparations for the divorce until she returned from the spa. It was now well into May, and in two weeks they would set off. Lately Constance had stopped referring to the all-consuming issue, and her aunt had begun to hope, faintly, that she would take her advice in the end.

One morning as they were sewing together in the living room, it became obvious that Aunt Wleügel had something on her mind.

In the course of a half hour she had changed her seat four times, dragging the large white cloth on which she had been sewing around the room with her. She cleared her throat, blew her nose, took off her glasses and replaced them for the seventh time, mumbling occasionally, "Dear me, dear me— one must do what's right."

Constance felt uneasy. What kind of torture was she going to be subjected to this time? She felt like a patient watching someone prepare to remove the bandages from a painful wound. Finally she couldn't stand it any longer.

"What are you brooding about, Aunt?" she said, tossing aside her sewing. "Is something wrong again?"

"No Constance—but I'm worried—Heaven knows how this is going to affect you," stammered Mrs. Wleügel.

"Well then say it; say it!" she cried like an impatient child.

"My goodness, you don't give me a chance to speak," her aunt said with an injured air. "It will bring back memories— promise you'll be calm, Constance."

"Is it Molde?" Constance asked quickly.

"Not at all. Well, it's the baby, you see."

"The baby," she repeated.

"The one—you know, Constance—the one she was expecting."

Constance turned toward the window, her back to her aunt. Blood rushed to her head.

"What about it?" she said, with a slight tremor in her voice.

"It died, and it's a blessing, really. . . . "

Constance didn't move.

"It was the best thing for the poor creature. Yes, for everybody," her aunt went on. "Ah yes, the Lord makes all things right in the end."

Constance crossed her arms on her breast and stared straight ahead.

"The mother," her aunt continued, hobbling around the room and flicking dust off the backs of the chairs with her fingertips, "has gone to America—imagine—with someone who wants to marry her. They were engaged—he was beside himself at first, I believe—but then he said if she could fall, she could rise again. Her mother told me about it—you remember, she's the housekeeper here. It certainly was very fine and Christian of him. And now Constance," she added in a softer voice, stopping right beside her, "now I think everything is quite different—yes, it's almost as if all these dreadful things have just been a dream." She rustled off again, tidying up, moving a few knickknacks from one spot to another.

"One must do what's right," she went on. "And it can never be right to push someone away who is lying at one's feet, repentant and imploring, especially someone so close—like Alette and the sailor, for instance. One isn't any happier for doing it." Mrs. Wleügel was straightening an antimacassar, which she couldn't get to lie flat. "I've never told you about myself, but I'll tell you now. I got a separation. Yes indeed, I did—I felt I would die if I didn't go through with it. But when it was done, I had no peace night or day—nothing but tears and pain. Being separated didn't help in the least. I had thought there would be some relief, some comfort in it, but I was wrong, as wrong as anybody could be—it was worse. I missed Wleügel—I had always felt unable to do anything without him. So after three months passed and I couldn't stand it any longer, I wrote to Wleügel and told him I would forgive him. I have never seen anybody so happy—he cried and carried me down to the carriage. When I got home I almost felt it was the happiest day of my life. Of course he had relapses, you understand." She stopped for a moment to dry her eyes. "Ah yes, the poor man—he always reproached himself so. But right then I wanted to thank God on my knees. He had taken both my little ones to Heaven, you see—little Conny had died too; it wasn't long after that." She couldn't speak through her tears. "Ah Constance, my dear, we all have our sorrows, don't you see? When we're young we scream and say we can't bear it—but then the Lord comes and shows us that there are many less fortunate than ourselves. Then we understand that punishment purifies us, and if we only try to do what's right, God makes everything turn out for the best in the end." She could force out the last words only with difficulty—her quiet weeping turned into racking sobs.

Her poor aunt, thought Constance; she certainly had had her share of suffering. But why were they always saying God sent it, as if He had anything to do with all these revolting things. She walked over to her aunt, put her arms around her, and gave her a heartfelt kiss. Then she went into her room and closed the door.

But in bed that night she asked herself, for the first time, if she could imagine the possibility of returning to Ring.

Everything in her rebelled at the thought, but the question kept returning. In the end she cried herself to sleep, grieving that she had not overcome this uncertainty, wondering what they might get her to do.

By the time their day of departure arrived, Constance had yielded to her aunt's fervent pleas: she would agree to see Ring before they left, but not until they were on the point of driving away.

He fell to his knees in a storm of emotion, cried and kissed her hands. Constance freed herself, said good-bye, and walked out.

He followed her into the hall, begging to be allowed to write to her. He pleaded fervently, assuring her that he would not expect any answer. Finally she yielded and said yes.

Every other day a letter arrived at Modum. After a few weeks of this, she let her aunt persuade her to send a few words in reply.

Ring's next letter was filled with rapture.

The stay at the spa did not have the desired effect upon Constance, although the doctor assured her aunt that improvement would not be long in coming.

But Constance grew thinner and remained weak and listless. Insomnia plagued her, and her nerves were in such a state that her eyes filled with tears at the slightest provocation.

Letters came regularly from Molde. In a letter to Aunt Wleügel, Constance's mother wrote that Blom had been ailing for some time and now was confined to bed. The doctor had said that his illness was a kind of progressive nervous fever.

"I think it's grief about Constance," she wrote. "He could probably recover if he had good news from her, but you mustn't try to talk her into it—her father doesn't want her to consider his feelings in any way."

Constance read this letter shortly before bed one evening. That night she didn't fall asleep until five o'clock in the morning.

She lay there struggling to work up her courage. If she went back to Ring now, it would make them all so happy—why shouldn't she do it? They all had the same opinion, so there must be some wisdom in it. Wasn't it just a meaningless formality after all? There was no question about living with him as his wife—she'd prefer death to that. And it didn't make any difference to her where she lived—there was nothing attracting her to any other place—dear God, life wasn't worth all the fuss—and she was tired, so tired. The whole world was against her, it was madness not to give in—and maybe it was just as they said, a matter of adjusting to circumstances.

By the time they left the spa, Constance had written to Ring and promised she would give up the divorce and return to him. There was one clear and definite condition: she would not come back as his wife; he would have to let her live as his sister or hostess.

Ring gave his joyful assent. Naturally, that went without saying, he wrote back to her. Strangely enough it made no dent in his happiness—a sign of how much he had changed. Constance would see that his terrible mental torment had left a mark on him. He swore eternal gratitude and devotion and called her his guardian angel.

Once Constance had made the decision, she felt greatly relieved. It was as if she were sailing into harbor after a troubled, dangerous journey. The praise and gratitude that her aunt showered on her, that overflowed from the letters of Marie and her parents, soothed her like incense. She was filled with a languorous self-satisfaction. When she thought about the sacrifice she had made, she was moved and exalted by her act.

16

EVERYTHING WAS FINE in the beginning. Ring was as happy as a lark, as humble as a servant restored to favor, ready to do everything in his power to win back the confidence his false step had cost him. In every conceivable way he showed his intention to please her. Anticipating her smallest wish, he slipped the footstool under her feet, took care that the newspaper was ready at precisely the time she liked to read it, brought her flowers and books; he was touched and grateful if she allowed him to kiss her hand when she said good-night.

Constance adjusted better than she had expected beforehand. If things remained as they were, she felt she could probably tolerate living with Ring.

But gradually, as Ring grew accustomed to the new arrangement, the joy and gratitude he had felt when Constance gave up the divorce was pushed into the background. It would have been an utterly senseless thing to do—to abandon her fine home, break up a well-ordered life for such an insignificant reason. Talk about making a mountain out of a molehill—this was certainly the perfect example. She had been stopped, luckily, and Ring congratulated himself on the part he had played in it.

These thoughts increased his confidence, and the mixture of embarrassment and deference that had initially marked his behavior toward Constance gradually began to disappear. He became more like his old self, and one night, after a few drinks, jokingly hinted that she should move in from the guest room—it was so disagreeable lying there in the big bedroom alone, he was afraid of the dark, and so on.

She pretended not to understand him and quickly changed the subject.

Some days later he returned to the topic. Constance was ashamed of him and gave him a look of such disgust and indignation that he didn't have the courage to proceed. But after a few days passed, he was on the attack again—complaining about his position, expressing his hopes and desires in the most explicit way. Constance refused, contemptuously, and asked if he had no sense of honor at all. Embarrassed, he remained silent for a few days, but then he began to coax and wheedle again. Constance reminded him angrily of their agreement and told him he would drive her to distraction if he didn't stop bothering her. Striking his hand to his forehead, he moaned that no man could bear what he was going through. Thus it went for several months. Little by little Constance's anger subsided under the dulling weight of custom. In the end she greeted his advances with the half-irritated, half-indulgent expression of an adult trying to ignore the pestering of an ill-bred child.

Often during this period, Ring was groggy when he went to bed. Constance could smell the liquor when he came in to say good night. On more than one occasion she heard him come in from stag parties so drunk that he had trouble finding his room.

One morning after such a party, he felt too ill to go to the office and had to lie down on the sofa as soon as he had dressed. Complaining of headache and dizziness, he remarked several times that he couldn't imagine what was wrong with him.

"It's easy enough to understand," Constance said indifferently. "When a man comes home in a state like that, naturally he'll wake up with a hangover."

"And what do you think causes it?" he said, turning dull eyes toward her. "What's a desperate man supposed to do? Oh Constance, it's your fault."

She clamped her lips together, measured him with a disdainful glance, and walked away.

Marie had persuaded Constance to join her at the charitable organization where she served as a member of the board. Constance plunged in eagerly. At this time, with friends rather uncertainly keeping their distance, she had nothing else to do. She sewed and knitted, not only at the weekly sewing circle, but also at home. She took walks with Marie, investigating conditions in their district. The work distracted her and kept her occupied; at times she found solace in forgetting her own cares in the misery of others.

One morning she and Marie went out to Ruseløkkveien to search for a family that had moved into the district and asked Reverend Huhn to sign their request for charity. He had asked Marie to find out if they were deserving poor. Marie had jotted down the name and address, so they found the place easily. It was a large tenement with many one-room apartments and kitchens shared by many families.

In front of the building stood a woman, barefoot except for wooden shoes, who was scrubbing woolen clothes in a cut-off barrel filled with murky grey wash water. A piece of ragged burlap with a large black number in one corner, obviously a remnant of a sack, served as her apron, and a blue checked handkerchief was knotted around her head. Her bare, knobby arms were streaked with dirty water. They asked her if she could tell them where to find the family in question.

With a sullen expression and a stabbing inquisitive stare, she pointed to a cellar window just at ground level to the left.

The two women thanked her, and gathering up their plissé skirts, descended the filthy stone steps.

Marie knocked on the door, which was partly ajar, and getting no answer, pushed it open and stepped over the threshold, with Constance behind her. The low, oblong room contained hardly any furniture except for a narrow bench in the far corner, where a curled-up figure lay snoring on a bed of straw. A shred of a decrepit blind hung in front of the lowest panes of the window, which began at the ceiling and extended half way down the wall. In the middle of the rubbish-strewn floor stood a rough wooden crate crammed with nondescript rags. A boy of five sat on one edge playing with a broken frying pan; his face was covered with a thick layer of dirt and his eyes were crusty and oozing. Beside the stove was an iron kettle that had been scraped clean, a wooden whisk inside it;

near the top, around the handles, traces of porridge still remained. A pale little girl sat on a chest under the window; her eyes were unnaturally large and her thin hair was tied in a pigtail with a piece of shoelace. Her bare feet were filthy; the back of her ragged dress was held together by a single hook. She was holding an infant on her lap, wrapped in what remained of a chocolate-colored shawl. The baby's head was a single crusty sore; he fretted and whined, sucking his fingers and staring dully out of rheumy eyes. The little girl was trying to soothe him, jiggling him up and down, forward and backwards, on her knees. A pestilential smell filled the room, and moisture had made broad streaks down the whitewashed walls.

"We're looking for a workman, Severin Bendiksen," Marie said, turning to the child on the chest. "Does he live here?"

"Yes," the girl answered, with a frightened sideways glance at the bed.

"Is he home?" Marie continued, looking around the room.

"N-no," she said hesitantly, glancing toward the bed again.

"He's the one sleeping over there, of course," Constance whispered. "Don't ask her again, the poor thing."

"The wife's name is Ellen Jakobsdatter," Marie said, holding the slip of paper in her hand. "Is she here?"

"No," was the reply.

"Is she at work?"

"She's out begging," whispered the child.

"Are these your brothers and sisters?" Marie continued, looking from the infant to the boy, who had come over to his sister and now was staring at the strangers, his coal black fingers in his mouth.

"Yes," was the answer.

"Isn't there another one?"

"No," the girl whispered.

"But it says here that there are four, *four* children unprovided for," Marie read.

"We are four with Fredrikke," stammered the child.

"Well where is Fredrikke then?" Marie asked.

"Out begging."

"Isn't she your sister?" Marie went on.

"Y-es," she drawled, looking at Marie with frightened eyes.

Constance was holding her handkerchief to her mouth, nearly nauseated by the stench.

"We can't get any more information here," she whispered. "That child is an idiot. Come on, let's go."

"Does your father have a job?" Marie asked as they were turning toward the door.

"No," whispered the child.

"He can't find anything?"

"Y-es," she glanced toward the bed again.

"Please ask your mother to come see me," Constance said, writing her name and address on a scrap of paper from Marie's notebook, "and I'll give her some clothes for you. She obviously doesn't understand a syllable," Constance muttered, turning toward Marie.

"Y-es," answered the child.

"Do you know anything about the people down there?" Marie asked the woman who was still outside washing when they came up to the street.

"Can't say as I do," she answered with a disdainful jerk of her head.

"They've just moved in, haven't they?" Marie continued.

"Aye, and with the Lord's help they'll soon be out of here, too," the woman remarked, looking as if she would have no hesitation about throwing them out.

"Is it unpleasant living in the same building with them?"

"It's unpleasant, all right," she retorted, scrubbing vigorously on a heavy workshirt.

"In what way? What do they do?" Marie asked condescendingly.

"Ask the landlord," the woman answered crossly.

"Fighting and carrying on?" Marie asked, shaking her head as if to say: I'm not surprised that you're angry.

"Since they moved in, we ain't had a night's peace." The woman pounded away on the wet clothes, splattering water in all directions. "Oh no, and we've got to put up with it, cause we're right on top of them."

"Does the husband drink?" Marie asked.

"Reckon they both do, God forbid," she said in a guarded tone.

"Oh no," Marie said, "that must be so awful for the rest of you."

"Wouldn't be so bad—grownups can look out fer themselves—but when they start yelling and beating them kids—swearing and crashing around—you'd think the house was coming down."

"Good heavens, how dreadful," Constance said with a sigh. "What do they live on?"

The woman looked at Constance for an instant. A scornful expression appeared on her wide coarse mouth.

"Live on?" she repeated. "You want to know what poor people live on?"

"I mean, don't they have any income?"

"And where would they get that? From charity maybe—how would I know."

"Doesn't the husband have a job?" Marie asked.

"Him! Wouldn't make any difference—he drinks up every shilling he lays his hands on."

"But if he were helped to find work, don't you think he would be all right?" Constance asked in a sympathetic tone.

Something covetous glittered in the woman's small, dull eyes. She shook the water off her hands, gripped the edge of the barrel, and turning to face the two women, said in a suddenly shrill voice, "That would really be a sin and a shame, a no-good like that, too lazy to lift a finger unless he's beating his wife! She's sleeping outside on the ground again, scared to let him see her—and that good-for-nothing, lying in there dead to the world—you can hear him snoring clear out here—a pig like that, with his shopgirl over in the basement—expecting, same as his wife—but that's the kind you always give the help to—while other poor, hard-working souls . . . " she had to stop and catch her breath.

Constance had grown quite pale. "That poor woman," she said with a shiver. "Something ought to be done for her."

"Her!" the woman cried. "Oh she's truly needy all right. She

141

goes out begging and comes back with her bags and baskets so full she and her brats can't hardly drag them in the door. Course she gets caught sometimes and turned in for stealing," she added, with a malicious glint in her eye.

"Come on, let's go," Constance whispered, tugging at Marie. "Don't stand there listening to that horrible woman."

Marie said good-bye; the woman scarcely responded, and the women hurried away from the dismal place.

"That Bendiksen family is the worst kind of trash," said Marie. "You can't call them deserving poor."

"The worse they are, the more they need help," Constance objected. "How awful and depressing it is to see such filth and misery—it's sickening! And imagine, this is only one family— there must be a thousand like them."

"You left a message for her to come to your house. What are you going to do with her?"

"Give her the clothes I have ready and whatever food and money I can scrape together."

"But you heard—she's a drunkard and a thief."

"What concern is that of mine? They're starving. I can see why they do those things."

"People who are energetic and hardworking don't go hungry; nobody can say we don't take care of our poor," Marie said firmly.

"Well, that's easy to say, but I don't believe all that rubbish about anyone being able to find work who wants it—not enough to live on, at least—and when there are so many children, and sickness—it's heartbreaking."

"The decent ones will always get help," Marie assured her. "We must trust in the Lord for that."

"The decent ones—born and bred in conditions like that! And the help you talk about is criminal! Bringing them up to live on charity—it's demoralizing; it teaches them to lie down like cattle and wait for more."

"But my goodness, what can we do?" Marie cried.

"I don't know—I just don't know—but what we're doing is wrong, terribly wrong."

"Really, Constance, I can tell from your voice that you're

crying. If you're going to act like this you aren't fit to go visiting people."

Constance didn't reply. She walked with her head bowed, the tears streaming down her face. Shortly afterwards they arrived at her house. She hurriedly said good-bye to Marie and went in.

That afternoon, when Ring had returned to his office and Constance was alone in the living room, the maid entered and said that a beggarwoman was asking to speak to her.

"Has she been here before?" Constance asked.

"I don't think so. She says you asked her to come."

"Ah, it's her," said Constance. "Show her into the dining room."

As Constance entered the room, she saw standing by the door a large, strongly built, but exceedingly thin woman whose sallow angular face was enveloped in a brown woolen hood. Around her shoulders she was wearing the chocolate colored shawl that had been wrapped around the infant that morning; on her feet were a pair of gaping, tattered men's boots. The hem of her black skirt was ragged and much shorter in the front than the back. She wore no apron, and her coarse bony hands were clasped above her sharply protruding belly.

"I'm the one the two ladies came to see this morning," she said obsequiously in an accent from Western Norway.

There was something feline and cunning in the way she tilted her head slightly as she talked; her eyes were shifty and uncertain. She had a crude, protruding lower jaw, and her mouth seemed to have spit out every gentle feeling.

Constance felt uneasy at the sight of her; she was reluctant to get involved and at a loss as to what to say.

"I'd like to give you a few clothes for the children," she said after a few minutes thought.

"Thank you, ma'am, that'll be a help, I'm sure," the woman said, one hand stroking the other restlessly.

Constance was astonished that she didn't seem more grateful.

"Beg pardon ma'am," she added immediately afterwards,

"do you know if they're going to help us?"

"I certainly hope so," Constance answered. "You must need it terribly."

"Yes ma'am. With my husband laid up and four hungry children, besides the one on the way," she added humbly.

"Is your husband crippled?"

"It's his right arm, you see—it's there on the application—he was at sea when it happened—he fell and broke his shoulderblade." Something in her voice begged the lady's pardon for bothering her with all this.

"Can't he do any work at all?" Constance asked.

"Oh no—Lord help us, what can a man do with one arm? He can carry fish for people—odd jobs like that—but now they've started delivering to the houses, there's no work left for the rest of us." She spoke in the same servile tone, her hands in constant motion.

"But how can you go on having all those children when you don't have any way to support them?" Constance asked disapprovingly.

"What's a poor soul to do?" the woman said, shaking her head piously. "It's God's will."

The answer irritated Constance.

"What about illegitimate children—do you think God sends them, too?" she asked.

"They must be a punishment for sin," sighed the woman meekly.

"Wouldn't you rather live alone, so you wouldn't have to have any more children?" Constance asked.

"When you're married before God, you have to live together. What God hath joined together, let no man put asunder." She sounded as if she were reading the words from a book.

Constance was nauseated by the sound of these words in the woman's mouth.

"But your husband isn't faithful to you," Constance said. "I've heard he has another woman."

"It's a sin of weakness, ma'am. The Bible tells us to forgive our erring brothers." The words were accompanied by a sanctimonious sigh.

Constance was going out to get the clothes when she suddenly remembered that there was one more question she wanted to ask.

"The little girl we met today mentioned someone called Fredrikke—is she your child?"

"No, he had her before we got married."

"Don't you think you would be better off if you left your husband and lived on your own?" Constance asked. It sounded more like she was thinking aloud than actually speaking to the woman.

She shook her head. "How could I expect help from either God or man if I did an unchristian thing like that?"

Constance handed her the bundle of clothing. The woman took it, thanked her, and tried to roll it up more tightly on her lap.

Constance looked in her change purse. A tense expression appeared on the woman's face; she didn't move her head, but her eager eyes followed every movement of Constance's fingers.

"Please, here's a little something for food," Constance said, holding out a five kroner note.

A dark flush suddenly swept over the sickly pallor of the woman's face, and a glimmer of surprise appeared in her eyes; her features quivered. As she was taking the money, she seized Constance's hand and pressed it to her cracked lips. Tears were streaming down her cheeks when she raised her head.

"God bless and reward you for eternity," she whimpered, drying her eyes with the back of her hand. "God strengthen you and bring you joy for the kindness you've shown a poor hungry soul."

Constance shivered, moved by the intensity of the woman's emotion, and her lips trembled. How much hunger and pain the poor creature must have suffered to collapse like that at the sight of a miserable five kroner note.

"I'll do what I can to help you get charity," she said, with a nod of dismissal.

"Oh thank you, thank you," the woman answered as she left

the room.

Constance was troubled. She couldn't free her mind of the things she had seen that day. The stinking cellar room and those miserable children were still present before her. That contemptible marriage—the drinking, the beatings, the debauchery—filled her with disgust.

She couldn't get rid of the feeling that she had been contaminated by her contact with those dreadful people, and several times she had to sniff at her dress to reassure herself that no odor clung to it.

This was a woman who accepted her husband's behavior as a part of marriage—without rebelling or leaving—who continued to bear his children, even though he mistreated her and carried on with another woman right before her eyes. Were hunger and need so powerful that they could destroy every bit of human feeling?

No concept of responsibility—not even toward the innocent creatures their careless appetites brought into the world, and turned loose in a life so filled with misery and pain! It was God's will—He was the one who sent the children, man had to accept His will—that was the only answer they had.

Didn't religion seem to turn people into dumb animals who didn't think beyond the food on which they gorged themselves at the moment?

These people lived like animals—what was the use of helping them? It was like trying to fill a bottomless pit—they just dug themselves deeper and deeper.

No, she would not go to visit the poor again. There was really nothing she could do except take their suffering upon herself, and that didn't help anybody. Marie could go alone! She was so matter of fact about it—her categories were all ready: deserving or undeserving. From now on she would send her gifts to charity and let others give them out to those who were truly in need.

When she had made this decision, she felt relieved. She went in and washed her hands, moistened her handkerchief with eau de toilette, then picked up a book and sat down to read.

17

ONE AFTERNOON TOWARD the end of October, Mrs. Wleügel came to visit Constance. Twilight was falling, but the tile stove cast such pleasant reflections around the room that Constance had not felt like ringing for the lamps.

Her aunt had brought her some used clothing for the poor, but Constance told her to send them to Marie instead. Mrs. Wleügel said she had received a letter from Molde and told her a little about its contents.

There was a pause. Mrs. Wleügel twisted nervously in her chair and softly cleared her throat a few times. Finally she said, "Your mother also wrote about how happy she is that everything is fine again between you and Ring. She can't stop thinking about it."

"Well, I'm glad they're happy," Constance said with a sigh.

"But if she were here and could see for herself, she'd be terribly concerned—yes she would, Constance."

"Why? They got what they wanted."

"Because Ring is in a bad way, Constance." Her aunt paused a moment to gather her courage. "I'm afraid he's going to the dogs over this," she said firmly.

"Going to the dogs—now? I thought you talked me into coming back to keep that from happening." There was an edge to her voice.

"You don't have your heart in it . . . " She broke off as the door opened and the maid came in carrying the lighted lamps.

"You've only gone half way, Constance," she went on when they were alone again. "One must do what's right, and it can never be right to be unyielding. Ring can't stand it, Constance —he's becoming a drunkard." She almost whispered the last words.

"Becoming?" Constance said disdainfully. "You've got your tenses wrong, Aunt. Past and present tense are closer to the truth."

"Oh no, Constance, this is quite different from taking a glass too many at a party. Quite different," she repeated, shaking her head.

"No, by heaven, it isn't," Constance answered indignantly. "He's never known how to control himself."

"But it's gotten worse—it's gotten much worse, Constance. He does it out of desperation," Mrs. Wleügel sighed. "Things can't go on like this," she continued imploringly. "You've got to move back in with him or he's going to become a complete drunkard—imagine what that would mean, being married to a drunkard. You've got to go all the way with this—forgive him completely and absolutely. One must do what's right, Constance."

"Has he complained to you?" Constance asked. Her voice cut like a knife.

"No indeed, he hasn't," said Mrs. Wleügel, a bit flustered, "but anyone can see that the man is bitterly unhappy. He's come to my house several times around seven o'clock, and he's been quite tipsy. That's terribly early in the evening."

Mrs. Wleügel was not telling the truth. Ring had expressly asked her to plead his case with Constance. He was waiting at her house to hear what happened.

"He knew what he was letting himself in for," Constance answered curtly.

"Yes, but the man's bound to be in torment. He couldn't help but be, unless he were superhuman—and he certainly isn't that."

"No, God knows!" Constance exclaimed scornfully.

"But you really can't reproach him for that," her aunt answered with a pained expression.

"When a man agrees to something, he should stick to it. He's despicable otherwise," Constance cried.

"Men are weak—Ring doesn't have your strength of character. We aren't all alike, Constance. One must do what's right."

Constance didn't answer. She sat with her elbows on her

148

knees, her face in her hands, rocking slowly back and forth.

Mrs. Wleügel hobbled over to her and put her hand on her shoulder.

"In a sense, I'm here in your mother's place, Constance," she said earnestly. "You must know that I want what's best for you."

"Oh yes, you all do, at least that's what you say." Her face was still hidden in her hands and her voice was muffled and unclear.

"Those of us who are older," her aunt went on, "have a better view of your welfare."

"Well, God knows if the things you make me do are so good for me," she almost shouted, jumping to her feet.

"Really Constance, how can you be so unkind."

"No, it's true," she cried. "You're destroying me—you're corrupting me completely—making me think life is just a sink of lies and misery. It's unreasonable to expect faithfulness and truth in marriage, you say. Ring's not an exception—far from it—the others are much worse. The terrible things you hear don't upset you—you, Marie, Reverend Huhn, Mother, and Father—all of you. You pretend to think it's terrible, for the sake of appearances, but there's nothing genuine about your anger. That's how it is, you say—men are so weak." She paced back and forth restlessly, stopping now and then for a moment to make a gesture with her hand, the words tumbling out in a torrent, her eyes ablaze. Suddenly she walked directly up to her aunt, stamped her foot, and raised her tightly clenched fists to her face. "Why do you all pretend to believe that idiotic talk about the good and the beautiful—the power of religion —that marriage is sacred and made by God. Sacred!" she repeated with a laugh. "I loathe the filthy institution—loathe and despise it. I despise everything—everything—and myself most of all, because I'm wretched enough to let you lead me by the nose, in spite of, yes *in spite of* my better judgement. Do you know what this means, Aunt? It means the end of me."

The old woman retreated a few steps. Constance's words whirled past her—she hadn't understood a syllable. But this violent revolt frightened her; leaning heavily on her cane, she stared at her, wide-eyed and speechless. When Constance stopped, her confusion gave way to tears.

Constance was suddenly calm.

"Forgive me for getting so angry, Aunt—that wasn't meant for you," she said in a dull voice. "It's not your fault, or anybody else's—it's the whole system, but you don't see that, Aunt."

Mrs. Wleügel continued to weep.

"Now don't be angry with me." She put her arm around her shoulders. "You mustn't cry, Auntie—you know I didn't mean you—there, there, stop crying."

Mrs. Wleügel slowly dried her eyes, blew her nose, and put away her handkerchief.

"You said such ugly things, Constance. You really frightened the life out of me. I know I've always wanted to do what's right." Her tears welled up again.

"Yes, I know, Aunt—and you have, too. You've done the best you could for me and everyone else." Constance patted her cheek.

"Well, I'd better be getting home," her aunt said, with the look of a child who had been scolded unjustly. She took a couple of steps and paused.

Constance stood there, pulling at her handkerchief with short deliberate jerks.

"Think about what we've been discussing, Constance," she pleaded timidly. "Believe me, it's best for both of you."

Unable to make herself say what her aunt wanted to hear, Constance made no reply.

But Mrs. Wleügel would not give up without some kind of promise. Ring was waiting at home, and he had called her his guardian angel.

"Promise me that you will forgive Ring completely," she implored. "Or at least, promise me you'll try."

At the word 'forgive,' Constance again felt her blood start to boil. Her tongue burned to reply that if she went ahead and forgave him, to use their words, it would just mean that she was deliberately throwing herself in the mud. But she repressed it. What was the use? This decent old soul whose original purity and refinement had been dulled by life—it was pointless to frighten her.

"Yes Aunt, I'll try," she said quietly, turning her face away.

"That's good of you, Constance—thank you for saying that. Now things will be much better, you'll see. You'll be so filled with happiness, and when you ask yourself why, you'll know it's because you did what was right."

Constance sighed deeply, but made no reply.

After Mrs. Wleügel had left, Constance sat down to think. She had felt all along that it would end like this, but she had lacked the courage to look the truth squarely in the face. There was no use in resisting any longer; since she had agreed to come back to him, there was nothing else to do. In the long run, her position was impossible. She was slipping downhill and there was no way of stopping herself. May as well let go!

She thought about Ring's infatuated antics, his vows of love, and shuddered. Agreeing to live with a man she despised! But perhaps it wouldn't be so bad when she got used to it. She had never really loved him! But she had made an honest attempt to love him. The idea that he could be unfaithful had never entered her mind. She had considered herself his property, regarded her marriage with respect, at least—and somehow, that had held things together—but now! She felt as if she were deliberately prostituting herself for her keep. "Yes, that's what it is!" she said to herself, clasping her head in her hands. "Well," she whispered a little later, "there are so many others who do it—it's no worse for you than for anyone else."

When she heard Ring in the hall, she picked up her work and was leaning over it when he came in.

He said a pleasant good evening and sat down in the armchair next to her.

"You're so industrious, Constance," he said admiringly. "Always busy—you look so sweet sitting there at your work."

She didn't answer.

"What are you knitting now?" His tone was unassuming, but very interested.

"Stockings."

"For the poor children?"

"Yes."

There was a pause.

"Do you know what day it is, Constance?" Ring asked, after clearing his throat a few times. His voice was timid and uncertain.

"No," she said curtly.

"It's the 26th of October, of course. Didn't you remember?"

"No," came the reply.

"But I thought . . . " He had very nearly blundered and revealed that he knew her aunt had been there. "Well," he continued, with a self-congratulatory smile at his excellent memory, "so you had forgotten—it's the day we became engaged, Constance," he added softly.

"Remembering that doesn't give me any pleasure, I'm afraid," she said dryly.

Ring sighed deeply.

"Ah well, Constance, that may be true, from your point of view. But as for me—well I can't help but think of it as the happiest day of my life, after our wedding day, of course."

"Oh hush!" she said, with an impatient gesture.

"All right, Constance, I'll be quiet if that's what you want—not a word without your permission. I'll do anything to please you." He leaned toward her with an imploring look; his voice was soft and timid.

She turned away, an expression of weariness on her face.

"Oh Constance, couldn't you bring yourself to give me a single little sign of affection, on this one day—it would be an act of kindness." His voice cracked; he held his hands to his eyes and drew a deep moaning breath.

Constance measured him with an appraising eye.

"He's drunk again, of course," she thought to herself.

He stood up, walked up and down the floor a few times, and sat down very quietly in the same place.

"I have had a vain hope," he began in a distressed voice. "I thought the memory of that day might soften you—oh Constance, you are being very cruel to me." He leaned forward, his elbow resting on one knee, his face in his hand.

"Tell me one thing," Constance said coldly. "What did you

really mean when you were so willing to take me back on the terms I set."

"What did I mean—I meant . . . " he stammered.

She looked him directly in the face. He was flustered.

"I don't understand," he broke off, lowering his head.

"You seemed to think it was so reasonable—you hadn't even imagined it could be otherwise. Do you remember?"

"I was perfectly sincere, Constance. I could understand very well that it wouldn't be right away—but I hoped, of course." He stopped and sighed.

"There was no talk about right away or later—no possibility of change in the future. You accepted my terms absolutely. When I think about the way you're behaving . . . " she stopped suddenly. "My God, aren't you ashamed of yourself?" she added, turning away.

"I love you so much, Constance," he moaned.

"Don't use that word; it's detestable coming from you," she said, her anger growing.

"I couldn't help thinking your feelings would soften in time!" he burst out, sitting up in his chair. "I hoped that some-day I would manage to win you back. If that's a crime, too—well . . . " he stopped.

"You counted on wearing me down, keeping at me until I finally gave in. That's why you started pestering me almost right away. You broke your word, right from the beginning. You don't have a grain of character."

"Demonstrating character isn't easy for a man in my posi-tion. Seeing you every day, being near you and never daring to touch you—oh Constance, you must end this—you must be-long to me again—you must, you must."

He sank to his knees and hid his face in her skirt.

"Get up," she said with distaste. "What are you doing down there?"

He obeyed immediately and sat down again in his chair.

"Your calculations weren't bad," she said, with a look of near hatred. "You knew what you were letting yourself in for, and that's more than I did. But I give up, I'm the one who drew the short straw. Go ahead—you can have it your way."

She had gotten up from her chair and now stood with her arms crossed, staring straight ahead of her.

He jumped to his feet.

"You'll be my wife again, just like before," he whispered, extending his hands to her. "Oh, Constance. . . . " A melting tone had come into his voice. "This is too much happiness; it's been too sudden." He gripped his head with his hands. "You forgive me completely . . . "

"I don't forgive you—*never*, do you understand?" She stepped nearer to him. "Beg the corpse of a person you've murdered for forgiveness, and see what it says. I'm doing this because I despise myself—do you hear me, I despise myself. It's what I get for being defeated, defeated when I gave up the divorce—it's my fault." Wringing her hands, she bolted past him. "It's no use trying to escape the consequences of what we do," she almost wailed, "they come after us and beat us down." She paced back and forth in a state of violent turmoil.

"Constance, once you came back, it had to end like this. The relationship you imagined was impossible—unnatural. But you'll see—things can still be good; I'll make you happy yet." He took a step closer to her.

"Happy!" she said scornfully. "Words like that have nothing to do with my situation. Let's see the thing as it is." She walked over to him. "Just now when I agreed to be your wife again," she said threateningly, "I didn't mean what you thought! Let me tell you something—for me this is no different than being forced by a stranger, do you understand, no different at all."

Ring flinched.

"Oh no, Constance—don't say such dreadful things. But it doesn't matter, not as long as I can have you back again. This is just a mood that will pass. Oh, Constance, I'd spend the night on my knees to thank you, if you'd let me—but you won't allow it, of course."

"I ask only one thing," Constance said, appearing not to have heard his last words, "and that is that you stop drinking."

"You can't say I drink too much, Constance," he said, crestfallen.

She waved her hand as if she did not care to discuss it.

"Do you remember how many times you've said that if you hadn't been tipsy, as you call it, you wouldn't have gotten involved with the maid?" asked Constance.

"And it's true, too," he said humbly.

"So from now on, will you stop getting tipsy, so there won't be any risk of drunken behavior?"

"With pleasure, Constance. You'll never see me touch that filth again. I'll be better off without it, too, and now that I have you back again, it will be easy—I won't have to deaden myself or pep myself up."

"Yes, all right—that will do," she said, walking out of the room. Needing to be alone, she went into her bedroom and paced up and down the floor; it seemed an eternity since she had spoken to her aunt. She couldn't believe it had just been that evening. Nevertheless she felt quite calm, so strangely unmoved inside; she must be getting hardened, she told herself; she felt neither desperate nor sad.

Ring was intoxicated with happiness. Finally, finally he had reached his goal. Tears of joy and excitement came into his eyes, and his chest swelled in a deep sigh of release. He went into the next room and lit one of his finest cigars—tonight—as early as tonight! He really had suffered terribly in the last three months—ever since it happened actually. It had been almost a year now. Surely he had been punished enough and he'd been more than patient. But now they would start a new life. A new life—praise God!

He couldn't stay still, he had to keep constantly on the move. There was something missing somehow, something he needed, but he couldn't quite put his finger on what it was.

A glass of that fine Champagne cognac with a little soda water—ah, that would hit the spot.

In exceedingly high spirits he shot through the living room, but then remembering his promise, he returned abruptly.

A little later, the urge came over him even more strongly than before. Tonight it could only have a beneficial effect on him—make his mood richer, his spirits even higher. It wouldn't go to his head on an occasion like this. If he just took a single glass tonight ... Again he started off, then turned around.

It was strange how intensely he needed it right now—perhaps it was because of the enormous strain he had been under all day. He felt so limp and weak—it would simply be a tonic for him.

It wouldn't make any difference if he drank just one glass. Constance really hadn't meant it like that. It went without saying that he wouldn't do anything reckless tonight.

Yes, he would do it—this one would be the last. He would simply raise one last glass to his old self. This was an important occasion really.

He had just poured it out and lifted the glass to his lips when he heard Constance come into the living room.

Hastily gulping the contents, he set the glass carefully down on the buffet.

"I was looking for the matches," he said as he came in from the dining room, red-faced, his features tense. "Always losing track of them," he mumbled, wandering into his study and making a show of looking around the room.

Constance looked at him in surprise; she had heard the clink of the glass as she entered the room, and now she went into the dining room to take a look. She picked up an empty glass that was standing beside the cognac bottle and sniffed it. Then she calmly set it down again and stood, lost in thought, her face stiff and expressionless.

After a little while, she pulled herself together, walked back into the living room and sat down to knit.

And after supper, when Ring put his arm around her waist and caressed her, she tolerated it with icy tranquility.

18

So THEY BEGAN AGAIN. Everything fell into the old patterns outwardly, and Ring felt like a man who had struggled against fate and gained his victory at last.

But he was not happy just the same. Constance's scornful behavior and icy coldness alternately hurt and infuriated him. He had hoped she would yield, that she would melt, finally, and show him some affection—occasionally, at least. But all his love and patience were completely wasted on her.

If only she would treat him the way she did in the first year of their marriage! In those days he had felt dissatisfied and abused, but now he would accept her as she was then with kisses of gratitude.

Gradually his behavior changed. He became brutal and bad-tempered. This stubborn female would never stop avenging herself—she could make an angel lose patience.

There were ugly scenes between them in which Constance threw her contempt and loathing in his face, demanding vehemently that he treat her politely, at least in the presence of other people. He would scornfully reply that his behavior was much too good for her—a woman who talked the way she did that time, as if she were a . . . well, he'd said quite enough—he would do what he pleased, etc.

In calmer moments Constance told herself, when she thought about it, that it really wasn't so strange that he dared to talk that way. He had lost respect for her precisely because she had given in—it had begun then.

But the years passed and time had its usual moderating effect. Gradually Ring got over the fixation that his wife had to love him, and he was easier to live with as a result. His own feelings had also cooled a bit, and so he was less inclined to pick a fight when Constance treated him coldly. Constance, in turn, had grown calmer and better adjusted to her life. She no longer sat brooding about a situation that, after all, could not be otherwise. She had told herself that this was the way matters stood, and then accepted her lot. She was tired of these skirmishes; they only made life uglier than it absolutely had to be. Desiring peace at any price, she became passive, even accommodating, about his caresses. It was better to have a husband in good spirits during the moments they spent together than someone disagreeable and full of vindictive feelings that he took particular pleasure in airing when other people were around. Ring rejoiced in the change, congratulating himself on the good effect he had finally had upon his wife. He was unaware that what he called his domestic happiness had grown on the grave where the innocence of her heart lay buried. He was not one to understand such things.

Once in awhile, of course, a minor skirmish would occur—a quick exchange, followed by a hostile glance—the words flying between them in rapid volleys. But this happened less and less frequently. Afterwards, Constance felt annoyed and ashamed of herself; she might just as well pick a fight with the postman.

Her ideal of marital existence had come to consist of both of them going their own ways in peace, speaking to each other courteously when they had to. And on the whole things were smooth and calm between them. They were busy in their own separate ways and didn't meddle in each other's business. Ring had his work and his boat, his stag dinners and his brandy. He also permitted himself occasional piquant little adventures with the singers at Tivoli. Lately he had been full of all sorts of wild schemes that amused him and kept him busy. Most recently, he had gotten hold of a camera, and for some time he was passionately devoted to his photographic experiments. He took pictures of Constance sitting in the living room, time and again, until finally she lost patience and refused to sit for him. So he beckoned to friends and acquaintances in the street or took pictures of the kitchen and the housemaid. His friends were relieved when the fever finally ran its course.

Constance, in turn, busied herself doing all the things that idle, well-to-do ladies find to pass the time. She read novels, crocheted lace, and embroidered cloth with golden thread. She stood in tableaus at charity bazaars, learned to ride a horse, subscribed to the theater, and went to balls and parties. There were also her male friends to look after, although they caused her constant trouble and irritation. They always fell in love with her, of course, and made declarations—or at least showed their feelings so plainly that it was intolerable to be near them. But she didn't care any more—what difference did it make to her if they deluded themselves, these stupid fellows—she only talked to them to fill the idle hours, and forgot them the instant she turned her back. They were useful, that was the main thing; they helped her overcome the boredom that was always lurking in the shadows.

During this period she was swept up in a continuous whirl of amusements. The Rings' house was more accessible and festive than ever before. And Constance was radiant with a vibrant, mature beauty. People talked about her a great deal; she was considered a very dangerous coquette.

Occasionally at parties Constance ran into Lorck. He had passed the final part of his examination with distinction and now was practicing medicine in the city. He had achieved a considerable reputation, and people spoke of him as one of the most competent of the young doctors.

Though he made no attempt to approach Constance, she had occasionally noticed his glance resting on her from a distance as she was chatting with one of her admirers. She had seen something hostile in his eyes—half derisive, half hurt—and it seemed like judgment, even condemnation. Once she asked why he never came to visit any more; he looked at her, his eyes flaring angrily, and made no reply. When she repeated the question, he said in a low voice, "I have no desire to witness what's going on *there*." He turned and walked away. Constance was simultaneously indignant at his presumption and deeply stung by it. She had a momentary impulse to vent her feelings—to scream or cry—but with a flippant remark and a burst of laughter she hid it under a mask of gaiety. At the supper table when the conversation turned to Meier, who was still studying at the conservatory abroad, she seized the opportunity and raved about his charm and good looks; she finished by asking Lorck to send him her regards when he wrote, and say she thought he was the sweetest person in the world. Whereupon Lorck retorted that she had better give that job to someone else.

19

THREE YEARS HAD PASSED since the twenty-sixth of October—the day, Constance reminded herself occasionally, that she had given up the battle for her human dignity.

For the last few months Ring had been very bad-tempered. His business affairs were going poorly, and it looked as if the iron mines might drive him into bankruptcy. After the purchase he had learned that they were worthless. The Swedes had duped him. If he couldn't find a way to extricate himself, he would be ruined. Luckily, Hansen, his legal adviser, had discovered a technical error in the purchase contracts, and on his advice, Ring had begun legal proceedings.

These developments had entailed several short trips to Sweden from which Ring always returned in a nasty temper. Constance had begun to regard the iron mines as the great bane of her life.

It was the end of October and the Rings, who had been staying in the country, had just moved back to town. The last few days had been damp and chilly and there was a strong hint of autumn in the air. Ring was leaving for Sweden again; he had planned to take the train to G•oteborg, but then a couple of beautiful days came along, with warm sunshine and a tempting westerly breeze. He suddenly felt an urge to sail his boat down the fjord for as long as the wind lasted and then go on by land. It would be the last trip of the year. He talked Lieutenant Fallesen into coming along and sent a messenger home to tell his wife that his clothes had to be ready by two o'clock. Sometime around two, he drove up in a cab and had it wait below.

"I'm taking the boat and here you've packed my train case,

dammit!"

"I thought you had finished your pleasure trips for the year."

"Blast it, this isn't a pleasure trip," he said, pulling the bell rope. "Those confounded mines!" He hurriedly opened the drawer of the writing table and took out some money.

"Here," he said to the maid, "take all this stuff out and put it in the other one—you know, the one with the compartments. Then take it down to the carriage."

The maid took the valise and went out.

"Oh by the way," he called after her, "we'll also take the two bottles of cognac from the buffet—and one last thing—a colored shirt. Let's see—the cigars," he muttered, pausing for an instant, his face wrinkled in concentration. "I think I have enough. . . . " He went into the next room again and came out shaking a cigar box up and down. "Mustn't forget the matches."

Constance handed him a few boxes.

"Hell's bells, my new pipe!" He rummaged in his pockets, then bustled around looking everywhere until he spotted it on the window sill.

"How long will you be gone?" Constance asked, when he had paused for a moment to light a cigar.

"Don't know," he answered, his cigar between his teeth and the burning match in his hand. "A week, maybe. Do you need money?"

"I just have five kroner in cash. You'd better give me some."

"Let's see, have I forgotten anything?" Ring said to himself. "My gear is on board—oh yes, the money, that's right." He took out his wallet and laid a couple of bills on the table.

"You can get by on twenty kroner, can't you? No? Well, all right—here's forty then."

"Are you going to wear your silk hat?" Constance inquired. He had just put it on.

Laughing at his own absent mindedness, he hurried out to the hall and looked on all the clothes hooks.

"Dammit! I can't find my stocking cap."

"You probably left it on the boat," Constance said coming

in to look.

"Oh yes, of course I did," he said, putting on a hat with a small round crown. "Now where the hell is my cigar holder? It was on the bookcase today."

Constance picked up an object from the floor and handed it to him.

"Nothing in this house is ever where it's supposed to be," he said, taking the mouthpiece.

He opened the door to leave. "My keys," he cried suddenly, clapping his hands to his pockets. "Damnation, wouldn't that be a fine thing ... "

Constance had already begun searching and found them for him.

"Nearly forgot to say good-bye," he said, coming back inside. He took the cigar out of his mouth to kiss his wife, replaced it immediately and went down the stairs smoking.

Constance stepped to the window to watch him drive away. After the carriage turned the corner, she turned her head and glanced back into the room. Heaving a sigh of relief, she began to straighten the room. It was always such a mess after Ring left on one of his trips.

She had received a postcard that morning from a childhood friend who was married to a minister named Sunde; now he was being transferred to a new parish, and she was passing through Kristiania on the journey. The parish was five hours by train from the city, and Mrs. Sunde was travelling ahead to prepare the house so that everything would be in order when her husband and children followed. Unless the steamship was late, she would be in Kristiania by dinnertime the next day.

The following day was overcast. The sky was dark and heavy, spotted here and there with thick black clouds with sallow, woolly edges. There was no wind, but people could feel something threatening in the air. They peered at the sky and then at the barometer, which had dropped unusually low, and predicted that a nasty storm was on the way.

Constance slept late the next morning. It was nearly noon by the time she had finished dressing, and just as she was fastening a broach at her throat, she heard a carriage stop outside and, a moment later, the ring of the doorbell. Rushing to the door, she arrived there before the maid, and threw her arms around her friend. As she was helping her take off her coat, Constance learned that she had to leave again at four o'clock. She was disappointed, having hoped to detain her for a few days. Ring was away and they could have had such a pleasant time.

"You haven't changed a bit, Constance," Mrs. Sunde said, looking at her friend with delight. "Although, no—you're really more beautiful."

"Oh, people don't age as fast these days as they used to," Constance answered, pouring out the hot chocolate and setting a cup in front of Mrs. Sunde.

"That depends—look at me! You wouldn't have recognized me again if you hadn't known—I'd bet my life on it."

"What a thing to say! It's nonsense, you haven't changed so much."

"Oh, I know it very well. If only I didn't look so awful, I wouldn't feel so old. But imagine—four babies in five years! You'll always look marvelous if you don't have. . . . Are you sorry about it?"

"Not at all! But other than that, what's it like to have children?"

"Exhausting; difficult; an endless struggle. And all those sleepless nights!"

"But what about the happiness, the joy that comes with motherhood—remember the lines in the Bible, 'for joy that a man is born into the world.' It must be very special, isn't it?"

"Yes it is, of course, but it's such a strain on our income." Mrs. Sunde sighed deeply.

"Is the salary very low, Rikke?"

"Oh yes—there's no money in such a poor parish."

"How much do you get?"

"Two thousand kroner, not counting an allowance for rent."

"No more than that?"

"No, that's the most. As long as there were just the two of us, we could make do, but we've really been pinched lately."

"How old is your youngest?" Constance asked.

"Nine months."

"Surely you don't want any more?"

"How could I want more!" Mrs Sunde said, rolling her eyes as if beseeching God to be her witness. "But what's the good of wishing—there's so much one could wish for." Her voice was dejected and she looked tired and worried.

They had left the table and gone into the living room.

"But now tell me a little about yourself, Constance. You're happy of course with all these lovely things." Her glance slid to the velvet upholstered furniture, the fine curtains, and the beautiful paintings.

"Happy," Constance said hesitantly. "That's a stupid word, basically."

Mrs. Sunde laughed. "I don't know," she said. "There are people who are happy, certainly."

"Do you think so? Well maybe—but surely they're fooling themselves."

"You have changed, Constance—inside, I mean."

"Yes, I certainly have. But come sit down, Rikke—tell me how satisfied you really are with your life."

"I can't complain. I have a kind husband and sweet children."

"Yes, yes, of course—aside from that—I mean, how do you feel about life?"

"If I had enough money and if everything weren't such a struggle—then—"

"Aren't you terribly disappointed? Did you really think it would be like this?"

"Well, now that you mention it, I do remember feeling that way in the beginning. I cried many times, believe me; but later on I got so busy with other things."

"I think life is completely empty," Constance said impatiently, "and it's astonishingly brutal besides. It runs its course, crushing us underfoot, utterly indifferent to how we feel about it."

"I think it would be good for you to have a child, Constance."

"Far from it! All that talk about children is a myth. If I had children I'd wish they were dead."

"No, that's horrible!"

"I would never have any peace until they were dead. There's so much evil in the world just waiting for them! Brr!" Constance pulled herself together with a shudder.

"God preserve me from seeing life like you do!" Mrs. Sunde said in astonishment. "What does your husband think about it?"

"Do you think I talk to him like this?"

"You must not be happy in your marriage, Constance."

"Oh really, Rikke, let's agree not to use that meaningless word. Besides, I'm happy enough—just like all the others."

"You both seemed so much in love at your wedding—Ring especially. I remember discussing—forgive me—how happy you both were."

"Did you?"

Mrs. Sunde was fiddling with a letter opener.

"I'm so afraid for you, Constance," she said hesitantly.

"For me? Why?"

"Because—well, you mustn't be angry—it's just that if you don't love your husband, some unprincipled man could come along and charm you."

Constance burst out laughing. "Your concern is very sweet, Rikke, but you don't have to worry! Men aren't like that. Unfortunately, I almost said."

"What a terrible thing to say! You don't mean it seriously?"

"Why not? At least that would be something."

"Really, there is nothing in the world more disgusting than a married woman who keeps a lover."

"Or a married woman who lets her husband love her in exchange for keep—it's the same thing," Constance said with a shrug.

"But isn't it a wife's duty to love her husband and let him keep her?"

"Yes, of course . . . " Constance looked bored with the subject. "Oh, you know," she rose abruptly, tossing aside the book of poetry she had been fingering, "marriage is an ugly in-

166

stitution, basically."

"Really Constance, you shouldn't talk like that about something established by God. Think what the world would be like without marriage."

"Well I've no idea, and I don't care either," Constance answered, and sat down again on the sofa.

"Surely you're not dreaming about free love?"

"Indeed not—but I'm not dreaming about love that's forced either. I'm not dreaming about anything."

"Free love is a sign of the worst depravity. Then fornication will become part of the social order, Sunde says."

"Does he?" Constance smiled wanly. "Surely, he's forgotten that fornication is already part of the social order, and it has been for ages."

Mrs. Sunde was too dumbfounded to reply.

"Anyhow it's ridiculous for us to be talking like this," Constance said, suddenly recollecting herself. "Love—what a topic it's become these days!"

"It's interesting enough, I suppose," said Mrs. Sunde, groping for something to say.

"Do you and your husband get along well, Rikke?" Constance asked in a completely altered tone.

"Why do you ask that?"

"Oh I just wondered—you don't have to answer if you don't want to."

"Well, yes, we get along quite well," said Mrs. Sunde. "Very well, actually—especially now that I know how Sunde wants things to be."

"Did you have trouble getting used to him?"

"Oh no—not so much. As long as I appear to give in and humor him a bit, I can get my way."

"Don't you ever quarrel?"

"Not any more. I don't have time, you see, except when I'm in bed with a new baby, and I'm not in the mood to quarrel then."

When the maid announced that dinner was on the table, the two women were shocked at how late it had become. There was barely enough time to eat, and they hastily drank their coffee while putting on their coats and hats. The maid had ordered a carriage, and Constance went along with her friend to the station.

"It was a pity I didn't get to see your husband, Constance," Mrs. Sunde said on the way. "You must give him my regards."

"We wouldn't have been able to talk so freely," Constance answered. "It was good, really, that he was away."

"Ah well, perhaps. Brr—what awful weather!"

It had begun to storm, and the street was filled with a haze of swirling dust, trash, and dry leaves. Even inside the carriage, the women had to rub their eyes continuously. Constance leaned forward to look at the sky. It was black and squally, and a few large raindrops had begun to fall.

"And your husband is out in his boat!"

"Oh he's looking after himself, you can be sure of that. He's in a harbor someplace with a cigar and a toddy."

They arrived at the station with scarcely enough time for Mrs. Sunde to buy a ticket and board the train before it began to pull away. Constance waved good-bye and stayed until the train was out of sight. The wind had strengthened and a driving rain had begun to fall.

When she arrived at home, she stretched out on the sofa and tried to sleep. It was no use. Her head ached from the strong wind, and she felt terribly depressed and lonely. She lay there listening to the wind howling, the rain beating violently against the window panes. When the wind came from that direction it blew so hard against the house that she could feel the room shaking. She paced up and down, unable to stay still. Finally she stopped by the window and stared down at the garden. It was a painful sight. Autumn had come suddenly and brought havoc and destruction in its wake. The once tall and beautiful lilac bush looked pitiful, prostrate on the ground in the side bed, its tattered leaves in the dirt, a few thin wisps of root still holding it in place. The dahlias were bowed to the earth. When the gusts blew in among them, they seemed to be shaking their dark brown heads in grief at their ruined beauty. The palms in the large yellow pots with white painted bases were snapped off in the middle and dangled by a few strands of fiber. The long thin fronds were snarled by the rain; sporadically the wind whipped them apart and they snaked around wildly, struggling to get loose. And how quickly the leaves had disappeared from the trees! There had been leaves there yesterday—now they were strewn across the garden and heaped beside the roads, dull and blackened. The wind had swept a huge pile up against the fence in the lower yard. It was slow work—the leaves were sodden and unyielding, sticking together in great clumps behind the tree trunks, the legs of benches, and on the arbor's latticed walls. Constance shuddered, feeling with a kind of desperation that she should go into the next room where it was warmer, or at least leave the window and its dismal spectacle. But it was as if she were held fast, as if some unseen power forced her to stay and watch as the wind whipped the rain, driving it in swirling gusts between sky and earth, smashing it down on each frail plant that still dared hold its head erect. With a kind of breathless tension, she followed the gusts as they died, then swelled again. They seemed to come from inside her—the drawn-out moans, the blasts that came with such fury—rising and subsiding, the mournful wail swelling into a demonic shriek. And in the midst of it, she could see her summer garden before her, fragrant and gleaming in the sunshine; and she saw herself sitting on a bench in the evening, the peaceful moonlight flooding through the branches of the trees onto the gravel paths, touching every flowerbed with silver.

It had become quite dark, but still she stood there. Her soul felt pierced with cold; her heart was a hard lump in her left side. Its weight was so great that she felt a need to vent her anguish, but she did not.

The maid came in and announced that tea was ready. Constance tore herself loose and went into the dining room where the lamps were lit and the samovar was hissing softly. It was good to get away from that violence in the sky. What had possessed her to stay there so long!

After supper she read a little of *Fromont jeune et Risler aîné*.[18] She had only the last chapter to finish. Poor Risler's dreadful death moved her greatly. Throwing down the book, she pressed her handkerchief to her eyes and wept for a moment.

Before going to bed she decided to take one last look at the weather; it seemed endlessly fascinating tonight. She went into the next room. The storm had subsided a bit, and for the moment the rain had stopped, though the sky was still threatening. Like a narrow segment of an orange, the moon hung in the sky, struggling to get a clear view from behind the tattered clouds racing past it. Now and then a weak whitish beam touched the ruined garden. Leaving the window, she walked into the adjoining room. A faint light seeped in from the open dining room door. In the center of the room she stopped and looked uncertainly up at the ceiling; stretching her arms over her head, she sighed softly. She slid into a chair, put her arms on the table and buried her face in them. She did not realize she was crying until she felt cold tears on her face; she did not bother to wipe them away.

The next day she learned that Ring had capsized in the storm. He and Lieutenant Fallesen had drowned, but the crewman had been rescued clinging to the hull. He was the one who brought the message to the office.

20

AFTER RING'S DEATH, Constance stayed on in the same house. She withdrew from society, closing herself off from every contact with the world, seeing none of her friends and acquaintances.

Initially she had felt numbed by the news of her husband's sudden death. It took time before she got it firmly in her mind that the hateful chains of marriage had fallen away and she was free of him forever.

When she was finally fully conscious of her freedom, she began to suffer remorse about the past.

Again and again she asked herself if things wouldn't have been better if she had devoted herself, right from the start, to being a good and loving wife. But how badly she had behaved!

She had ignored her duty as if it had been no concern of hers, excusing herself by saying she couldn't help it. She had gone into her marriage as if it were a party, thinking of only one thing: her own satisfaction; valuing only one person: herself.

She bitterly reproached herself, finding a grudging satisfaction in painting herself in the worst light possible.

She dragged old memories out of oblivion, little things from their first year of marriage when Ring had been touchingly grateful for her smallest kindness. She remembered apologizing once for being cross and unreasonable all day long. Tears had come to his eyes; he had taken her hands and kissed them again and again, murmuring softly, "My sweet Constance, you've done nothing at all."

It pained her to the soul to think about these things when

he was lying at the bottom of the sea, and she would never have a chance to tell him that she knew she had been unfair.

As long as she was occupied with these thoughts, she had a powerful need to be alone. Later, when her incessant brooding had squeezed the last bit of life from her memories and they stood around her like mute shadows, she had grown so accustomed to solitude that it had become precious to her, and she was unwilling to give it up for any price.

The distractions life could offer had lost their appeal. They seemed like pleasures that belonged to childhood, nothing that an adult would want to be concerned with.

Little by little, she sank into a dull kind of indolence, an ennui that was strongly akin to depression. People thought it grief and praised her faithfulness; but her closest friends shook their heads and said it was a pity to see her go on like this. She was obsessed—there was no other way to describe this misanthropic withdrawal. And it could turn into genuine mental illness.

Constance didn't care what people said about her. All she wanted was to be left in peace.

After Ring died, Lorck had come to the house several times, but had not been admitted. So he wrote a note asking if Constance would permit him to see her. She answered that she was receiving no visitors. One afternoon he saw her on the street and tried to speak to her, but she greeted him unwillingly and walked quickly past.

His long-nourished passion for Constance had never been extinguished, and it blazed up the moment he knew she was free. In the past year, he had fought in vain to overcome what he regarded as his fatal passion. He had plunged into his work with ferocious energy, abandoned himself to reading and study; he had thrown himself into affairs with other women and feverishly avoided idleness. Wanting to hate and despise her, he told himself a hundred times that she wasn't worth a particle of the agony he suffered—she had stayed in that filthy marriage—but it was no use. His love was like a weed that grew more vigorously the more it was trampled upon. It had begun the night she rejected him. His stupendous blunder of blindly judging her in terms of his own crude theories had made him look at life with new eyes.

Now, when he thought of the bold and reckless way he had broken into her private world, he felt like sinking into the ground with embarrassment. The further removed he was from his former modes of thought, the more outrageous his behavior seemed to him. In his blundering ignorance, he had thought he knew all the answers, but in truth, he had been a ridiculous buffoon. It had been a painful time for him, but he told himself that through this pain he had become a man. At moments he was even thankful that it had happened. If Constance had been the kind of woman he thought she was, if she had thrown herself into his arms that time, he would never have learned what love was, never have come to regard life with respect. Through the two-fold anguish of his hopeless love and the painful self-knowledge gained when she refused him, he learned for the first time to make finer moral discriminations in every sphere.

In the meantime his reputation as a skillful doctor was growing. A couple of lucky cures under difficult circumstances made him popular right from the start, and his serious, calm demeanor inspired confidence in people. The general opinion among his friends was that he was a completely altered person, and they spoke of him with respect.

His father, a wealthy merchant, had died almost two years after Ring, leaving Lorck a considerable fortune by local standards.

A couple of times in the two and a half years since Ring's death, Constance had yielded to Marie and Hansen's earnest entreaties that she join them at one of their parties. She had been so uncomfortable that she swore she would never go again. The more she weaned herself from people, the worse their company became. Their conversation was alien to her. The flighty way they talked, leaping from one thing to another, so familiar to her once, now confused and depressed her. She sat among them, understanding nothing, feeling bored and disgusted.

At one of these parties, she had met Lorck. Constance could

see he was thinking about approaching her, and she turned away in a kind of terror. Later that evening, she was sitting by herself in a side room near a rather deaf old lady who was leafing through an album and asking her an occasional question about the portraits. The other guests were watching the young people dance.

Suddenly Lorck was in the room. For an instant she thought of running but she decided against it and pretended to be busy with the old woman and the pictures.

"You aren't dancing, Mrs. Ring?" he asked, seating himself some distance from her.

"No," she answered without moving.

"You don't enjoy that any more?"

"No."

The old woman asked a question which Constance answered, bending very close to her and raising her voice.

"It's so seldom anyone sees you," Lorck said. "One would think you weren't in town."

"I stay home most of the time."

"All winter I've done hardly anything but look for you—don't be angry," he added, responding to the glance she directed at him. "That's just the way it is."

She turned her head away and bent over the album.

"I know I'm bothering you," he said apologetically. "But what else can I do? I want to talk to you. I must—now, while I have the chance."

She gave him a quick glance.

"What do you want with me?" she asked coldly.

"I have something serious to say, but you must give me permission first." His voice was earnest and intense.

A maid came in to announce that the old woman's carriage had arrived. She stood up immediately, said a friendly good evening to Constance, paid her respects to Lorck, and left.

Constance would have followed but Lorck stepped in her path.

"You mustn't go," he said in a strangely constricted voice. "Don't be afraid," he went on apologetically. "And don't stand there like you're about to run away. What I have to say can't

174

insult or hurt you. It's just that I'm not the same," he stopped and took a deep breath "as I was that time I offended you. Do you believe me?"

There was something about him that impressed her.

"I forgot all that a long time ago. Let's not drag it up again," she said in a tired voice.

"No, no, not drag it up again—but you don't know how that scene is burned into me—your helplessness, your pain, your unspoken appeal for compassion. I was a beast. I didn't think it was possible for something to affect me like this. Do you remember in Bjørnson's *The King*—the way he changes toward Klara—something like that has happened to me. Do you believe me?"

"Yes," she said calmly.

"You've got to know," he said passionately, "that I'm not the man you've been despising all these years—you have no right to do that, no right at all."

"I haven't been despising you—I just haven't thought about it."

"No, I've been too unimportant to you." A spasm passed over his face. "But give me your hand now and say you've forgiven me for my disgusting behavior that night." His voice was supplicating.

"I have nothing against you, be assured of that," she said mildly, extending her hand to him and meeting his gaze.

He squeezed her hand for an instant. "Thank you," he whispered and walked out of the room. He went directly home.

Some weeks later, Constance ran into him on the street. After he had approached her and greetings had been exchanged, he asked if she would permit him to come and visit her.

Constance had given him a frightened look and hesitated before saying that if he wanted to, he could.

The next day he came and spoke quietly with her for an hour. Trying to be as entertaining as possible, he talked to her about the Swedish actors and a concert by some Polish musicians. He urged her to go hear the French singers at Tivoli, but she wasn't interested. He wanted to talk about anything that would amuse her, and he felt that luck was with him. She listened amiably, inquired about this and that, and as he was leaving thanked him for his visit. He left with the feeling that his presence had at least not been disagreeable to her. As he descended the stairs he was thinking about how soon he might come again.

He waited two weeks. She was at home and received him politely, but it was impossible for him to tell from her appearance whether or not she was glad to see him. He had hoped to get somewhat closer to her this time, but he was disappointed. He tried to arouse her interest in activities around town, in people's interests and occupations, but her responses were so reserved that he was afraid of boring her. He stopped talking, hoping she would change the subject, but she just made a few comments about the weather, and an awkward pause followed. He steered the conversation to the theater, but when she replied that she never went and had no interest in it, his heart sank. What could he do to reach this withdrawn, mysterious woman? He left with the melancholy feeling that he was farther from her than ever.

After he had gone, Constance sat and thought about how handsome and pleasant he was. He certainly made a completely different impression than he had before. Her ill will had disappeared, and when she considered everything, she almost felt a kind of fondness for him.

Still, she really did not want him to visit her. She preferred to be free. It was too much of a strain to have to sit there, answering his questions, trying to find a topic of conversation. The truth was, she didn't like being distracted when she was occupied with her own thoughts. Why couldn't they leave her in peace?

She walked out of the living room and opened the kitchen door.

"Are you there, Johanne?"

Johanne appeared at the door of her room.

"Would you recognize the man you let in today?"

"Dr. Lorck? Good heavens yes."

"If he comes again, say I'm not at home. Now don't forget."

"No, I'll remember all right."

A month passed. Lorck had tried three times to see Constance, with no success. Then one day, the following letter arrived for her:

Mrs. Constance Ring:

I have come to your house several times without seeing you, so I will try to write. I am so afraid of offending or frightening you that I don't know how I will find the words. What I want to say is this—for a long time I have thought deeply about myself and you. I know from the bottom of my soul that I love you, and that my love is worthy of you. All my happiness in life lies in your hands. If you refuse to see me, I won't find it in this world. If you could learn to trust me, don't you think that possibly, in time, I could win your love?

Your most devoted,
Niels Lorck

She was extremely surprised by his letter, but when she gave it some thought she felt stupid that she hadn't seen earlier what he had in mind.

She replied immediately:

Dear Dr. Lorck:

You must not be angry with me, but I believe you would be wasting your time if you tried to win my love. It would be disgraceful if I used you in an experiment, just to provide some variety in my dull life. Because it couldn't be anything more than that if I let you make the attempt. I respect you too much to use you that way, and besides, I haven't the slightest desire to do it. Don't think I harbor any ill will toward you, quite the contrary. You may be sure of that.

Yours,
Constance Ring

21

Six months passed. Early in the winter old Judge Blom died, and Mrs. Blom moved in with her youngest daughter, whose husband was a minister in Nordfjordeid. So the childhood home disintegrated: the two brothers settled in different places, and the middle sister moved in with her fiancés family in Molde.

Constance was painfully affected by the news of her father's death. It was as if the images of her happy childhood and early youth were lost at that moment. Now her dear father was in his grave, and the other occupants of her beloved home were scattered to the four winds. There was no longer a fixed spot to which she could tie her dreams and longings, no protected place for her thoughts to turn in her most dejected moments. Everything had been swept away; she felt naked and deprived, her life such a meaningless waste that death often seemed preferable.

Sometimes she was so tired and bored that she seriously tried to decide the easiest way to take her life. But then night would come, and she could go to bed and sleep. It was a relief to sleep.

Sitting at home during the long, long afternoons—and she was always at home—she felt as though the hours would never pass. Loneliness tormented her, but seeking out other people seemed more terrifying still.

It was a wet, unpleasant day in March, with icy winds blowing in from the northwest. The snow remaining on the ground was filthy grey and streaked with brown.

Constance had been trying to stitch a strip of embroidery from her sewing basket. She had long ago forgotten what she planned to do with it. She had read for awhile, tossed the book aside, paced up and down the floor, and sat down again to sew a few more stitches. Suddenly she flung down her embroidery, swung her chair completely around and leaned her elbows on the windowsill. Propping her face in her hands, she stared out at the street with bored, apathetic eyes.

It was not a cheerful sight.

The people looked miserable as they hurried through the slushy streets. Some walked in pairs, tormenting each other, no doubt; others were alone. Some dashed off in a hurry; others drifted aimlessly along.

There was the bread boy coming around the corner with his dark green scarf wrapped around his neck and the familiar violet mittens that were supposed to compensate for the ragged, outgrown clothes he was wearing in the bitter cold. He was so thin, so blue with cold; he looked as old and troubled as a man of sixty. It must be deadly to come here every single day, around the same corner, in the same cart, delivering the same bread to the same houses for the same price. "Ah," she said, sighing deeply, "what a miserable spectacle."

Next came the brewer's man with his cart. Thank heaven, it must be five-thirty. He was wearing decent clothes, but dear Lord, how weather-beaten he looked—his shoulders were as stooped as if he had been in irons.

No, the street was unendurable. She turned her back to it, and let her hands fall to her knees.

No doubt she should go out for awhile; she should take a walk and try to get rid of this heartburn.

She thought about standing up, putting on her outer clothes, walking out the door and down the steps, but oh, the street was so wet and nasty, and the main roads were even more disgusting. She said aloud, "No, I won't go out."

If only she could have a hot cup of tea! But no, then Johanne would be running around with the tray, asking those infuriating questions that were her specialty.

She couldn't understand it, but whenever she heard Johanne coming in from the next room to ask one thing or another, an insane horror at having to listen and reply seized her, and she felt a desperate impulse to throw herself out the window, just to get free. She began to pace up and down the room, placing each foot carefully in a square on the patterned rug. Then she stopped in front of the mirror and examined her hair style. They said it looked so old-fashioned. What if she tried knotting it lower down on her neck. No, definitely not, what was the point of that!

Better to darn the hole in her stocking that had been bothering her all day. She bent down to slip the stocking off her foot and remained in that position, as if a spell had turned her to stone.

One picture after another came and went—no, not pictures exactly, a swaying dissolving jumble of memories that flickered, then slipped away, scenes forming and floating away in an instant, and interspersed among them, snatches of songs, opera melodies, dance music—various bits and pieces—all of it so sluggish and lifeless that it bored her to distraction.

But finally with a powerful effort she straightened up, shuddering as if she were shaking off something repulsive. She pulled her stocking back up; it was too dark now to fix it and there was no yarn handy anyhow. She walked over to the shallow easy chair by the stove and sat down.

She always sat there during the long, twilight hours of the winter day.

And here in the peaceful dusk, where the last gleams of daylight slanted in to meet the rosy glow of the coke stove, she gave herself up completely to the fruitless tumult of her thoughts.

The fragrance of primroses and hyacinths hung in the air—Marie had sent them for her birthday the other day—intermingled with her own perfume and the scent of the sandalwood box from the corner of the étagère. Long shafts of light played around the madonna above the sofa—the expression on her face seemed to alter in the flickering light. The fluttering outlines of Beethoven and Mozart danced against the window while Minerva stood, proud and unmoving, on the shadowed writing table. The bookcase was in darkness, but the mirror between the windows caught the glimmering restless fire, and the shattered multi-colored brilliance of the prisms in the chandelier. Now and then a pinkish golden shaft fell upon a beaded pillow, the corner of an afghan, or a piece of red drapery, appearing and disappearing sporadically.

The only sounds were the ticking of the clock on the table, muffled by the velvet upholstered stillness, and the rattle of coal in the stove when the bottom layer burned to ash and the top layer tumbled down.

These twilight moments were all her own. She could rest in them, yield to her despondency and her weariness with life, freeing herself from the shadow of control that her reason still exercised over her activities. Sometimes she pondered about how different life was from the way she had been taught. It was a shame that the old deceived the young; for they had to know the truth. Why lie and pretend life was something it never had been or ever could be? And the lies were everywhere—in the books they read, in their lessons at school, in the pictures they were shown, in the way the adults talked about everything.

She was amazed that the rest of them seemed to manage their lives so well. Hadn't they, too, been crushed with disappointment? Either they were satisfied because they didn't know any better or they pretended to other people and themselves that nothing was the matter. She thought of the future with painful anxiety; she couldn't imagine how she was going to endure the burden of her life.

But Johanne considered her mistress a pathetic creature for allowing herself to drift through the Lord's precious days so aimlessly. It was a pity that some people had everything in the world while others had nothing but drudgery from morning to night. She herself, for example. She would never feel any different—if they covered her with gold and threw shiny kroner in her path, she'd have nothing to do with menfolk.

Johanne spat into the slop basin and dashed off so carelessly with the freshly-washed cups that it was a wonder they didn't break.

Her mistress was a constant source of irritation. She could not understand her.

That some poor creature could shut herself in and care about nothing, she could well imagine. But Mrs. Ring certainly didn't need money or anything else! The puzzle was impossible for Johanne to solve, no matter how hard she tried.

If she were stingy or religious—but that wasn't the case—many little things proved otherwise.

But there had to be some explanation for her behavior. Finally she decided that the mistress must have something on her conscience.

If only she could find out what it was.

Johanne was unhappy in service; it was so deadly dull it could drive a healthy person mad. And people said her job was easy. That was what was so aggravating.

If only they knew how little time she had to sew anything for herself. It wouldn't be so bad if the mistress behaved like other people! But as it was, she had to spend the entire morning just sitting around waiting to serve her.

Johanne was only a simple housemaid, but she knew one thing for sure, she wouldn't be able to hold up her head in the world if she carried on like Mrs. Ring did—dawdling and talking to herself, taking all morning to put her clothes on.

If she were sleeping late, Johanne could understand it. But to get up at nine and not let her maid into the bedroom before twelve—that was disgraceful.

If only there was a decent stove in the house, she could put the coffee pot there—but that round monstrosity! Oh, very fancy of course. So she had trouble keeping the coffee hot. Not that it mattered—the mistress never scolded her if it was cold—but Johanne had too much self-respect to take advantage of her. And that nonsense about setting the table in the dining room—she'd stopped that long ago. Breakfast couldn't just sit there all morning long.

After all, a person had to have some standards of decency.

Now she took the mistress her breakfast on a tray.

Once in a while Johanne would have an urge to know what in the world she was doing in there hour after hour, and she would peek through the keyhole. Often she would see the mistress sitting bolt upright, a shoe in her hand and one foot resting on her other knee. Johanne would go in suddenly on some pretext, and the mistress would jump like she'd been caught red-handed and quickly put on her shoe. After awhile, when the silence inside made Johanne suspicious, she would again creep up to the keyhole in her stocking feet, and there the mistress would be, sitting in the same position, except now she was in a trance over her other foot.

As anybody could see, there was no way of dealing with her.

Or she might be sitting in front of the mirror combing her hair. It seemed as if her arm would fall asleep, it went up and down so slowly, until it fell to the table and lay there, and she sat with her head hanging forward, as if she had been struck from behind.

Then she would suddenly throw back her head and plunge her outstretched fingers into her hair, pulling it tightly back away from her face. When she put her elbows on the table and began to stare at herself intently in the mirror, Johanne knew it was safe to go and take a nap for an hour—she would find the mistress in the same position when she came back.

A charming lady, Mrs. Ring.

She was that way about everything, even waking up in the morning. "My soul, she doesn't open her eyes, just lies there squeezing them shut so she won't have to let on it's broad daylight," Johanne would tell the maid downstairs.

There were other things that irritated Johanne, as well. Having to tell lies, for instance—the mistress wasn't home, she was supposed to say, when God knew she was loafing in there with her book or her crocheting—though nobody could make her believe they weren't just for show.

"I'm not home," or "Don't let anybody come in, I have a headache." Oh, when she heard those messages she wanted to throw up. She mimicked them out in the kitchen, spitting them out in an unflattering imitation of her mistress's voice.

"God help me, it's the worst kind of laziness," she often growled at the end of her scandalized reflections. "It would do her good to get that body of hers moving once in a while," she said, making a gesture as if she were cracking a whip.

When the doorbell rang the mistress often came running

into the kitchen, shaking her head as if to reinforce her orders. That was the only way Johanne could tell that something wasn't wrong with her legs—she had begun to wonder, since she appeared to have so much trouble dragging herself from the living room to the dining room and back again.

It was impossible to remain in such a house. The eternal silence affected her ears, and she was so nervous that she jumped up in terror whenever the clock struck, trembling like somebody wanted by the police.

In the fall she would leave. She got no particular thanks for everything she put up with—Mrs. Ring wouldn't give her so much as a grateful word.

In actual fact, Johanne's situation was better by far than she was accustomed to.

But she was bored.

She had an active and energetic temperament, and in the past she had waged furious battles with her mistresses.

But here she had no opportunity for that kind of thing.

Imagine going on like this all year round, with nothing happening whatever! She would rather have household brawls every day.

But Mrs. Ring was as meek as a new lodger. She gave Johanne the money necessary for the household and let her arrange things the way she wanted.

The first two weeks she was in service, Johanne had regularly asked each morning what they should have for dinner. Just as regularly she had received the answer: "Fix whatever you want."

So she had stopped asking.

Once she had tried to provoke her by serving the same food three days in a row, but she got no response. Mrs. Ring had eaten as usual, without saying a word.

Oh, even a stone would be irritated.

♦

In the living room the darkness was growing deeper. The coal was nearly gone and Constance sat there, shrinking from the thought that she would have to get up if she didn't want the fire to go out. When she heard the doorbell ring she shot to her feet. She mustn't let them in! Gripping the knob of the dining room door, she remained in place, her ears straining, her head stretched forward. She listened with a desperate intensity, as if her life were at stake.

"Yes, somebody's coming. . . ." Cat-like she slipped through the door.

"Are you sitting in the dark, Constance?"

The words rolled into the warm perfumed air, bringing with them the damp chill of a March day.

"Please say something. You're going to make me bump into something." The intruder took a few steps forward and banged into a chair. "Well really!" Turning, she fumbled nervously toward the door and hurried out, as if something evil were hot on her heels.

Constance, crouching in the most distant corner of the dining room, realized that Johanne, once having opened hostilities, would not give up; she would come back with a lamp. She stood up and paused for a moment to compose her features. That was Marie's voice she had heard. As she walked in, Marie and Johanne were coming through the opposite door, the latter armed with a small lamp.

"Were you here?" Marie asked, with something like indignation in her voice.

"No, I was in there," Constance said, turning her head toward the door behind her.

"And I was in here talking to myself in the pitch dark. Oh, that's creepy!"

"Light the lamp, Johanne, and take that one out—surely you can see it's smoking," Constance reprimanded.

Clamping her lips together to conceal a malicious smile, Johanne cast a telling glance from the lamp to her mistress, plainly indicating her opinion that the business about the smoke was nonsense. Outside, she tossed her head and mumbled to herself, "Why should I lie for her—it'll do her good to have to move that numb mouth of hers."

"My goodness, it's so warm in here," Marie gasped.

Constance suggested that she unfasten her coat; her friend remarked that she would need to if she didn't want to risk getting sick.

Constance rolled down the venetian blinds, then walked over to help her with her coat.

"Thanks, I won't take it off. I can just stay a minute." She slipped it off her shoulders before sitting down.

Constance sat down also and picked up her work. She talked about the weather and asked about the children, without paying any attention to the answers.

Marie had pulled off her gloves. She sat there uneasily smoothing them out with a kind of absentminded thoroughness. She asked Constance about the heartburn and learned it was just the same.

"Of course sitting indoors all day, it's no wonder."

Constance drew back in her chair and turned aside slightly as if she were trying to evade her.

"How is the bazaar going?" she asked in an effort to keep the conversation alive.

"Splendidly. We've gotten lots of things and they're still pouring in."

"That's nice," Constance said smothering a yawn.

"You really should join us—but you never go anywhere these days." It had a casual sound, as if she hadn't intended to say it; she still seemed preoccupied with her gloves.

"Now let's not start *that* again."

"No, let's not. I'm not really in the mood for that tonight."

Constance felt a moment of surprise at Marie's mildness. Merciful heaven, what a torrent of words the subject usually evoked.

"Have you been to the theater lately?" Constance asked, searching for something to say.

"No, oh what am I saying—I saw *A Bankruptcy*[19] just the other day."

"Did you like it?"

"Yes; well, I mean it was very moving." She had picked up her handkerchief and absently pressed it to her nose. Now she was pleating it into narrow folds which she struggled to make straight. "It's terrible when the family learns they are completely destitute," she continued, "but still, some things are worse than poverty."

"That's true," remarked Constance.

"Of course that's easy to say, you know, but suppose it happened to—to you, for example, Constance." She sounded as if she needed to say it quickly, and her voice quavered slightly.

"Suppose what happened?" Constance's expression flickered and her voice was a little unsteady.

"That you were poor, say—that you had lost everything." The words came out in a rush.

"Has something happened with the lawsuit?" Constance asked, sitting up in her chair.

"Have you really not noticed? Haven't you seen how upset I've been?" Marie took a deep breath and exhaled it.

"Well say it then! What is it? Have they come to a decision?"

"Yes, I'm afraid so. I suppose you've guessed—they wrote and said that you—well, to be blunt, the case is lost."

"But that's impossible!" Her voice seemed to catch in her throat.

"That's what Rikard said, too, but I'm afraid you're in for it now. He got a telegram first, and a letter came today."

"And it said the case was lost? It was quite clear?"

"It was quite clear—I read the letter myself. Rikard would have been here but he thought it would be best if I came and prepared you."

"You might have told me earlier," Constance said in a subdued voice. "I must say, it's very strange."

"I could hardly tell you until I knew, don't forget."

"That this was brewing, I mean; then it wouldn't have come as such a shock. Though I suppose it wouldn't have made any difference." She threw herself back in the chair and crossed her arms on her chest.

"We get our bad news fast enough. I didn't want to frighten you before it was settled."

"And you're quite sure there's no mistake."

Marie shook her head.

"So I'm poor then—haven't got a pin—quite simply a beggar."

"Now you have to be brave, Constance. Besides, I don't really know if everything is lost."

"But I know very well. Ring told me when he began the suit—Hansen said so, too—we'd be completely ruined if we lost. But he was so sure it was impossible."

"Lawsuits are tricky; people should never get involved with them."

"But this one has been very useful, since I've had money to live on these years—otherwise every shilling would have gone to those precious iron mines. What a clever move that was, a real work of genius!" She had been moving around nervously as she spoke, apparently unaware of what she was doing. Now she sat down in a low rocking chair and rocked restlessly back and forth.

"What are you going to do now, Constance?"

"Do? Forgive me, but that's a very strange question."

"I mean, how do you plan to support yourself?"

"Plan to support myself? How do you suppose I'll support myself? Will you tell me that?" She looked like she was about to boil over.

"The first thing, of course, is to give notice on this apartment and sell your furniture," Marie said, with a strained expression on her face.

"And then?"

"Well you'll have to see if you can find a position as a teacher, or as a housekeeper for a widower, or you could set up a business at home."

"Or I could become a minister in a parish, or join the circus, or be a midwife," Constance interjected. "Oh there are lots of things I can do!"

"I don't think the situation is anything to joke about, but of course if you can be in good spirits, so can I." Marie rose and pulled her coat up over her shoulders.

Constance seemed lost in thought. She was staring into space, with her brows contracted, a grim expression in her dark eyes.

"When you get right down to it, Constance," Marie continued as she bent down to fasten the bottom button on her coat, "as sorry as I am for you—now please don't be angry—I really think this will be good for you."

"Oh yes, when all is said and done, we'll see what a great stroke of luck this is," Constance said.

"Well you can say what you please, but you've been living a wretched life, just the same," Marie continued, slowly pulling on her gloves and smoothing them out one finger at a time. "You haven't been interested in anything, and you haven't wanted to do anything." She smoothed her right hand over the upturned palm of her left one. "Take the bazaar we've all been working on, for example—you haven't been willing to lift a finger, even when we begged you. Behaving like that— well, it serves no purpose, it's just plain wrong. And it brings its own punishment."

"So it seems," Constance answered, "and isn't it fine that justice is being done."

"You are taking this very strangely. You actually seem angry, as if there were something I could do about it."

"My God, Marie, surely you can understand that it's not very pleasant to discover I'm going to be starving sometime in the near future."

"Now listen, I can't get a decent word out of you. It's pointless trying to reason with you when you're being so—I don't know how to describe it—hot-headed!"

"Perhaps you expected me to jump with joy at this bit of news? Isn't a person allowed to lose her head in circumstances like these?" The chair had been motionless while she was talking, but now she began to rock as rapidly as before.

"If it did any good."

"It does as much good as anything else. It doesn't make any difference."

"If only I could make you understand that you simply must do something."

"But dear God, can't I be allowed to gather my wits? Surely you don't expect me to drag all my furniture down to the auction hall on the spur of the moment!" The chair had stopped again, then immediately was set in motion.

"It's impossible to get through to you tonight. I hardly dare give you Rikard's message—it's from me too, of course."

"What was the message?"

"We would be very glad to have you move in with us until everything is settled—in short, we want very much to help and advise you."

"Well, thank you; I know that, of course."

"We're really very concerned about you, both Rikard and I."

"Oh I'll find a way out all right." She nodded grimly.

"Do you have anything particular in mind?"

"Nothing at all! If things get too bad I can always kill myself. That's always a way out."

"Don't say such ugly things. Though you don't scare me—everybody knows that the ones who are really serious don't talk about it."

Constance mumbled something through clenched teeth and nodded, her face rigid.

Marie was ready to leave. She had hesitantly picked up her muff and now stood patting the soft fur with her gloved hand.

"There is something I would like to ask you, but you've got to promise not to be angry, Constance."

"Go ahead and ask," Constance said dully, without removing her eyes from the pattern she was studying in the curtain.

"Why did you turn Lorck down? I'm just asking out of friendship," she went on hurriedly, when Constance suddenly twisted around in her chair.

"Lorck," she said. "What do you know about that? It's all gossip anyhow."

"No Constance, I don't believe that. Remember Lorck is Rikard's good friend, and mine too for that matter—and there has been something between you, I'm sure of it. But I want you to know that if you've turned him down, I'm just speechless."

"Then it doesn't make any difference," Constance said, calmly settling back in the chair again.

"I'm not just thinking of the practical side of the thing—his excellent position, his reputation, his money and looks—all those things aside, it's still inconceivable."

"Yes, I imagine so."

"Now listen, Constance—just this once. You do plan to marry again, I assume."

"Don't you think one marriage is enough?"

"Enough! Yes, if you had something to occupy you, but look at the way you've been living! Have you really thought for one minute that you could continue to lie around like this for the rest of your life?"

"I don't know what I've imagined," Constance answered, with a motion of boredom and fatigue.

"No that's just the trouble. Listen, Constance, couldn't you write to Lorck . . . "

"And ask him to propose again?"

"Well you could do worse things. Just make an overture— you would find the right words."

"Now that I've fallen so low in the world," she smiled bitterly. "Yes I suppose I could."

"That's not the issue. He doesn't need money, and when a man is so much in love, there's no shame in meeting him half way."

"Let's not talk about it, Marie!" Constance was exhausted.

"Well, all right, but you shouldn't be so proud, Constance. The day will come when you'll regret it, believe me, and it may be too late then."

Constance made a gesture of dismissal and appeared unwilling to discuss it further. Mrs. Hansen said good-night and left the room.

Constance followed mechanically and lit her way down the stairs.

22

W HEN CONSTANCE CAME BACK into the living room, she placed a large pink shade over the lamp. Slumping down on the sofa, she buried her face in one of the pillows and lay there uncomfortably, her feet on the floor. She didn't move or cry. She tried to think about her situation but could only make false starts that dissolved and were gone like soap bubbles. She couldn't form a proper chain of thought, couldn't get hold of a coherent idea.

Lorck appeared and disappeared, but his image was dull and indistinct, fragmented by the riot of other images that jostled against it.

What if she had married him! Oh no—she hadn't wanted to. But she would have been safe then—and he did love her. Oh nonsense! What kind of love were men capable of? They flitted around, strewing fine words and sentiments that were as shopworn as common harlots—and then they came to offer themselves in marriage. Their love was disgusting. They loved one woman and lived with someone else. Not that it really mattered—maybe that was all right, perhaps it wasn't as squalid as it seemed. She had no wish to condemn anybody—she just wanted to keep her distance from it.

She had brief glimpses of her dead husband—he disappeared then returned, again and again. Broken pieces of their life together, tangled and ever changing, drifted into memory. She felt sickened by it. They were inconsequential things—she had no wish to remember them—but they continued to come, like shadows cast by trees in moonlight, their branches bending slowly up and down in the wind.

Johanne announced that tea was on the table, would the

mistress please come in and eat. Constance jumped to her feet and thanked her, then instantly resumed the same position as before.

What would become of her now? Living on the charity of relatives in some rented garret on the edge of town? Rent? She had no way to pay it—and what would happen when her clothes were worn out and she needed new ones? That nonsense about going out to be a teacher—she didn't *know* anything. Or keeping house for a widower—never in the world! All that talk they threw at her—all the talk, talk, talk. No, the only thing to do was kill herself. It was her duty, really, a question of honor. She was so sick of everything. She had often thought seriously about taking this way out. What was there to live for, anyhow? Wait for death to come and toss her through the door, whether she wanted it or not? It was better to go freely.

How could she be such a coward as to fear a little pain! Oh, but it would be awful after she swallowed the poison. It would start right away—her breast heaving, her face turning black, the rattling in her throat; she would foam at the mouth—wasn't froth the right word for that? And she would be so disfigured, so ugly afterwards.

Someone would find her on the sofa—that would give the family a shock—they would all come running and then lift, very slowly, the cloth the doctor had laid across her face.

She had a bottle of cyanide that her husband had used during his photography mania. There had been a skull and crossbones on it, so she had put it away for safekeeping.

Yes, she would do it tonight. Actually it was good this had happened, otherwise she probably would have been capable of living out this disgusting life to the end, some way or other. And even if it were painful—dying was never pleasant—besides, she would lose consciousness right away.

If she could just get Johanne out of the house; she had to be alone in the apartment. She really ought to send Dr. Blunck a letter and ask him to come. Yes of course, she would have to do that. Sitting down at the writing table, she finished the letter in a few minutes.

Dear Dr. Blunck,

Come in the morning as early as possible, and be discreet when you see what has happened, for the sake of our old friendship.

Yours,

Constance Ring

"He'll say I died of a heart attack—it's appropriate, really—and then there won't be any fuss about the burial." She wrote the address on the envelope and went out to the kitchen. Johanne was eating her supper at a small table in the corner.

"Take this letter to the mailbox, Johanne. Here is ten øre for a stamp."

Johanne gulped down the rest of her tea and stood up.

"If you have something to do tonight, you can take the evening off," she added, straightening a hairpin that seemed to be bothering her.

Something in the mistress's voice startled Johanne. Just the way she said "Johanne"—she seemed so strange, almost moved.

"Well thanks, then I'll look in on my sister. She had a baby a few days ago." She hurriedly stacked the cups and saucers and began to clear the table.

"Well then you had better leave right away, Johanne. I'm so afraid they'll close and you won't be able to get a stamp."

"But shouldn't I clear the table and get the bedroom ready?"

"I'll take care of it myself. You needn't come in again tonight. I have a headache, and I'm going to bed. Do you hear, Johanne?"

"Yes ma'am," Johanne said with a nod.

Constance walked back into the living room again, and started rummaging through her writing table, tossing letters and papers carelessly into a heap beside her. The pile grew larger. Some receipts and an insurance policy that had lapsed a year before went back into their places.

The doorbell rang. Terrified she sprang up and locked the door, but then she remembered—Johanne wasn't home; no power on earth could let them in. For a moment an expression

194

of contentment appeared on her face. In a second she realized that it was just the paper boy ringing; she wouldn't go out to get the paper tonight.

But was she absolutely sure Johanne had gone? She needed to make sure; it would be too risky otherwise. Holding the lamp in her hand, she went out to look. The kitchen was empty; she peeked into the maid's room—yes, she had gone. Walking quickly, she crossed the kitchen, but as her hand touched the doorknob, she glanced back at the warm cozy room and felt strangely touched by it. The white cafe curtains were pulled firmly together and the valence above was caught up in the middle by a rosette of blue silk ribbon. The long work table over by the window was covered by a white cotton cloth, and on it, a blue anemone drooped in a water glass. There was a peculiar odor, a mixture of burnt coffee and Russian soap, which she found so agreeable that she stood and inhaled it. The towels were hanging in their usual places—the lamp towel over in the corner with the glass brush and lamp scissors, the one for the knives nearer the window, and the other two, close to the pantry door. On the stove, the brightly polished tea kettle was simmering. The recessed shelves above the table were covered with white paper—Johanne had clipped the edges into a scalloped pattern that she had seen on funeral clothes. The brass coffee pot shone from between two polished mortars. Under the stove there was a pile of kindling wood and the two green watering cans were hanging over the sink. The floor was scrubbed clean, and on a mat in front of the kitchen door, the cat lay dozing.

She hadn't imagined that a kitchen could be so appealing. It was like a bit of enchanted land—she had a sudden awareness of many moments of rest and comfort amid this order and cleanliness, after the work was done.

Suddenly the cat flew across the room—a hissing, snapping ball—and planted its claws in a mouse. With a muffled scream she bolted out of the kitchen and hurried back to her letters.

Kneeling down, she started gathering them into her lap. When she had the whole pile, she walked over to the stove and stuffed them in by the handful. The fire had gone out. She struck a match, but the fire just smoldered without kindling until she poked it to let in some air; then it burned brightly to ash. She stared mournfully into the fire as though she were witnessing a cremation, sitting there before the beloved old stove where she had spent so much of her dreary life.

She continued putting things in order and began to tidy her sewing basket. Her hand fell on the still unfinished strip of embroidery; absently, almost tenderly, she let it slip through her fingers before starting to roll it up. Dear God, those days hadn't really been so bad. Those days—it was just yesterday, this morning even—but years seemed to have passed since then.

Quickly, without a backward glance, she walked to the bedroom. A window was open and she peeked out at the sky. It had cleared now; the sky was filled with wispy clouds and large patches of blue; a half moon was shining. She adjusted the blinds so the light didn't come through the green wooden slats; and dragging the chaise longue out of the corner, placed it so that the light would fall on the face of someone lying there in the morning when the blinds were rolled up. She sat very straight on the chaise longue, gripping its upholstered edge, as if she needed the support. Head bowed, she sat for a long time without moving. Time and again she was on the point of getting up, but she continued to sit there just the same.

The clock on the table began to strike. Startled, she counted the chimes one by one. Eleven! She got up quickly, took off her dress, corset, and shoes, then put on her robe and slippers. Her eyes had looked blank and dead, but now that she felt the soft robe on her limbs, a gentler expression appeared on her face. She looked around at all the old familiar objects, mute servants that had been so faithful and quiet in their actions. Memories loomed up, attached to everything. Suddenly she was filled with a piercing grief, an inexpressible self-pity at having to leave all this when she loved it after all. She was being forced to do it, forced! Yes, there was nothing else she could do—she had to get away. The hour had come, there was no way out. And really she deserved to die—she had been living like an animal, simply sleeping and eating. That was what she had accomplished. That was what she was so afraid to leave behind.

With resolute steps, she approached the chiffonier where the bottle was locked away. Inserting the key in the top drawer, she unlocked it.

At that moment, she heard something in the kitchen. Startled, she began to tremble violently. Johanne had come back before she was finished. It was eleven thirty. Remembering the letter, she went in to ask if Johanne had taken care of it.

No, Johanne had not gotten a stamp; the shop had been closed.

Constance felt strangely relieved.

"If you want the doctor, ma'am, I can go down there early in the morning," Johanne said.

"Oh well, that's soon enough. Let me have it back in the meantime."

Johanne reached into her pocket. "Here's another one," she said. "I met the postman on the steps, so I thought I'd better take the letter, since you didn't want to be disturbed."

Constance gave the envelope a quick glance. It had a French postmark and she felt as if she ought to recognize the hand-writing. When she got back to the living room, she tore open the envelope and saw it was from Lorck.

She glanced through it eagerly, then tossed it on the table and walked up and down the room, bumping into chairs and footstools, and shoving them aside to make a path for herself. She went on like this far into the night, now and then picking up the letter to reread parts of it, then starting to walk again.

I'm bothering you again, in spite of myself. Ever since I left Norway I've done little else than try to convince myself that it would be foolish and intrusive to write to you again. Nevertheless, I'm doing it, just the same. I have to try one more time. This is how matters stand. My mind is so set on you that I don't see how I can ever be free again. I can't be happy unless I can spend my life with you. Is it still inconceivable that you could give me any hope? I can't help thinking about how different things might be. It's on my mind constantly, torturing me day and night. Are you absolutely sure that you have no use for me at all, for my love, and my honorable desire to do everything within my power for you? I can only think of one thing—how can I make you my wife? I am in Paris now; if by some miracle you give me the answer I'm hoping for, I will come for you immediately and bring you back to Paris, where I plan to continue my studies for some time.

Niels Lorck

When Constance went to bed at five that morning to try to get a few hours of sleep, she had already made her decision. The letter to Lorck was finished on the writing table. She had asked him to meet her in Copenhagen where they could have the wedding and then go wherever he wanted.

She had wept while she was writing the letter, struggling with a multitude of feelings. At some deep level she rejoiced in her rescue, but she was filled with a powerful awareness of the torment she had suffered and a feeling of pity for the miserable desolation of her life. She felt anxiety about her coming marriage and fear and uncertainty about herself; yet hand and hand with these came a dawning hope for the future, gratitude toward Lorck for loving her, and a deep desire for a fully human life. She felt tranquil, almost contented. It was going to be a busy time, and there was always some value in keeping busy. The newest Paris fashions, which had been sent to her the other day, paraded past her, and she pondered for a moment about whether she should buy her new spring dress at Bon Marché when she arrived in Paris, or at that other large store, what was its name?

Yes, of course marriage was better than some hideous death by her own hand. She had been married before, so at least she knew what to expect. Besides, now that she was not so idealistic, she would see things very differently. It would make a big difference.

It really isn't so easy to die, Constance said to herself, lying in bed with sleepless eyes, her cheeks suddenly pale and thin. With a sigh that sounded like a sob, she turned on her side and pressed her face into the pillow; "When it comes right down to it, marriage is better," she mumbled.

23

LORCK AND CONSTANCE were in Lausanne. They wanted to take in the glorious Swiss September air before setting out for Norway, and they intended to stay as long as the summer weather lasted.

They had been travelling for nearly a year and a half now, spending the first two months in Paris, moving on to a spa in the south of France and then to Italy. They had passed the winter in Rome and had been travelling toward home all summer.

Recently Lorck had begun to miss his work; he longed to be active again and to settle into a normal home life with Constance. Constance also thought it would be good to settle somewhere. Lorck had written to the young doctor who was managing his practice and told him that they would be back in Kristiania in October.

At the beginning of their marriage, Constance had had trouble adjusting. She was withdrawn and shy with Lorck and found it hard to talk to him.

When she sat within the circle of his arms and he poured out his soul, confiding as he stroked her hand and kissed her hair, how much he had suffered for her love, she didn't know what to say to him. Understanding that her silence was not indifference, Lorck did not try to force her to talk. He hoped that the time would soon come when she would feel safe and relaxed with him, and he could afford to wait. Constance often felt sad and half-ashamed that she could not respond to him. She tried in vain to overcome it, but her embarrassment was so acute that it was painful to sit alone at the table with him. She could hardly bring herself to ask for money to buy the things she needed. Lorck had to remember on his own to keep her supplied with pocket money, as he discovered accidently one day, when he needed some change to pay for something and found she didn't have a shilling.

Just the same, Lorck was happy. That his wife was not as ardent as himself did not diminish the joy he felt at finally having in his arms the object of his dreams and longings. He knew she hadn't loved him when he married her, but she had told him she wanted with all her soul to love him, and on that promise he had built his hopes. He had entered his new life with the honorable intention of devoting his future to her, and he had no doubt that finally he would win her heart. Every opportunity that a husband with plenty of money and time alone with his wife could use to endear himself, he exploited like a miser. His whole being was a well of tenderness—every word, every glance declared his love. He was careful about how he expressed his passion, so that his caresses did not frighten or offend her. He wrapped her in an atmosphere of love and adoration, and she lived within it, at first without reflection, then in timid wonder, and finally drunk with happiness. For it did happen. She was in love before she even had time to know how it began. When she thought of how different her first marriage had been, the way she had struggled to make herself love Ring, she closed her eyes and smiled in joy and gratitude.

Never had Constance dreamed life could be so filled with joy; never had the inconsequential pursuits of daily life seemed so amusing. Each small chore was filled with pleasure. Her youthful cheerfulness returned, born of the inner contentment of her soul, and she went humming through the days, with sunny, smiling eyes. There was a strange, quiet pleasure in walking beside him—no special destination, just walking endlessly and feeling the gentle pressure of his arm when she made a comment that pleased him or asked a question that rang agreeably in his ear. And when he turned his head and looked into her eyes, his smile intoxicated with happiness, a warm current of rapture ran through her. If they were on a lonely road, the smile would become a kiss, ending in a giddy little laugh; their kisses were brief, because they could afford so many. More and still more. She lived from day to day in a soft embrace of happiness and love, enclosed in a world where it was good to be.

But imperceptibly their relationship began to change. When Lorck felt that he fully possessed her love, he relaxed, conscious that he had won what he longed for most in the world. An inexpressible peace filled his mind. Nothing before his marriage mattered to him any more. His relationship with Constance had become his life's central meaning, the fixed point from which he lived, acted, and experienced everything. He felt like a man who after many years of being a passenger on a common steamship, suddenly had a first-class sailing ship of his own.

At times he thought of himself as a conqueror, with a right to rest on his laurels. Almost without realizing it he shifted to wanting to be the recipient of love; and he enjoyed her nearness and devotion in full measure. He loved her just as sincerely, more deeply and truly, he told himself, but there was no longer a treasure to fight for, and so his behavior took a more passive form.

Constance noticed the change and felt the absence of their former state of rapture. Life had become quieter around her. She felt as if the ship of their love was becalmed, and occasionally, that the voyage was becoming a little monotonous.

During the last few weeks before they stopped in Lausanne, Constance had not been really well. She was bothered by nausea and faintness, and occasionally, for no apparent reason, little fits of nervous weeping. In Lausanne, she finally realized what was wrong. She had been reading a French book that she had found by accident in the sun-room of the hotel. The title was *Health Care for Young Mothers*. There could be no doubt—she had all the symptoms. A giddy feeling of happiness swept over her; her first thought was to dash upstairs and tell Lorck. But when she went into the bedroom where he was changing his collar, she suddenly became shy and blushed furiously. When Lorck smiled and turned toward her expectantly, she threw herself in his arms and hid her face in his chest. So it emerged in whispers, in veiled phrases, like a timid confession of a dangerous secret. Lorck didn't understand right away. Constance had to tweak his ear and scold him for being so dull-witted. When it finally penetrated, he was speechless with joy. In the early days of their marriage, he had waited with eager impatience to share this happiness, but now he was unprepared for it. He held her at arms length, regarding her with an expression that Constance had never seen on his face before. She lowered her eyes and again wanted to hide her face in his chest, but he lifted her in his arms and carried her triumphantly around the room, beside himself with joy.

One morning a few days later, Lorck was sitting in the sun-room reading a newspaper while he waited for Constance to finish dressing. Suddenly, he was surprised to hear a voice that sounded familiar. Turning his head in the direction of the sound, he saw through the open door of the restaurant a tall, broad-shouldered figure in a grey summer suit and straw hat speaking to a waiter. Before he had time to collect himself, the figure turned on his heels and walked into the sun-room.

"What the devil, is that you, Meier?" Lorck cried, getting to his feet.

Meier stepped back in amazement and stared at Lorck for a moment as though he didn't believe his senses.

"Well, well," he said with a shrug, as if trying to gather his wits. "It's not so astonishing, really—you were just as likely to be here as anywhere else."

"Wonderful to see you, old boy," Lorck said, shaking his hand heartily. "I thought you were in Norway. The paper said you had come home."

"I did, but that was ages ago—no reason not to go abroad again."

"It's so strange to run into you. When did you get here?"

"Last night—with Jenny. I've been escorting her."

"So your sister is along—that will be nice for Constance. . . . "

"I've already dropped her off. She decided she wants to learn French, so of course she's staying in a pension."

"And what will you do now?" asked Lorck.

"Anything that turns up. I've got a month of vacation that

I've got to kill somewhere."

"Well how are you? Tell me a little about yourself."

"There's not much to tell. I dabble at giving music lessons, go home to number 19 Pilestredet, and live on melancholy and money troubles."

"You've become famous since the last time we met," Lorck cried. "You haven't said anything about that."

Meier shrugged his shoulders.

"Famous . . . " he said dejectedly. "You can't eat fame."

"But the performance of your composition was a great success."

"Pah." Meier grimaced. "That doesn't mean a thing if someone has the bad luck to be born in a country like Norway. The conditions for music are so miserable," he said with a wave of his hand. "May as well go home and go to bed."

"But once you get a little recognition, it's not so bad, is it?" Lorck said.

"Recognition! What the hell does recognition mean in Norway? There aren't any positions, so what is there to do?"

"But you're a composer!"

"A composer," he sneered. "What's the point of putting together a bit of music that will be played once, twice at the most, in a provincial city like Kristiania."

"But it was performed in Copenhagen and Dresden."

"And praised in the newspapers," Meier interrupted, with an ironic laugh. "Yes, what a success!"

"But you'll keep on working of course—you have plenty of time."

"Keep on working! Plunking at the piano with amateurs— grinding out harmonies with people who have no talent."

"Oh nonsense," Lorck laughed. "Don't you do any composing at all?"

"Where would I find the time? Unless a man has a fortune, he's doomed to failure the way things are today."

"What's happened to you? You used to be so—"

"Oh yes, such an optimistic young man," Meier interrupted. "That gets worn away."

As they stood there, Lorck looked at his watch.

"Have you had breakfast?" he asked.

"No I haven't—God knows, I'm hungry as a wolf."

"Let's eat together," Lorck said. "Or perhaps you are meeting someone?" he added when Meier appeared to hesitate.

"Oh nothing like that; I'm completely at liberty."

"I can't wait to see my wife's face when she sees you," Lorck said.

At that moment the door opened and Constance walked into the room. Lorck smiled and watched her expectantly.

Meier grew pale and ran his hand through his hair. Constance paused, looked at Meier incredulously, and a pleased smile spread across her face.

"No really, is it Meier?" she cried, clapping her hands together with unrestrained pleasure. "How in the world did you get here?"

"You may well ask, Constance," Lorck said. "I'm sitting here, not suspecting a thing, when I hear this fellow talking inside—isn't that amazing?"

"The surprise is mutual," Meier said, taking her outstretched hand. "I didn't have the faintest inkling of what was in store for me."

"How wonderful to run into you," Constance exclaimed. "How are you?"

"I'm fine thanks. There's no need for anybody to ask you that."

"You must stay on here for a few days, Meier."

"Yes, you really must," Constance added.

"We'll take some excursions," said Lorck.

"And have a wonderful time together," Constance finished.

That afternoon Meier picked up his sister at the pension to take her on the outing he had arranged with the Lorcks. They had driven out to a cliff above Lake Geneva, where there was a delightful view, and decided to walk back. They had all had tea together at the hotel, and afterwards he had taken his sister back to the pension. He was on his way back home now, glad to be alone so he could collect himself after the day's events.

The sudden meeting with Constance had affected him like scraping the scab off an old wound. The woman was his destiny. The thought of her had inspired him to write his long composition. He had written the rough draft long ago, but he had begun to work on it in earnest when he heard that Ring was dead. His sister had written to him about the isolated life Constance was leading. Without really intending to, he had nourished his hopes anew on the image of loneliness that his sister's words had painted for him. Restlessly he worked on. As soon as he had done something to show his worth, he would go home, declare his love for her, and ask her to marry him. With her, he could fight his way forward, become someone worthy and great. He felt bold and confident. He had always loved her, believed in her, understood her better than anyone else did. This was his pride and happiness. When he thought that someday he might rest his head on her breast, his heart swelled with longing and happiness. Then, just as he was putting the final touches on his work, the news arrived of her marriage to Lorck. It utterly crushed him. He shut himself in during the daytime and roamed around at night until he collapsed in exhaustion. He would lie for hours on the sofa, weeping like a small child. His sister had written to him about Constance's financial situation—that the lawsuit was lost—and it was not until then, people said, that she had accepted Lorck's proposal.

If only he had arrived in time, everything could have been saved—this was the thought that rankled so painfully in his heart. Lorck had taken her away from him, taken her with the help of a piece of blind luck. Lorck, who had so little understanding of her true value—in the beginning, at least. Of course, he had come to see him later to say that he owed it to Mrs. Ring and the truth to confess that he had been a fool; he had been completely wrong about her. He remembered the affection he had felt for Lorck from that day on. He could have hugged him with gratitude; the camaraderie of earlier days developed into close friendship. Now he hated Lorck. He begrudged him his happiness; he wasn't good enough for her—nobody was, not even himself—nobody.

Everything had fallen apart for him the moment he knew she was lost. He cursed the brutality of fate; life did not seem worth living to him. His work became distasteful to him—what was there to struggle for now? What was there to win?

Sometime afterwards he received the news of his father's death. In the state of mind he was in, it made a relatively small impression; but then his monthly checks stopped, and he had to return home again. There was no inheritance to speak of. His mother was left with her widow's pension and two unmarried daughters whom an uncle had promised to look after.

So he had begun his work in Kristiania, struggling through life from day to day, bored and tired and discontented.

It seemed to him that he had become more tranquil lately; he had begun to forget. Then fate tossed her suddenly down in front of him.

Now it had all boiled up again—the love, the sorrow, the torment of knowing she was in another man's arms. It was intolerable, impossible to witness it—he had to get away before he became so miserable that he couldn't hide it any longer. Today he had conducted himself well; they hadn't noticed the slightest thing. Obviously Lorck had no idea of his state of mind. But how he had struggled!

He had arrived at the hotel. Without looking either to the right or left, he ran up the stairs to his room.

24

MEANWHILE LORCK AND CONSTANCE had seated themselves in an arbor in a corner of the hotel's spacious garden. It was a cool, quiet evening. Lorck was overheated after the trip and he was drinking iced red wine to cool himself. Constance was leaning back on a comfortable garden bench, her shoulders wrapped in a large black lace shawl. The garden was filled with pale shafts of moonlight and sharply etched shadows. Within the arbor the dim light filtered through gaps in the vine leaves, tracing a pattern of innumerable streaks and slashes upon the table and along the floor.

They were talking about Meier, exhilarated at having run into him. Constance thought he had changed a great deal, and not for the better. He was so cynical and derisive about himself and everything else. Lorck replied that this was what happened to artists doomed to live in Norway. "Just the same, it's a pity," he added. "He's a fine boy. I've always liked him."

"Yes, I have too," said Constance. "I wish he'd marry a rich woman."

"Shall we put our heads together and see if we can find him one?" Lorck said with a smile.

Constance laughed.

"When we get home we'll be very cordial to him, Constance. I think he likes being with us."

"Yes, we'll be very cordial," Constance answered.

"He certainly was crazy about you for a while. Didn't you know it?"

"I had no idea."

"Didn't he ever give you a hint?"

"Never!" answered Constance.

He's a cultured, well-bred person, Lorck thought, sighing at the memory of his own behavior.

"Well, it was probably just a passing fancy," he said aloud.

"Did he say anything to you about it?" Constance asked with a shy, teasing smile.

"No, not the slightest thing," he asserted. "I could just as well have imagined it. I always thought everybody was in love with you."

They were both quiet for a few moments.

"What are you thinking about, my dear Conny," Lorck asked, taking her hand.

"Oh, nothing really," she said sweetly.

"Come on, tell me now," he said, pulling her closer.

"It's not so easy to do. Sometimes my thoughts race around so wildly, or they come in bits and pieces and won't fit together, or some goblin carries me away and I can't find the words."

He had put his arm around her waist, and with his other hand pressed her head to his chest. They sat there without speaking, holding each other tightly.

"Now I know what I was thinking about," Constance whispered, pressing her lips to his beard.

"What is it, Conny?"

"Oh, it's what we've talked about so many times—how happy you've made me, all our blessings, the things we've shared, the love you've made me feel for you, and especially, oh you know, what—what's going to be coming soon."

"My sweet darling," Lorck said, pulling her closer to him, "you make me so happy—your words are adorable and your caresses are so sweet."

"And you were so afraid to marry me . . . " he added tenderly a little while later.

"Not you any more than anyone else. There was nothing I wanted—everything seemed disgusting."

"You wouldn't have anything to do with me, you naughty thing. Do you remember how hard I had to struggle? And if that letter hadn't—ah, I can't bear to think about it."

"It was a terrible time," Constance said. "I had gotten myself into such a state. And to think that you really wanted to marry me—that was so good of you," she said, clinging to him.

"I loved you, Conny."

"And do you remember how stupid I was when we were first married—completely wretched with embarrassment."

"You must admit, Conny, I really have been quite persistent—you did everything in your power to discourage me, but I was in love with you. I never loved anyone until I loved you."

"Is that really true, Niels—tell me, is it true?"

"Yes, my dear, I know that now. If you hadn't existed I never would have learned what love was. And now that our treasure is on the way, I'm filled with joy, Conny."

"But still, you've loved other women; I mean, had relationships with them?"

"They were all meaningless, Conny. It wasn't until I met you that I really began to live."

"And that's the way it is for you, too, Conny," he went on a little later. "Your life began with me, isn't that right?"

She didn't answer.

"Because you love me—tell me you love me."

"You know that, of course, Niels," she said softly.

"But say it anyhow—it's so sweet to hear it."

A strange feeling came over her. She wanted to shake off his arms and run away. It was as if something ghostly was creeping up on her in the dark, something she did not dare turn and face. She shivered. And then at that moment she remembered the sweet pleasure that had stolen over her when Meier quite accidently happened to lay his arm on the back of her chair. But she wanted to get away from all that now, and in a single bound be safe inside the circle of love and happiness that had enclosed her for so many months. She wrapped herself protectively in memories—the tender hours, the fascination of the little things that had taken place between herself and Lorck. She wanted to be happy, *was* happy.

"I love you," she said, "love, love, you," and her kiss and embrace were more intense than ever before.

With an enraptured smile on his lips, Lorck pulled her to his heart. She buried her face in his soft thick beard.

"What in the world," he said with a sudden jerk. "I feel sick." Clutching her hand, he bent over with a groan. He was shivering violently.

"The ice has given you a chill," Constance said. "Come on, we'll go upstairs."

He stood up with difficulty, and supporting himself on Constance's arm walked through the garden into the hotel, stopping occasionally because of the pain.

By the time they reached the room, Constance was frightened by his pallor; there was cold sweat on his forehead, and he was complaining of unbearable nausea. She sent for a doctor immediately.

The doctor was a middle-aged, stocky little Frenchman with abundant grey hair and a beard. He told Constance that her husband had caught a severe cold, but he hoped it would not get worse. He promised to send some medicine and return in the morning.

25

LORCK WAS CONFINED to bed with gastric fever, and Constance cared for him tirelessly. Most of the time he didn't recognize her, taking her for someone else; often he called her Kristine.

The doctor found a nurse to relieve Constance at his bedside every other night. It would be three or four weeks before they could even think about travelling home; still, there was no danger if caution was observed.

Meier had given up the thought of leaving for the present and had told Constance he would stay as long as he could be of any use to her. Constance had thanked him heartily, making no attempt to conceal her pleasure at his decision.

He gave her daily help and encouragement, fetching medicine from the pharmacy and remaining constantly on hand to perform small services. Every day he brought flowers or fruit and made her go out for a bit of fresh air in the garden. Sometimes he had to come as many as five times to suggest a walk before she would agree to it, since she refused to go out unless Lorck was sleeping. Then a girl who was watching over someone in the next room came in; she had orders to fetch the mistress the instant the master awoke.

When Lorck's mind was clear, Meier occasionally went in to inquire about his condition. Lorck always nodded, gave him a feeble smile, and said he was feeling better. Once in awhile he asked about the newspapers, and Meier told him some small tidbit of news. When he began to get stronger, Meier read to him until he fell asleep or said he was tired.

One day, after thanking Meier for his great kindness to Constance and himself, he said it was a comfort to know that

Constance could turn to him.

Two weeks after Lorck fell ill, Constance was sitting in a large armchair at the head of his bed. All morning he had been restless, hallucinating at intervals. The doctor had given him some medicine to quiet him, and late in the afternoon he had fallen asleep. Constance had taken her usual walk in the garden and found Lorck still sleeping when she returned. She had sunk back in fatigue. The book she had been reading was in her lap; her hands had loosened their grip and lay beside it. Hearing something from the next room, she got up and peeked through the half-opened door. It was the maid bringing in the mail. Signaling for her to put it on the table, she sat down again to doze.

Not until Lorck had taken his evening medicine and had been prepared for the night did she remember that there might be newspapers and letters from home. Then she would have something to pass the time while it was her turn to keep watch.

There was a lot of mail today; not only a pile of newspapers, but a package and a letter, both addressed to Lorck.

Constance saw that the letter was from Hansen—who was looking after their financial affairs—and thinking it might require an answer, opened it.

She was sitting in the outer room. Lorck's door was open; from her place in the low armchair by the round table, she could see him in bed and be ready at his slightest movement. The evening was still so mild that the door to the balcony was open; the scent of stock and roses wafted up from outside, filling the room with fragrance. A lamp with a large paper shade glowed dimly, barely illuminating half of the spacious room.

When Constance had read a little of the letter, she turned very pale and her hands trembled so violently that the characters seemed to jump on the page. She placed the sheet on the table in front of her and put both hands to her head. Breathing as rapidly as if she had been running, with color coming and going in her face, she read the letter through, again and again. Gradually her composure returned. At last she folded the letter, stuffed it into its envelope, and walked out on the balcony.

It was a beautiful evening. The moonlight cast the shadow of
the hotel out upon the open square below their room, gleaming down on a fountain topped by a balloon-cheeked cherub
that stood near the entrance of one of the main streets. Moonlight illuminated one side of the great monument at the left of
the marketplace, marking figures of remarkable shapes and
sizes. Further on was Lake Geneva, its surface shimmering and
silvery where the moonlight struck it, and coal black on the far
side near the high ground. Several boats of singing, laughing
people glided back and forth, and the sound of music drifted
up from a public garden nearby.

Constance, however, was quite untouched by the evening's
harmonious delights. She stood with crossed arms, staring
straight ahead, pierced with anguish.

The letter had said:

> Dear Lorck:
>
> Kristine has just brought a package that she
> begged me to send to you. At first I thought I'd
> leave it until you returned, but since I don't know
> how long that will be, and it seemed so urgent to
> her that you get it right away, I'm sending it on to
> you. She told me that the little boy is dead, and I
> can only congratulate you about getting the child
> off your neck, especially given your situation at the
> moment. She said the package contained a few
> farewell words. She didn't say what else was in it
> and I didn't ask. She said she wouldn't be coming
> for money any longer and wanted to thank me for
> the money she had gotten over the years, and for my
> trouble as well. I felt sorry for her, the poor thing. I
> offered her the usual amount for next month, since I
> thought she might need it and I knew you wouldn't
> object—but she wouldn't take it.

Then came a reckoning of the money he had paid for the
child's support during Lorck's absence, a friendly greeting to
Constance, and an appeal to be sure and come home some
day.

Constance had no idea that Lorck had a child. This sudden discovery overwhelmed her, throbbed continuously like a painful wound. With all her might she tried to thrust the pain away. It was unbearable. He hadn't told her because he wanted to spare her, of course—what would be the point? There was no deceit in that. She had never for a moment imagined he had lived a celibate life; at least she ought to have considered that he *might* have a child.

What if he had more than one, with other women! The thought was unendurable; she screamed, pressing her hands to her eyes, and stamped her foot. The idea twisted and gnawed inside her.

And now *she* was bringing his child into the world. Oh, how disgusting—a child with God knew how many brothers and sisters, brats wandering around the streets. If only she could get out of this! Imagine, just a few weeks ago she had felt so jubilant about it. But perhaps she had been mistaken! She clung passionately to the thought.

Suddenly a faint sound came from his room. She straightened up, dropped her arms and listened. He was ill, of course; she had completely forgotten.

She hurried inside, but paused in the next room. She felt reluctant to see him now, to hear his voice. What if he didn't recognize her and called her Kristine—Kristine! Ah, she put her hand to her heart—so that was it. The sound came again. She stretched her hands out in front of her, clenched them violently together, and mumbling something that sounded like a prayer, went in to him.

He was sitting up in bed staring anxiously toward the door. He looked ghostly in the clear moonlight.

"Conny," he implored reproachfully, "I've been waiting for you." He reached out his hand to her, but it immediately fell back on the blanket. She noticed that he was completely rational.

"Do you want me to light the night lamp?" she asked without approaching him.

He sank slowly back onto the pillow.

"Why won't you come over to me?"

She drew nearer to the bed. "Are you feeling better now?" she asked.

"As long as you are here, I'm fine. Let me feel your hands on my forehead."

"They're so cold. It will chill you."

"No, it will soothe me."

She stroked his forehead with one hand.

"Both of them," he said in a weak voice.

After awhile he moved her hands to his lips and kissed them. Then he put them back on his forehead.

"Sit with me, Conny—I'm so tired." He groped for her skirt to pull her closer to the bed. "You mustn't leave me. Ah well, go on then, just go . . . " he said suddenly in a completely different tone. "I can see perfectly well that I'm a burden to you—naturally it's more pleasant to go walking with Meier." He spoke haltingly, with a peevish ring in his tone.

Constance was so amazed at this unexpected reversal that she couldn't think of an answer. Lorck, who had expected her to respond with reassurances and loving words became even more disturbed by her silence.

"Why haven't you given me my medicine? I'm supposed to have a spoonful when I wake up; I heard it very clearly. How can anyone get well like this?" His voice was hoarse and he groaned from the effort.

Constance went over to get the medicine bottle.

"No thanks, just leave it—leave it," he complained.

"Come Niels, take your medicine nicely, like a good boy." She poured him a spoonful.

He lay there sulking for a few minutes and then took it.

"Why don't you say anything? Why don't you tell me I'm wrong—why don't you kiss me?" he said fretfully. "Kiss me." His voice was tender suddenly.

She bent over and touched her lips to his. His breath was foul, and she turned away involuntarily.

"You need rest; you have to sleep," she said, stroking his curly hair to soothe him. Slowly, gently, she lulled him to sleep. That night Lorck slept quietly without interruption for the first time since he had been confined to bed. His illness had clearly taken a turn for the better.

But Constance could not sleep. She wanted so much to forget the pain she was suffering. She closed her eyes and lay still, very still; shifting her position now and then, she lay on her back with her knees drawn up in an arch, turned and buried her head in the pillow, but nothing helped. Finally she got up and went into the next room. If she walked up and down until she was cold or exhausted, maybe she could sleep then. She slipped her bare feet into a pair of slippers, threw on a skirt and a bed-jacket, and crept softly out of the bedroom.

A strange pale light, dead and still, filled the room. Through the open balcony door the chirping song of a great choir of birds could be heard. She walked out on the balcony. It was wet with dew and the sky was blue-grey and hazy. There wasn't a breath of wind. The trees and plants seemed asleep, and the lake stretched out in profound repose. In the eastern sky there were narrow golden stripes—the sun would soon be up. The stillness was oppressive, and Constance shuddered. Her thoughts circled around one thing—this one thing—this woman he had loved and lived with, who had given him a child.

She wondered if he had loved Kristine the way he now loved her! What if he had—what if he had? She writhed at the thought.

Suddenly she remembered the package—it had to be letters. Hansen had mentioned some parting words.

"Oh dear God," she whispered, "there are letters—letters!" She raised her eyebrows and opened her eyes wide as if in terror; pursing her lips, she whistled softly. A kind of rapturous agony seized her; she would throw herself on the letters and read like someone possessed. She didn't waver an instant or feel a shadow of doubt; on the contrary, she knew nothing in the world could hinder or stop her. Her mouth twisted cruelly; the blood hammered in her temples and her hands trembled as she tore off the wrappings.

On top was a crudely written letter, with highly irregular spelling:

Dear Niels,

Please forgive me for daring to write after such a long time, but I have to tell you that God has taken our beloved son home, and even though I know very well it was the best thing for my poor blessed Anton, a fatherless boy, with his father still living, even worse, I still feel bitter sorrow that he's passed away. He was my pride and joy, the picture of his father, even though you don't like to hear that now that you're married and don't love me any more; but it made my heart glad to see the likeness because I couldn't stop loving you when you left me and gave your heart to someone else. It was bad luck for me, my pain but also my happiness, because I love you just as much today as when you called me your kitten and said my love was your comfort and happiness. Whenever I think of those wonderful nights I spent with you, my tears flow, and they always will because I'll never forget you as long as I live. But enough of that—my sweet darling boy died eight days ago today and was buried five days later. His coffin was so pretty—it was filled with flowers; he was only one year and eight months old—he was born in January, after the October you left, if you remember. He had typhoid fever and he suffered terribly. Right before he died he opened his eyes and looked at me like he wanted to complain, and I felt stabbed to the heart because I brought him into the world so shamefully; I bent down to talk to him, I couldn't stop crying, and then he smiled at me sweetly, took a deep breath and died. I thought my heart was going to break right then, but we can bear more suffering than we think possible. So now I'm saying good-bye for the last time; I'm leaving for Drammen where my family lives; I think I'll be able to find work there. I won't ever see you again in this life, but I will think about you often and also about the little one I suffered and grieved for. I sincerely hope you will always be happy and that your wife will love you as much as I did, so you will never be without love. So for the last time, thank you for everything. Because of you I've tasted happiness in life, and even though it just lasted a little while and ended in bitter sorrow, I wouldn't have traded it for anything in the world, no never. And bless you for providing so well for our child. Keep well and be happy.

Your old and faithful friend,
Kristine

When Constance had read the letter she put her face down in her hands and sobbed. That poor woman and her child. Why had she been cast off? By what right did men behave that way? They used up the youth, the health, the love of these women, as if they had been created for one purpose, used them until they had their fill. If they saw something more desirable, they cast them aside, leaving them to the fate their ruthless male egotism had prepared for them. She felt a strange compassion for this patient sufferer who was so filled with goodness and resignation, and at the same time, a raging bitterness against the callous society that made it so safe and comfortable for men to indulge their sexual desires.

She no longer felt jealous; the nature of her pain was something different. She felt a sudden violent aversion to her husband; she couldn't stand the thought of him.

The remaining letters were from Lorck to Kristine. They were numbered and she read them in order. She saw a relationship that had lasted several years, during which time he had had love affairs on the side—this was evident from his responses to Kristine's reproaches and jealous outbursts. One of these rivals had been a married woman who was obviously a member of Lorck's own set. In one of the letters Lorck had written:

My beloved Kristine,
Now calm yourself, I'm coming back to you. You shouldn't be bothered about this silly episode. If

you hadn't accidently found out about it, it wouldn't have hurt you in the least. To tell the truth, I'm tired of constantly having to be on the lookout for her husband; and when it comes right down to it, she's never been able to take me away from you completely. I would never have given her a thought if she hadn't thrown herself at me. I'm happiest in your arms, you must remember and believe that. I really love you, Kristine. You are so good and sweet and lovely—especially when you're in a good mood, not sulking and crying in that unbecoming way, do you hear me, kitten?

For the most part the letters consisted of making arrangements about when she should come to his house. They were filled with the same kinds of endearments he had spoken to Constance, sometimes even the exact words, and they went through her like a sword.

Then came an interval of several months during which no letters were exchanged, and then a letter that began:

Yes my love, of course you may come back to me if you are still as fresh and sweet as you were—I'd like nothing better. When I advised you to accept that fellow's proposal, I thought it was the best thing for your happiness; now that you've turned him loose, there's nothing to keep us apart. You must realize that I didn't let you slip out of my arms with a light heart. The things I've had to resort to in the meantime have not been amusing, and a lovesick woman that I got involved with out of sheer boredom is leaving the city any day now. I'll be happy to have you back. Come tomorrow evening at ten if you can. If I'm not home, just lie down quietly and go to sleep like you used to in the old days when I would wake you with a kiss; you still have your little key. And I've fixed up the bathroom; it's very enticing—you'll see what an excellent bath attendant I can be.

A sequence of letters followed, more loving and affectionate than ever, but with an undercurrent of sadness. She was his comfort and refuge, he wrote. Constance estimated that they were written around the time he had proposed to her. And then came the time period when Kristine had been pregnant. Constance read his apologies, which revealed a sincere compassion larded with cliches he assumed would be consoling.

At last she came to the final letter. Inside was a brief farewell—he was leaving the country and wasn't sure when he would come home, or if he ever would at all. He told her to draw a monthly sum from his lawyer, Hansen, who knew the situation and had orders to begin payments whenever she asked. Finally, he advised her to marry a man who had made her an offer of marriage, and declared his willingness to give her money for a trousseau.

When Constance had finished reading, she cut the broken seal off the wrapper and packed the letters up carefully. She found some string, wrapped it around the package, and locked it with Hansen's letter in a drawer. She sat down with her elbows on the table and her face in her hands. For over ten minutes she remained unmoving. Suddenly she appeared to collect herself and stood up. Her cheeks looked ashy grey and her lips were queerly compressed; her fingers fumbled with the tablecloth as if she were dimly trying to catch hold of something. If Lorck had seen her at that moment, he would have had difficulty recognizing his wife in this rigid figure with the sagging features and the deep furrows between her staring eyes. Quietly she crept back into the bedroom, but in spite of her caution the door squeaked and Lorck woke up.

"Are you up already, Conny?" he asked drowsily.

"No, I'm coming back to bed," she answered quickly. "I couldn't sleep, but I'm sleepy now."

Her head was already on the pillow of the bed beside his.

"I had such a lovely sleep, Conny. I feel so much stronger—give me your hand . . . " His voice died away and he was asleep again.

But Constance was still wide awake. Her icy fingers lay in his, but as soon as she knew he was asleep, she freed them. She was suffering intensely, the burning pain in her heart waxing and waning as her thoughts circled the images called forth by the letters. Again and again she imagined him caressing these women. He had gone from one to the other; now it was her turn, that was all there was to it. She asked herself why it hurt so much—she had never imagined that she was the first and only one he had loved. Why did she let it have the power to wound her so deeply? She was the one he loved now; there was nobody else. But her happiness had collapsed; his love had no special value any more—at least, not like before. She was just like all the rest of them, and that took the glory away. Half unconsciously, she had thought of herself as an exception, as someone special in his life; now she saw that this wasn't the case. There had been so many of them. He had called them all by the same pet names he now gave her, been their Niels— "your Niels"—what did it mean when he said he was hers? How long would it last? The bond of marriage was no obstacle to him—he had robbed other men of their possessions; why hadn't he let them keep their wives in peace! She remembered his attempt to seduce her when she was married to Ring, and that coupled with the knowledge she now possessed made her almost think of him with loathing. What did it matter to men like that if they were married—had obligations to a woman—a woman! In matters like these honor did not apply. It consoled her to imagine him as depraved as possible—it made her colder and calmer. She would bear her misfortune with dignity. She had married a bad person, that was all there was to it. She would say nothing to him. It was out of the question for a mature person to make a fuss about something like this—it would make her look ridiculous. She would withdraw into herself and behave as if nothing had happened. But her love was gone. She didn't love this man; the man to whom she believed she had given her soul was someone else. That was all over now; he would just have to put up with it. No one could reap what he hadn't sown. Things would be very different between them from now on, perhaps not on the outside, but different nevertheless.

26

STILL, IT WASN'T as easy as Constance had imagined to calm herself. Each day the pain erupted all over again; whenever the inflection of one of Lorck's words reminded her of something they used to laugh about, or when he called her a pet name that had always been a prelude to a kiss, she could have screamed in her despair at having lost him. The nights were the worst—she lay sleepless hour after hour—a helpless victim of tormenting thoughts.

Lately she had refused to go for walks with Meier. One day, however, she decided she would go with him; when Meier had anxiously asked about the change in her appearance, she told him she had been suffering from headaches and insomnia. Gradually as Lorck recovered he began to dimly perceive that his wife had changed. When he caressed her, he would suddenly let go of her in amazement; it was like holding a strange woman in his arms. It began to upset him that their relationship was not as it had been before. What could be the reason? She received his kisses but did not return them unless he asked her, and then it was without warmth. He became more reserved and waited expectantly for her to notice, to miss his tenderness and come seek him of her own free will. But that didn't happen. Days passed in which they didn't exchange a kiss; and it struck him with painful astonishment that it was at precisely these times that her manner was most conspicuously lively and charming, as if she wanted to cover her coldness with high spirits, pull the wool over his eyes, in a way.

Every day that passed seemed increasingly to harden this new form their life together had taken. It began to be agony for him. Something watchful and nervous came into his manner—occasionally he was touchy and quick-tempered, and afterwards seemed plunged in helpless melancholy.

One morning Constance felt so ill that she stayed in bed until late in the morning. During the night she had suffered from violent waves of stomach cramps. When Lorck asked her what was wrong, she told him she had a headache and wanted to sleep. She didn't feel like telling him just then that she had miscarried during the night.

She lay with her eyes closed, feeling a faint satisfaction at what had happened. This was what she had wanted—she had half expected it. The violent mental turmoil she had experienced recently was more than sufficient cause. A feeling of freedom and relief swept over her; now she didn't have to bring into the world a symbol of a love she no longer felt. She told herself that the crisis had passed in her feelings for Lorck. It was so stupid and futile to grieve about his past. Actually, this was something that shouldn't concern her. She had succeeded in suppressing both pain and dislike, now only resignation and indifference remained—it was certainly possible to have a good life together; people didn't have to love so intensely. The last bit of despondency, the slight bitterness and irritation she still felt deep inside would surely wear away. He had not betrayed her. On the contrary, she was the one who had been too naive, too quick to surrender to dreams of happiness that she now understood did not exist, *could* not exist. Men were men, and women were utterly different—so ill-equipped, so full of vague ideas. It had been sheer lunacy, this fleeting illusion that his love for her was special, of a higher nature. What nonsense! Now she knew the truth. She had shed her illusions, slipped them off like a coat, and she was ready to take life as it was given. All things considered, it was better like this. Now she had her feet on the ground. And perhaps it was nonsense to think that these affairs of the heart, in all their guises, degraded a person, or hurt anyone. Take Lorck, for example—he was a splendid man in every respect; his friends, everybody who knew him, agreed on that. Now she could see for herself how quickly love could fall apart. What if she fell in love with someone else? Well, why not!

From this day on, she began to be happy about having Meier as a daily companion. When she was oppressed by her husband's company, Meier's arrival seemed like liberation. In the end his presence was a necessity to her and she longed for him when he wasn't there. Lorck, who had finally come to believe that Meier was responsible for the change in Constance's behavior, concealed his jealousy and was always perfectly courteous and agreeable, but there was a certain stiffness in his manner that he couldn't hide.

Constance no longer felt like being alone with her husband: she was shy with him, and sometimes suddenly left the room and busied herself with the clothes just to get away for a while.

Once Lorck, who was now up all day, peeked into the bedroom to see what she was doing, and she leaped to her feet and started pulling her large trunk away from the wall.

"Really, Constance, remember your condition," he said in a concerned, somewhat brusque tone.

She straightened up and looked at him for a moment.

"That's all over," she replied coldly. "That was why I was sick the other day." She took hold of the trunk again.

Her triumphant, almost hostile, expression struck him like a fist. He stumbled back a step.

"And you tell me like this?" His voice betrayed his shock and pain.

"It's nothing to make such a fuss about," she said with indifference.

Staring at Constance in helpless amazement, Lorck groped for the door to support himself. She was a mystery to him; his head was swimming—what on earth had happened to her? For a moment he wanted to grab her and shake an explanation out of her, but he felt so weak and sick at heart that he didn't have the strength.

Without another word, he went in and sat down on the sofa; he leaned his head back on the pillows and wept.

27

CONSTANCE WAS WALKING with Meier in the garden while Lorck took his usual long afternoon nap, the last remaining sign of his convalescence.

"Were you really serious about leaving, Meier?" Constance asked.

"Well now that Lorck is better, you don't need me any more."

"Of course I need you. Who will take walks with me in the afternoon?"

"I really ought to be on my way," Meier said with a melancholy smile.

"Oh no, you mustn't!" Constance interrupted, suddenly coming to a halt.

"You want me to stay then, stay on?"

"Yes, for as long as we're here."

For a moment he walked beside her in silence.

"I can just as easily stay as leave," he said despondently.

"You see, I've gotten so used to you now." Her tone was that of a child who sees she's getting her way, but goes on wheedling nonetheless.

"So I still have some purpose," he continued.

"You're talking so strangely," Constance said disapprovingly. "You're not the same as before."

"My life is so aimless," he answered. "Imagine a fellow who would as soon lie down in Babylon as do anything else."

"I hate it that you'll never talk seriously, Meier. Mocking everything is a bad habit."

"Mocking—" he said looking at her. "I thought you could see through all that."

"When you say something, I never really know if it's serious or a joke," she said, shaking her head.

"Hmm! Well, nothing could make me leave as long as you want me to stay—and I'm serious when I say that." He looked up at the sky and took a deep soundless breath.

She looked at him shyly. His face was composed, almost somber.

"Let's be friends, Meier," she said warmly. "We've always had a good time talking together."

A good time, he thought with a wan smile.

"Don't you agree?" she said immediately.

"It's been something quite different and more than a good time, on my part," he replied with a slight tremor in his voice.

"We can enjoy ourselves together, as friends, I mean. Don't you think so?"

"Friendship between the two of us?" His tone was almost harsh. "What do you mean by that?"

"Friendship is just friendship—I don't think the word needs to be defined more precisely."

Meier walked along, jabbing his stick into the gravel path, jerking it up again with each step, and leaving in his wake a deep track in the fine sand.

"For you, friendship is a luxury—a little thing on the side; for me it's something else. It's not a fair exchange."

"That sounds awfully calculating," Constance said, trying to strike a teasing tone.

"Well you don't have anything to lose," he continued, sending up spurts of sand with his stick. "You have house and home, fields and pastures, livestock and spouse, and all the rest of it. No doubt you're also quite happy." He suddenly turned towards her.

Constance blushed.

"Oh nonsense!" she said quickly. "Let's not talk about happiness." The instant she spoke she realized she was being disloyal to Lorck, but then the thought stuck her that she was not accountable to him.

Meier gave her a quick searching glance.

"Oh, it always crumbles into bits and pieces," she continued in a brusque tone, "if it doesn't turn into sheer misery, which is the usual thing."

Meier couldn't understand why he was suddenly so happy. He had to force himself not to leap into the air.

"I see," he said, trying to look indifferent. Not for anything in the world would he try to make her say more than she wanted.

The sun had gone down now and the light was softer and more subdued. The trees looked taller and the leaves had taken on a darker hue.

"How lovely it is here," Constance said. "Such deep peace— just smell the flowers."

"On an evening like this it's good to be alive," Meier said, taking a deep breath.

"You said your life was aimless," Constance began after a moment's pause. "Why do you say things like that?"

"Because the only thing I value is closed off from me forever," he answered.

"But with your talents, Meier ... "

"Yes, and my future," he interrupted, "with my ability as a composer, my worth as a performer—I know the speech by heart."

"Oh hush! Why do you pretend to have no respect for yourself?"

"Oh I respect myself, well enough—but it's disgusting, this talk about what people expect of me! I'm offended by people's willingness to assign me a place in their expectations. They can wait until I ask for their testimonials."

"Now I know what to say when I want to put you in a really charming mood."

"Well, I don't care about any of it," Meier burst out. "You know the story about the baby who was visited at his cradle by a fairy who said he would have everything in life except the one thing he wanted most." He spoke softly and there was a ring of hopelessness in his voice.

Constance felt strangely moved.

"Your symphony is so beautiful," she said quietly. "Being able to create it must have given you great happiness."

"But you haven't heard it," he blurted in surprise.

"Oh yes I have—in Rome. Do you remember Miss Schwartz? She brought it with her and played it at gatherings of the Scandinavian Society."

"Really! And my work truly pleased you?"

"I'm sure it's silly, but it seemed as if every bit of me was there in the music—everything I've experienced. But you aren't listening to me."

"You're wrong," he said softly. "I hear every syllable—tell me more."

"There really isn't anything more—except for the ending, I really didn't understand it. What did you mean by the ending?"

"It's a poem about my life, a fantasy about what the fairy said I would never possess." The deep sorrow in his voice pierced Constance to the quick.

"Never possess," she repeated. "You aren't alone in that Meier; none of us gets what we want most."

"Yes they do," he said vehemently. "That's just what's so terrible—seeing somebody else go off with it."

"But you are still so young, Meier. You don't know what life has in store for you."

He suddenly stopped walking and looked at her. He extended his arms, tilted back his head, and whispered, "Constance."

A tremor went through her. For a second she seemed to lean toward him, but then she drew back almost immediately.

"Let's not hurt each other Meier," she said in a trembling tone.

"No, not hurt . . . " he repeated, letting his arms fall.

They strolled on with downcast eyes, their pace slow and lingering. Suddenly Lorck was in front of them. They had been so absorbed in each other that they hadn't seen him appear from around a bend in the path. There was a moment of embarrassment at the unexpected meeting.

"Are you up already?" Constance said quickly. "I thought you were asleep."

"Do you by any chance know what time it is?"

"No, what time is it?"

"Eight-thirty."

"Really!" she cried. "My goodness." He took her arm and placed it through his. "Would you like to walk a bit more?" he asked.

"Whatever you want," she answered.

"It's a lovely evening," Meier remarked. "It's so mild and still."

"The air is a bit cool," Lorck answered. "I think we should go in and have tea."

They started toward the hotel. "Have you seen the most recent newspapers, Meier?" Lorck asked.

"No," he answered.

"The weather is rotten at home, and now there's a row about elections all over the country. They're whipping people up and creating marshmen[20] right and left."

"But it won't do any good in Kristiania; it's such a stuffy city."

The conversation came to a halt. In his heart of hearts, Lorck wished Meier were miles away, but he forced himself to hide it.

"Meier and I have been quarreling," Constance said, now quite composed and trying to ease things among them.

"Oh yes?" Lorck said dryly.

"Quarreling—oh, not really."

"Didn't you get angry because I dared in all modesty to say your music is something to live for?"

Meier felt a shock of displeasure. For him, their conversation had a value that he thought was his alone.

"I was just joking about that," he said haughtily. "It's an act I put on when I don't feel like talking about something."

Now it was her turn to be offended. She had taken every word seriously, and now he had reduced it all to empty phrases.

"It must be convenient to have an act all prepared," she said in an uninterested tone.

"Oh, yes indeed," he replied coldly.

"I just got a letter from Hansen," Lorck said. "He's ranting

230

and raving about the Left. By the way, Constance, he mentioned sending a letter and a package. Did anything come while I was sick?"

The blood rushed to Constance's face and then receded. Her knees trembled.

"No," she managed with difficulty.

"That's odd," Lorck said.

They had come up onto the lighted veranda outside the sunroom. Lorck felt her arm tremble in his, and he gave her a searching look. It was only momentary, but it was long enough to let him guess the truth. So this was the reason for the change in her. Thank God it was nothing else, he thought, feeling the need to take her in his arms and kiss her. This was something he should be able to make her understand. And here he had suspected Meier!

"I'll be glad to go to the post office to find out," Meier said in a conciliatory tone.

"I wouldn't think of it," Lorck replied in a suddenly elated voice. "It's closed anyhow."

An effusive friendliness welled up in Lorck. Meier was a fine fellow—a splendid chap. It was so good not to have to regard him as a secret enemy.

"You aren't serious about leaving tomorrow, are you Meier?" he said.

"Am I leaving tomorrow?"

"You said so yesterday. But you must wait and go with us—it's the only sensible thing."

Constance was amazed. She had instinctively perceived his aversion for Meier and with a kind of satisfaction understood the reason for it.

"With the greatest pleasure," Meier answered. "That is, if you'll be leaving before too long."

"The sooner the better, for us. I'm just waiting for you to name the day, Constance."

"Tomorrow is fine with me," she answered, "if you feel strong enough."

"Shall we say Friday? Does that suit you, Meier?"

"Any day suits me."

"Well, Friday then."

They had eaten supper and chatted awhile with some Germans who had shared their table with them. Lorck was longing to be alone with Constance, and so did not ask Meier to join him on the balcony for a cigar and sherry as he had done for the past few nights. Apologizing for being tired, he extended a friendly hand to Meier, said good-night, and nodded to Constance, who immediately rose and followed him.

The lamp was lit upstairs, but the room still seemed dark after the blinding gaslight of the hallway. Constance hung her hat and coat in the bedroom wardrobe, walked over to the window and looked out. She could no longer postpone telling Lorck the truth. She had intended giving him the package and letter as soon as they came upstairs, but now it seemed so difficult. The words she needed were like lead on her tongue. It would be better to wait until morning.

"Won't you come in and sit down, Constance?"

She turned and saw Lorck standing in the open doorway.

Without replying, she walked over to him. He took her hand and led her to the little corner sofa and pulled her down beside him. Putting his arm around her waist, he placed her head on his shoulder.

"Constance, my dear, show me what Hansen sent. You have it," he whispered.

She was startled and a bit ashamed, but the feeling passed quickly.

Without making the slightest movement, she answered, "Yes, it came while you had the fever."

He patted her head tenderly, "And so you read the letter—you must have. My poor, sweet Conny."

"I thought it was business and needed an answer."

"Of course, of course," he said mildly.

"I'll go get it for you." She started to get up.

"Oh no, wait awhile—sit still. I want to talk to you. Lean your head back again."

"I'd prefer to sit up—I can hear better then."

He held her hand in both of his, "Have you taken this to heart, my little Conny?"

She didn't answer.

"Have you taken this to heart?" he repeated, kissing her hands.

Quickly turning her head away, she said reluctantly, "There's no use in talking about it—I'd rather not."

"You mustn't think about it any more, or let it affect your love for me. There's no reason for it. It's behind us—it has nothing to do with us."

She had drawn away and now sat at an angle to him, with her elbow on the table and her cheek resting on her hand. The lamplight fell on one side of her face. She was pale and the expression on her lips was an indefinable mixture: pain and contempt, defiance and embarrassment, repugnance and a kind of hardened resolution.

"Constance," he continued softly, "you know that men don't live like monks—they *can't*, they *shouldn't*. Constance, you didn't marry me with any illusions on that point, did you?"

She still sat without moving. He waited for her to say something.

"It's so odd to be sitting here talking to you and not get a single word in reply. Don't you have anything to say, Constance?"

She waved a hand in dismissal. "I hear you, but I don't have anything to say."

"All young men get involved in these casual relationships with some young girl or another," Lorck went on, "not to mention the merely sexual liaisons. They really don't mean very much—and the latter mean nothing at all. There's a need for a surrogate, if you will, and it doesn't have the slightest influence on a man's capacity to feel true love later on." He paused and stroked her shoulder, then her arm, very slowly and gently, again and again. "Don't you understand, Constance?"

She made the same deprecating gesture as before.

"We think about this so differently," she said. "I mean, you just can't understand what it's like for me."

All of a sudden she burst into tears.

He let her cry. It just lasted for a minute or two and then she sat as unmoving as before.

"But that's absurd—it's idiotic and unreasonable," he said, a little impatiently. "If you don't get over this, it could completely destroy our life. You should be a little careful, it seems to me."

The same odd expression played around her mouth, and her eyebrows rose slightly.

"Don't you think I'm capable of loving you completely, Constance? Don't you think I love you as much as anybody could?" he asked earnestly.

"I don't know," she answered in a tired voice.

"You don't know!" He stood up suddenly. His voice was completely altered. "Then I can assure you that my love for you is as strong and pure as you could wish it to be."

She didn't answer. He paced silently back and forth across the room several times.

Then he knelt on a footstool at her feet and took her hands in his. "My Conny, I realize how this has hurt you. Now that I understand why you've been behaving so strangely, I'm relieved, because there has to be a remedy for this. Oh Constance, don't you know how I've suffered? I've been miserably jealous—imagine, jealous!" He kissed her hands and looked at her for an answer, but she didn't open her mouth.

"It was as if a stone fell from my heart," he went on. "The moment I saw your face and made the connection, my pain was gone. Constance, you won't think about the past, will you? Just about the present. It belongs to you. You must know how much I longed for you, how tired I was of everything else. My real life began with you—I've said it so often. You mustn't turn against me because of some fantasy."

"I haven't turned against you," she said tonelessly.

"But what is it then? Why are you so different from the way you were before?"

"Because everything is changed. The joy I felt in your love is gone. It's faded and it will never bloom again. That's what's happened. Nothing else."

"But it will recover. I won't give up until I've nursed it back to health. It will be stronger and more robust than ever before."

He stood up to kiss her, but she tilted her head slightly so that he could only reach her cheek.

"Why do you turn away from me? Don't you like me to kiss you?"

She had gotten up and was standing before him with averted eyes, her arms hanging at her sides. If only he would stop this inquisition—it was unbearable, she thought.

"Of course," she said in a low voice, "kiss me all you want."

He turned abruptly and went into the bedroom. She heard him undress and get into bed.

Constance leaned back on the sofa, crossed her arms over her chest and stayed there for a long time. She thought about Lorck's calm self-confidence, his certainty that everything could be straightened out as long as nothing was wrong with him or with his love for her, his inability to understand the simple fact that she no longer loved him. But before she knew it, she was thinking back over her conversation with Meier, smiling faintly when it occurred to her that she was much more interested in him than in this thing with Lorck. She was glad about that; the agony she had suffered in the beginning was unendurable. Meier was a fascinating man—the sound of his voice, the smile that came so rarely and lit up every recess of his face—his smile was adorable. What would it be like to be loved by him. . . . She closed her eyes and put her hands to her face—it felt burning hot and her temples were throbbing.

28

A COUPLE OF DAYS later they were on their way home. Lorck had not raised the subject of their relationship again. He thought it best not to discuss the matter; if Constance were left in peace, her mood would probably pass. She was a sensible woman, quite free of the sentimental notions that could harm a marriage.

He was in an affectionate mood during this period, not only toward Constance, but also toward Meier. He was bursting with news, with topics for them to talk about. Every day found him in a good humor, constantly on the alert for a chance to make himself agreeable—not in a conspicuous fashion, but quite the opposite, modestly and quietly, without calling attention to himself. Something gentle and very pleasing had come into his manner; even his voice had taken on a milder tone.

They had spent a couple of days in Copenhagen. The weather had been terrible and Constance was tired, so they stayed quietly at the hotel, going out only at night to the theater. Now the barometer was climbing, the wind and rain seemed to have blown away, and though it was mid-October, the sky was clear and the air was as mild as summer. They decided to go directly back to Kristiania by sea.

The day on the steamship passed very pleasantly. That evening they sat on the deck after supper, Lorck and Meier with a toddy, and Constance with a glass of sherry and soda. They talked about the pleasant days they had spent together, assuring each other that their friendship would continue. Finally they drank to an early meeting in Kristiania and a pleasant winter for all of them. Then they separated and said goodnight.

There were a great many passengers, and Lorck had not been able to get a separate stateroom. Constance would be sleeping in the women's cabin.

It was suffocatingly hot below deck, and a baby who wouldn't keep still was grunting and whimpering incessantly. Constance couldn't sleep. She twisted and turned on the narrow bunk until she was so hot she couldn't bear it. She got up, threw on some clothes, wrapped herself in her long, soft traveling coat, and went up on deck. The weather was glorious. She strolled back and forth, trying to imagine what it would be like to get home. She thought back over the things that had happened during the long period they had been away. She had been happy, really happy—yes, back when she had been in love with Lorck. Oh that seemed like such a long time ago. The future had seemed so beautiful and alluring; she had so looked forward to it—but now that future seemed as far away as ever. Although no, there was a difference now. At least she was married to a man she liked, even if she didn't exactly love him—and of course she had Meier. . . .

A figure suddenly appeared before her. She knew it was Meier before she saw him.

"I was hoping you would come up again," he said in a voice that betrayed his joy.

Her heart was beating violently and there was a rushing sound in her ears.

"It was impossible to sleep—a crying baby, and that stifling heat."

They walked slowly, side by side. He began to tell her about a steamship that had been so overloaded that people had to sleep in the rigging. Amused by his description she told him a few tales of the same sort.

One by one, the few stragglers still scattered around the deck finished their drinks and cigars and went below. Now the two were alone with the helmsman. The night was warm and still; myriads of stars shed a pale, glimmering light around them. The regular throb of the propeller, the sound of the wheel spinning, the soft hiss of water against the hull filled both of them with quiet pleasure.

"Let's sit down for a while," Meier said.

"I really should go below now," Constance mumbled, sitting down nevertheless on a bench at right angles to the wall of the smoking salon.

"Oh well," Meier said with a sigh, "everything comes to an end." It sounded like the conclusion to some previous line of thought.

She didn't ask what he meant, but said sadly, "I was thinking about that, too."

"Being with you has made me so happy," he went on. "What a shame it has to end."

"But it's not going to," she said almost vehemently.

"It will be different, just the same. Seeing you once in a while, observing all the social disguises—oh! it will be disgusting."

"Of course you can come to our house whenever you want," she said.

"But your husband will be there," he almost moaned.

She was startled. "I thought you liked him," she said, in confusion.

"I would, if he weren't your husband."

Constance felt suddenly giddy. She wasn't sure if it was fear or joy.

"You're joking," she said, trying to conceal the emotion his words aroused in her.

"Do me the favor of not insulting me—I never joke about things like that."

Constance racked her brain for something to say. Finally a thought struck her.

"Will you start giving lessons right away?" she asked.

"Yes," he answered curtly.

"It must be hard at the beginning, before one gets into it," she went on.

"Yes," he repeated.

Constance thought she should go. She kept imagining it to herself—she would stand up, say good-night, and go below—really, she couldn't understand why she didn't go down to the cabin instead of staying right where she was. She summoned her courage, and set out to do it in earnest.

"Do you have many pupils?" came out instead.

"More than enough," he said with an impatient shrug.

There was a pause. "What's the point of talking about this?" he demanded suddenly.

"What's the point?" she repeated timidly.

"Actually I think I'll be going abroad again," he said a few minutes later. "Life at home isn't exactly a cheery winter's day—not a summer's day either, for that matter. And now . . . " His voice trailed off.

"Don't go!" she said, with a start.

"Why do you say that?" he asked, bending toward her. The anxiety and seriousness in his tone frightened her.

"Because it's so boring to have friends go away," she said in a dry, nervous voice.

That stung him. Was she really a coquette after all, and simply toying with him? Or was she just so frivolous that, to her, everything was a game? It didn't fit his image of her, but maybe he had been wrong.

"Oh nonsense, is that all?" he said scornfully. "You'll always have enough to spare."

A wave of pain suddenly swept over Constance; it seemed composed, drop by drop, of every tear she had ever shed in her life. What had she accomplished for herself? Where were the blessings of life, the good things that should have come to her—what had become of them? It had all come to nothing. It had been a humiliating effort to muddle through her life, to fight her way forward from day to day. She longed to be back in her husband's arms—no! not in his arms, back in the time when she had been happy there, but no, a thousand times no! Why wish for that—a bubble she had been foolish enough to believe was firm ground, something strong enough to build a life on—a bubble that *had* to end by bursting. And now she was attracted to another man, another man! Wanting, and needing, to throw herself in his arms, to tell him she was his. The thought of being an unfaithful wife stabbed through her; so it had come to that. "An unfaithful wife!" She covered her face with her hands and burst into tears.

"Mrs . . . Constance," he whispered, touching her shoulder with his hand. She continued to cry. "Did I offend you?" he asked tenderly. "Forgive me—I beg you." He took her hand and pressed it to his lips, again and again.

His kisses soothed her, but the tears continued to flow. At last she dried her face.

"You mustn't worry yourself about this," she said in a low voice. "It just came over me—it's over now. But—but—life isn't very easy." Her breast heaved convulsively.

Her sudden outburst had affected him deeply. He could have knelt before her and covered the hem of her dress with kisses. At that moment he was utterly certain of the role they would play in each other's lives. He was sure now that she was not indifferent to him. He knew with a dizzying exultation that some day he would hold her in his arms, just as he had always dreamed. Pressing his hand to his chest to quiet the passionate beating of his heart, he waited a moment before answering, "No, it's not very easy, except for people who are lucky in love."

A man came to take his turn at the helm. They both jumped at the sound of his steps.

"Now you must go rest, Constance," Meier said, getting up. He began to pull off her gloves. She did not protest. He tucked them away and took her hands in his. His fingers touched her wrist and softly slid down to her fingertips. He held them against his face, pressed them to his mouth, and kissed them inside and out.

"Good night, Constance," he said in an unsteady voice as he let her go.

Without a backward glance, she went to her bunk below.

Meier lit a cigar and stayed on the deck for a long time. The hours passed like minutes. He was filled with the transcendent feeling of having left his old self behind. He had no particular idea, not even a coherent line of thought. He was filled with a sense of boundless joy; life seemed suddenly lovely and inviting.

It was almost morning when he finally stretched out on his bunk; he said to himself, again and again, "This is happiness."

Constance looked pale and exhausted in the morning. When Meier came up to say good-bye, Lorck shook his hand vigorously and told him not to wait too long before he paid them a visit. On the dock Meier turned and waved at Constance one last time. She was strangely stirred by the way he stood there, bare-headed and lost in thought, until Lorck took her by the arm and said that the luggage was through customs and everything was in the carriage. But on the way home, and for a long time afterwards, she kept remembering the way he looked when he said good-bye, and every time, she felt a shiver go through her.

29

THEY STAYED AT THE Grand Hotel while they were making arrangements to move into their home. Mrs. Hansen had rented an apartment for them in Homansby, not far from Constance's former building. She had hung curtains in all the rooms, moved in Lorck's and Constance's furniture, and put the kitchen and dining room in order.

They still had to buy a few things, hang the paintings, fill the bookcases, and arrange the bric-a-brac.

They had been back for three days. Constance finished straightening a few things on her writing table and gave the room an appraising glance. She went into the living room; it was very snug and comfortable. The dining room was large and bright, its two bay windows decorated with masses of green and flowering potted plants.

She also cast a quick glance into the bedroom—everything was perfect. She walked back into the living room and settled herself in a chair, the same armchair where she used to sit in the old days, dreaming the afternoons away in front of the tile stove. Sighing, she closed her eyes; she wanted to think about the past and the present, but Meier intervened. She went back over each of their meetings from the very beginning. Why hadn't she been in love with him then—because now . . . Oh if she had been free, she knew how things would have gone. Would have gone? Hadn't they gone too far already? No, no, no! She had always been a respectable woman; she would not let herself be anything else.

But she could enjoy his friendship—there was nothing wrong in that. It would add a kind of richness to her life, reconcile her to all the rest.

Then she remembered the night on the deck—the way he had kissed her hands, the sound of his voice, the words he had spoken, his farewell glance. Warmth flooded through her at the memory.

The sound of the front doorbell broke the stillness, jerking her violently back to the present. The maid came in and said a gentleman was asking to pay his respects. Constance took the card she handed to her.

"Send him in," she said breathlessly, fumbling for something in her pocket. In the minute that passed before Meier appeared in the doorway, Constance stood up and sat down several times.

She stretched out her hand to him.

"It's good to see you," she said nervously. "How are you?"

Meier squeezed her warm hand in his icy fingers, and stood there, struggling with something in his throat that kept him from speaking. "I ran into your husband a little while ago; he told me to come up and see your new home."

"You hadn't thought of that on your own?"

"I didn't know—I thought—Have you got everything arranged?"

Constance had regained her self-assurance; her face had lost its pallor; a fine pink color had come into her cheeks, and her eyes were shining.

"Completely," she answered. "This is my sitting room, would you like to see the rest?"

She walked on ahead of him. "This is Lorck's office," she said as they walked through the dining room. "Here you see the waiting room, the examining room, and the study." The latter was a little room with a window overlooking a side street, crammed with books and handsome upholstered oak furniture.

"And this is your territory?" Meier asked when they were finished with the inspection.

"Yes, this is my room. Isn't it pleasant?"

"Marvelous! And it's yours. I don't know if it's because the room belongs to *you* or because you belong to *it* that it seems so enchanting."

She bowed her head and brushed a speck of dust off her dress.

"Shall we sit down and try it out?" she said, pushing a chair towards him.

"Can you believe that we've only been back three days," Meier began as he sat down.

"Yes, can you believe it," Constance interrupted, "it seems like months."

"An eternity!" He waved his hand. "Yesterday and today seemed endless—it's because I haven't seen you, Constance."

She shifted slightly in her chair. "It seems like a long time to me, too," she said.

"I've had fantasies about coming here," he began again, "and I've been longing for you so intensely that I got used to it, finally, and decided it was good to have something to long for."

"You talk as if you've been doing it for years," she said with a smile.

"You're in my thoughts constantly, the way you were on deck that night—constantly," he repeated with emphasis.

"You've got to forget that, Meier." There was something imploring in her voice. "We'll be friends, just friends—promise you'll treat me that way." She lifted her eyes and fastened them on him.

Meier didn't answer immediately. He was lost in her beauty; it was so sweet to hear her voice, to be so near her, to feel her eyes on his face.

"You'll promise me, won't you?" she added.

"Oh no, don't make me do that. I can't just decide ahead of time to act this way or that towards you." His tone was aggrieved.

She weighed his words, staring straight ahead, and shook her head anxiously.

"I've loved you all my life—from the very first moment I saw you—and I've suffered more than you can ever imagine. Please let me act the way I have to." He had gotten to his feet and now stood before her. "I don't want to hurt you." A plaintive note had come into his voice. "Surely you don't believe I do?"

She looked down; her fingers picked at the lace on her dress.

"You don't believe that?" he said more fervently.

She looked up at him with a sad smile.

"No," she said, slowly shaking her head. "But Meier, Meier, where is it going to end?" She got up and walked quickly across the room.

"End? Why worry about that? Let whatever happens, happen," he cried passionately. "I'm yours—I belong to you, Constance, do you hear? I belong to you!"

Shaking her head, she pressed her hands to her ears and looked at him with frightened eyes.

"You mustn't be afraid, Constance," he said more calmly, walking closer to her. "Do I look like a bandit or a thief? I'd sooner chop off my right hand than touch you against your will."

She began to pace the floor, and Meier could see her struggling with herself.

"You'll learn to feel safe with me, Constance—nobody in the world could feel more tenderness for you than I do." He held out his hands to her.

She stopped in front of him, took both his hands, and squeezed them a moment.

"You'll be good, Meier—only good," she said in a low voice, looking anxiously into his eyes. Then she released his hands and began walking back and forth again.

"Constance, I have a favor to ask you: call me Harold when we're alone," he begged. "Oh do it, Constance."

She nodded and continued to walk.

"Someone is coming." She walked over to the door and opened it.

"Hasn't Meier been here?" Lorck called in from the hall.

"He's here now," she answered. She glanced back over her shoulder at Meier, signaling him to sit down. He felt a jolt of pleasure at this confirmation of their secret understanding.

"What do you say, Meier, it's quite habitable in here, don't you think?"

Lorck walked in and looked around with satisfaction.

They talked for a while about the splendid situation of the room, the benefits of morning sun, and things of a similar sort.

"So we'll move in tonight then, Constance," Lorck said after Meier had left. "Will you come down to the hotel with me to pick up our things?"

"All right, let's go now," she answered.

"Oh no, wait a bit—it's so pleasant here." He began to open the doors. "It's positively elegant when the doors of all the rooms are open." Rubbing his hands in satisfaction, he sat down to survey it all.

"And how clever you've been! Come over here, Constance. Isn't it wonderful to be alone in our own lovely home?"

"Yes," she said absentmindedly.

Setting her on his knee, he took her hands and began to bounce her slowly up and down as he hummed a little nursery tune.

"No, no! Stop, I have to speak to the maid." She hurriedly broke free.

He sat there, sick at heart. Since that evening in Lausanne he had not forced his caresses on her. He had waited for her to come to him. She loved him, after all, and that love was surely his greatest ally. If he could appeal to that, surely he could bridge the gap this ridiculous accident had opened between them.

Since the day he learned the truth, he had been courting her. Her slightest smile had made him happy; that was the harvest he reaped for his efforts. Each squeeze of the hand, each glance, each carefully devised situation had to show how much he longed for her.

His disposition had been so gentle, so earnest; he could clearly see that his way of dealing with the situation had made him into a better person. This had been beneficial. When Constance recovered, she would fervently thank him for saving their happiness. She would put her arms around him and press her lips to his—over and over again. And he would answer, "I wanted to teach you, Conny, how true my love was."

But now two weeks had passed during which she had made not the slightest sign of approaching him. After their arrival in Kristiania, he had thought he detected favorable symptoms. Something melancholy and virginal had come over her. Her voice was so soft and gentle; when she was sitting by herself, she seemed so distracted and dreamy. He had thought he was near his goal.

Now his courage was beginning to fail; a moment ago she had been sitting on his knee, as cold and unyielding as a statue. Was her love gone, then? Impossible! Nothing had happened that could justify such a change. It must be some experiment of hers to get even with him, to make herself feel more important somehow. He became bitter towards her; she was a hard woman, a sphinx. Maybe she could just not be won by care and tenderness; maybe she was a woman who had to be mastered. He would pit firmness against firmness, let her feel his disapproval, his coldness, until she came and begged him to love her. He would give in then, of course; he would let her enjoy in full measure the happiness of being in his arms again.

Constance had put on her coat; she was standing in the hall, unable to bring herself to open the door and tell Lorck she was ready to go. It was the height of stupidity to stand there dreading to call him—it was like the early days of their marriage when she was uncomfortable in his presence. She started arranging something in front of the mirror, then went into the bedroom and sat on the edge of a chair. She would wait until he came and looked for her. But the minutes passed, and finally it occurred to her that perhaps he had fallen asleep. She would have to go look.

He was sitting in the same chair, with his head tilted back, his eyes wide open, and his hands folded across his chest. There was something rigid about his face; his lower lip was pulled in at the corners, and his expression was dark and forbidding.

Constance started involuntarily, struck by how old and weak he appeared.

Straightening up, Lorck regarded Constance with a mixture of pleasure and anger. The dress suited her so well, with its fine black cloth, its lace and satin ribbons, and its stylish modern cut. She was wearing a soft black felt hat with a long bronze ostrich feather, and a coat of thick black silk, with a froth of lace around her throat and over her breast. The long French gloves were the same color as the feather, and they were smooth and taut around her fingers. In her hand she held a black satin parasol trimmed with lace and lined with golden-brown silk. Lorck thought about how lovely she looked, and sighed.

"Shall we go?" Constance asked from the doorway.

"Yes," he answered curtly, standing up.

That evening, while Constance sat arranging her hair in front of the bedroom mirror, Lorck paced back and forth in his examining room, smoking his cigar furiously, contrary to custom. All evening he had not addressed a word to Constance. They had eaten their meal in silence. When Constance had asked him something, or made a remark, he had answered in monosyllables, as grudgingly as possible. After a while Constance had gotten up, and with a curt "I'm going to bed," had left him.

Hurt by her indifference, Lorck pondered about what he could do to conquer her. If coldness didn't work he would have to try something else. He decided to be inconsiderate for a while. He would go out at completely unreasonable times, fail to come home for meals, stay out half the night, and if she asked where he'd been, tell her it was no concern of hers. He would treat her as if she were the most insignificant person in the world to him.

Suddenly he paused. Suppose she was already asleep—he would miss a chance to show her that he was going to bed without saying good-night. He tossed aside the cigar and hurried into her room.

When he came in Constance had just finished her hair. He was seized by the desire to go and take her in his arms, but he repressed it and turned away, hurriedly starting to undress. Sitting there on the edge of the bed she looked so gentle and sad. He watched her steadily while he wound the clock. He couldn't resist any longer. Gone were his plans about education and discipline. Before he realized it he was sitting beside her, his arm around her waist, pulling her close to him.

"Constance," he whispered, "how long can this go on?"

"What do you mean?" she mumbled, her head averted, groping for the edge of the bed.

"Your coldness, this distance. Aren't we going to live to-gether like people who love each other?"

At this moment, she felt more clearly than ever before that her love was dead, and that she should tell him so, directly. But she didn't have the courage. He had pressed her head against his chest, so her face was hidden. Had Lorck been able to see the expression in her eyes, he would perhaps have let her go. Now he took her passive acceptance of his caresses to be something different than it was.

But the next morning when Lorck had gone, Constance kneeled at the head of the bed and wept into her pillow, just as in the early days of her first marriage.

30

WINTER WAS OVER. This year it had been milder and shorter than usual, and already by March a breath of spring was in the air. Without the usual ice skating and sleigh rides, the city's social set had blossomed into vigorous activity, especially during the last few months. People were acting in private theatricals, giving balls, and arranging tableaus for charity bazaars. The climax would be the art-society carnival.

The Lorcks had been in the thick of things; they had even given a few parties themselves.

During the course of the winter, Lorck had tried every expedient to make Constance behave like her old self. He had neglected her, done everything an inconsiderate husband could think of to destroy the pleasure of everyday life, but it was all in vain. From the start, Constance had greeted his behavior with undisturbed tranquility. Nothing seemed to penetrate the barricade of indifference around her. Always the same polite manner—obliging and unwilling simultaneously.

But secretly she was hurt by his behavior. It was painful to be in the same room with him when every movement radiated disapproval, every glance was charged with hostility. Especially sitting with him at the table! Oh how she hated those silent mealtimes! When she wanted to pass him something, she could hardly find the words. Gradually she began to develop a violent distaste for him, mixed with fear and timidity. She heaved a deep breath when he went out and felt a stab of aversion when she heard him return.

Often she would dash out of the living room to avoid him when he came in. Sometimes days would pass when they would not exchange a word. If she asked him for something, he would give her a grudging answer.

She began to suffer from nervousness and palpitations. Finally the tumult of indignation overflowed. He was treating her like a poor relation, or like some misbehaving subordinate who deserved the punishment of her master's displeasure. She wouldn't take it any longer; she would give it back to him in kind. At first Lorck was astounded, then furious. On one occasion when she answered him sharply, he faced her and said she was a spiteful woman.

"I don't know what you're talking about," she answered coldly.

"Your deliberate coldness is driving me crazy!" he burst out. "Why are you behaving like this?"

"You're quite mistaken—you're just imagining things." She shrugged her shoulders, "I haven't done any of the things you've accused me of."

"Aren't you the one who's causing all the discord around here? Are you really not aware of it?" he asked.

"It's not me," she said curtly. "You're the one who's being tyrannical."

Lorck rolled his eyes toward the ceiling. "Tyrannical?" he repeated.

"You are doing everything in your power to force me to be different from the way I am or want to be; you wouldn't dare treat anyone else the way you're treating me." She looked at him defiantly.

"But why are you so cold to me, Constance? Don't you understand how much I'm suffering? Our life together is not the way I dreamed it would be," he said somberly.

"Can't you understand that it's foolish to try to scold love into existence?" She turned away impatiently. He gave her a wounded look and walked quietly out of the room.

Her words impressed him deeply. They continued to reverberate in his ears with a sound that was as sharp and chilling to his nerves as the scraping of fingernails on a blackboard.

After that Lorck stopped experimenting. He took refuge in his work, throwing himself into tireless activity. In addition to his large practice, he was vice-chairman of the medical association, the editor of a medical journal, and an active participant in community affairs. He thought things were better this way; there wasn't as much time to brood about circumstances at home. But the hope of winning back his wife's love had still not left him. He could push it into the back of his mind, but he couldn't escape it completely. Time would bring a remedy; there was no use in forcing himself on her.

He was sometimes tormented with jealousy. It was unbearable to think that Constance might prefer someone else. When he saw her talking to men at parties, looking so animated and captivating, he felt like a knife was piercing his heart. But he always controlled himself. On no account would he let anybody see his weakness. Besides, it was folly to object to his wife talking to other men. The incidents were only momentary, after all.

It was harder with Meier, who had become a familiar figure in the house, and whose company was obviously dear to Constance. After his afternoon office hours, when Lorck would go in to see Constance before making his house calls, Meier was often with her. Occupied with his work, Lorck was seldom able to join them.

It became more and more intolerable to him to know that Meier was spending so much time with her. Nevertheless, he was not seriously alarmed; that his wife could harbor, much less express, anything resembling love toward another man was impossible for him to imagine. He comforted himself with the thought that Constance was basically cold-natured; she had very little tenderness to spare. And, of course, she was a respectable woman; to suspect her would be an insult.

Meier was another story. Lorck knew men; he knew how far they could be trusted in matters like these. A couple of times he had detected a telltale glint in Meier's eyes as they followed Constance around the room, and he felt profoundly uneasy about it. He would have given half his fortune to send him away, at least from the house, but his fear of looking ridiculous restrained him. Then too, the friendly tone that had always prevailed between Meier and himself made it difficult to change.

In the meantime, Meier was so absorbed in his relationship with Constance that he was oblivious to Lorck's mood. Constance had long ago confessed she loved him, but she had also vowed to do everything possible to overcome it. She had told him there was no reason why they couldn't be friends, of course, but she would despise herself if she were unfaithful; she begged him to agree that this was the best way. Meier had replied that it broke his heart to possess only her friendship, but her will was his law. In fact, he had tried faithfully to comply. When she felt safe with him at last, she accepted their new relationship with overflowing confidence. He felt so rich and happy that for a time it was easy for him to control himself. His love was a kind of worship—it was special merely to sit by her side and listen to her voice, to exchange a few words, however ordinary. And the small signs of favor and distinction that a woman can quietly bestow on her favorite were so captivating to him that there were times when he felt he would never want more. He was filled with her, living from day to day on what he had won in his relationship with her, and on the certainty of seeing her soon again. Life had become something new for him; it was glorious being near her, and the time he spent working seemed like storing up his happiness. Sometimes, of course, he felt bitterness that this woman, the only person in the world he cared about, was another man's wife. A couple of times he had even vented his feelings to Constance, but one beseeching look had been sufficient to remind him of their agreement and to make him stop.

Once he had reproached her for behaving as she did; he didn't understand her. She didn't love Lorck, after all, she loved him; why then didn't she grant him her love? Why was she trying to ease her conscience? Surely the infidelity consisted of withdrawing her love from Lorck and giving it to someone else. With an anguished expression, Constance had sat there, rocking back and forth, moaning softly. Finally she answered in a low voice that there was a difference between infidelity and adultery. Meier repeated what he had often said before—he didn't want her love if she didn't give it freely and without remorse.

But when he left her that day, something in her behavior assured him that soon the hour would come when she would embrace him and say "I belong to you."

The day before the carnival arrived. Pressed by friends on the committee, Lorck had reluctantly promised that he and his wife would attend.

Constance was in the dining room sewing her carnival costume. She had been helping her seamstress Emma all day; she enjoyed working with the modest girl, who was so clever and resourceful. She was twenty years old, with curly blond hair swept up in an elaborate braided knot; her cheeks were pink and healthy and her blue eyes had a deep liquid sheen. It was impossible not to admire her figure: her back especially, strong and straight, yet fine-lined; her curved waist and beautifully rounded bosom.

Constance looked at the clock; she was expecting Meier. Lorck was out making house calls and would not be home until ten; he had a great many patients these days.

"Well, there's nothing left to do but sew on the buttons and fasten the straps to the bucket," Constance said, putting away the needle and thimble, and taking off the large apron she had been wearing. "It's all right if I leave you now, isn't it, Emma?"

"Yes, ma'am of course," Emma answered with a shy smile.

Constance heard someone enter the living room and peeked through the half-opened door.

"Good evening, Meier!" she cried out. "Come in here, I want to show you something."

In a moment he was beside her.

"Here's the skirt," she said, "red silk with a gold border; the stockings are a little too light, but I couldn't get the right color; and the shoes, see how elegant they are, with those little gold buckles. And don't you think the apron is charming? The little pocket is so sweet. I'll carry the milk bucket on my back—see the straps, they smell like Russian leather—and the bonnet is so becoming." She put it on for a second, then took it off immediately. "Let me have the bodice for a second—good heavens, Emma, you're putting the buttons on the back!" Constance laughed. Emma sat there, her face suffused with blood, picking at the buttons with trembling fingers. Constance could not imagine what was wrong with her. Taking the bodice, she showed it to Meier who had bent over to pick up the shoe that he had dropped on the floor. For a moment Constance was startled—she had felt something, but she wasn't sure what it was.

With a crash, Emma overturned the sewing basket and spools of thread onto the floor; Constance and Meier jumped up. Emma was already on her knees gathering them up again.

"Do you know my seamstress Emma?" Constance asked when they were seated in the living room.

"Why do you ask?"

"She was behaving so strangely—did you see her blushing?"

"I believe I've seen her a couple of times at my mother's," Meier replied after a moment's thought.

"Well that's modesty, I must say! But she's a sweet little girl, really," Constance remarked. "What are you wearing tomorrow?"

"A domino."

"But then I won't be able to tell you from all the rest of them."

"That doesn't matter—I'll know you, of course. Is that Lorck coming in?"

"No, it's Emma leaving," Constance answered, getting up and walking into the dining room. Meier followed her. Constance put the masquerade costume into a large oblong basket. He watched as she smoothed out the pieces, gently straightening the folds. The soft movements of her hands, her lingering air, mesmerized him.

"Will you do me a great favor?" he asked as she was on the point of covering the basket.

"A favor?" She turned quickly.

"Put the dress on and let me see you in it."

She smiled and seemed to consider.

"Oh do, Constance," he begged. "I'd like it so terribly much."

"Well out you go then," she cried cheerfully. "I can't get

dressed with you hanging over me."

With a happy nod he thanked her and went into the next room.

After a time she came out in her full costume, holding the mask in her hand. She looked splendid—every part of the costume accentuated the beauty of her figure—from the little Paris shoes that showed the beautiful shape of her ankles, to the multiple chains of pearls around her bare throat. The short jacket with its little puff sleeves was tight around her waist. Her heavy, shining hair hung loose on her back and shoulders, and the dark color looked beautiful against the red and gold ribbons of her bonnet.

Captivated, Meier stood there, his head tilted back in astonishment.

Constance felt a bit embarrassed in this unfamiliar situation.

"The milk bucket is the sweetest part of all," she said, turning her back so he could see it.

"It's all charming—charming," he repeated slowly. "You look so different—it's hard to imagine you could look like that—"

"Like what?" she asked.

"A fairy tale or a folk story, with princesses in disguise. Oh, nonsense—you're much more lovely than that."

"You're teasing," Constance said, pink-cheeked and laughing. "But look now!"

She put on the black silk mask and walked over to the mirror.

"What do you want with that little black thing!" He walked over to her, seized the rubber hooks that encircled her ears and pulled off the mask.

"Ouch!" Constance yelped. "Are you crazy, Meier?"

"Did I pull your hair? I'm so sorry, does it really hurt?" He seemed crushed.

"You should just feel it," she complained.

He brushed her hair behind her ear and stroked it tenderly.

As she touched the sore place, her fingers met his. Seizing her hand, he pressed it against his eyes, then nibbled it gently with his lips.

Constance stood before him with downcast eyes. Like a wounded bird, she hung her head, and her face grew pale. She looked up at him timidly and saw in his glance an inexpressible mixture of pain and tenderness.

A jolt ran through her body, willing her to retreat, but in an instant she surrendered to an irresistible desire. She threw her arms around his neck and leaned against him.

Dizzily he took her in his arms and pressed her against his chest. With a deep sigh of deliverance and relief, he buried his face in her neck.

His intensity frightened her. She wanted to free herself.

"A moment—just a moment," he whispered, holding her tightly. "There," he said, letting his arms slip down slowly until he could grasp her hands.

"Dearest—sweetheart," he whispered.

"No, no you mustn't," Constance cried in terror and ran out of the room.

Meier slid down into a chair and covered his face.

He could feel her fine, firm body in his arms, feel the breath from her soft throat, the warm pressure of her lips burning his cheek. He felt like he was drunk, and he reveled in it.

A door opened. He raised his head. It was Constance in her everyday clothes. She paused for a few seconds, shivering at the enraptured expression on Meier's face. For a moment she almost did not recognize him. She sat down and picked up her work.

"Are you angry at me, Constance? You look so sad." His voice was very tender.

"Not angry, really," she said pensively. "I couldn't help it," she added immediately, in a defensive tone.

He got up and walked over to her, wanting to see her face, but she had bent forward over her crocheting; he knelt and leaned toward her, trying to catch her eye. Letting her hands fall, she turned her face away.

"You have done me so much good, Constance, such indescribable good. Don't let it frighten you. The caress you gave me was like dew from heaven. You must say 'du' to me. You must say 'du'," he repeated.

She nodded.

"I've earned some confidence, haven't I, Constance?" he said softly.

She nodded again and smiled faintly.

He laid his head on her knees and sighed. She ran her fingers through his hair, tenderly, again and again. Closing his eyes, he let his head slide further into her lap.

"Harold, you have to go now," she said after a while. "I don't think you should stay this evening."

"Whatever you want," he answered without moving.

"You have to go now," she repeated.

He covered her hands with kisses and stood up at last.

"Remember the dances you promised me," he said.

"The first and the last," she answered with a smile.

"You should dance every one with me—can't you tell the rest of them no?"

She shook her head.

"I can't do that," she replied.

"But would you like to, Constance?"

"Of course, how could I want anything else?"

He pressed one last kiss on her hand and left.

31

"Constance, promise me you won't run around too much with Meier tomorrow," Lorck said that evening, after Constance had read him the carnival arrangements in *Aftenposten*.[21]

Constance blushed. "Why do you say that?" she asked.

"Because I want you to be careful."

"Do you have a special reason for reminding me about that?" she asked.

"Yes. You spend much more time with Meier than is suitable if you want to keep your reputation intact."

"This is something new," she said.

"You're wrong, my dear. For a long time I've had misgivings about the nature of your relationship with Meier—not for my sake, but for yours."

She shrugged her shoulders.

"And I just thought that tonight would be a good opportunity to say something," he continued after a moment.

"Why tonight?"

"Because I'm thinking about the carnival, and I want to warn you. People are talking about you and Meier in a way that makes me very uncomfortable."

"People. What do they have to do with us?"

"Your reputation is something that concerns both of us." He walked slowly back and forth across the room. She was staring at the newspaper, with her cheek propped on her hand.

"Who's been talking to you about this?"

"Someone who wishes us both well. But I'll be glad to tell you—it was Hansen."

"I might have known, that busybody."

"He was right to do it. I would have done exactly the same in his place," Lorck said dryly.

"Go tattling to your friend about his wife?"

Lorck shook his head impatiently. "It wasn't like that at all. He gave me a tip, out of friendship, so I could try to stop something that he believed was dangerous for you."

"But it can't be stopped now," Constance said.

Lorck abruptly came to a halt. "What do you mean by that?"

"I mean that Meier's company amuses and entertains me, and I don't intend to let people's gossip deprive me of it."

He stood quietly in front of her. "You're forgetting about me," he said somewhat gruffly.

"Do you intend to forbid me to see Meier?"

"I'd like to, frankly, but I only insist that you show some regard for rules that can't be ignored with impunity."

"And what does this regard entail?"

"You'll have to set the limits yourself. You aren't so inexperienced that I have to give you a lecture about it."

There was a pause. Seating himself beside her, Lorck took her hand and spoke in an earnest, kindly tone.

"Constance, you know that my dearest wish is to see you cheerful and happy. There is nothing I want less than to restrain or bother you. Don't you know that?"

"I've never complained," she answered curtly.

"I'm not jealous, Constance; I refuse to be—I know you too well for that. But other people judge things differently."

"Nobody is safe from gossip and slander. You shouldn't pay any attention to it." She pulled her hand away.

"You always do this, Constance. You intentionally try to avoid conversations with me. It's this distance between us that hurts more than anything else."

Propping her elbow on the table, she lifted her right hand toward her face and examined her fingernails.

"There is no confidence between us," Lorck went on sadly, "no joy in our relationship; you never share anything with me—we go our own separate ways."

"I told you in Lausanne that the joy was gone, for me at least," she answered calmly without raising her eyes from her nails.

A pained expression came over his face.

"Don't be so harsh, Constance. I can't stop longing for you," he entreated.

"I can't help it," she answered somberly. "That's just the way it is."

He was suddenly furious with her. How completely heartless and vindictive she was. She simply pushed aside all his tenderness and love—crushed it into the dust and walked on past with smiling lips and indifferent eyes. His faithfulness was contemptible to her—she didn't *see* it—his hard, honorable battle to win her back had come to nothing. Her friendship with Meier, everything she did, was one continuing insult to him—the man who loved her.

"Your behavior is outrageous!" he almost screamed at her. "If you can't control your spiteful nature, you might as well kill yourself."

With a shudder, she threw back her head and gave him a frightened look. She made no sound, but it seemed to Lorck as if she had uttered a cry.

She got up and walked to the door. Pausing at the threshold, she turned her head toward him. With an icy smile and an odd stabbing look, she said slowly and calmly, "Of course I could always run off with a lover instead of killing myself— there's that way out, too."

Lorck felt like he'd been stabbed in the back. Blood rushed to his head and the veins in his forehead bulged. It took a while before he found his voice.

"You're talking nonsense," he said. "Sit down and calm yourself, you can't go to bed in this state of mind." He took a step toward her.

She glided noiselessly through the door and closed it behind her.

Lorck sat there for a long time; a host of conflicting feelings preyed on him. What should he do? Try to make her jealous? Who could he use for such a purpose? Maybe he would have a chance at the carnival tomorrow. Oh no, he couldn't do it; he was tired of all that. Besides, she probably wouldn't even notice.

His thoughts wandered back to the old days, to the time when he had Kristine. A boundless, humble, and utterly self-less love had been laid at his feet; she had come and gone at his slightest gesture, gratefully accepting whatever he gave her. There had been beauty and joy in his relationship with her. It was a treasure to have a love like that once in a man's life; perhaps it was against the rules for it to happen twice. He had thrown it away to win Constance, a cold, unloving woman with no capacity to value what he offered her. So this was his lot—to go through life, a man without a home, rejected by the only woman he cared about—the woman to whom he'd bound his life and future. He thought about what Kristine must have suffered and his heart ached for her. The poor miserable girl. He could have knelt and begged for forgiveness. If he ever saw her again he would do it.

He asked himself if he really could imagine having Kristine as his lover again, with her committed, and him free. But no—there hadn't been any real satisfaction in it; he had just been aimlessly drifting through life. If he had married Kristine, she would have understood his past—her own was no different really—and similarity on this issue was certainly important. She knew the value of things, could tell the difference between real love and a relationship that was merely sexual. Constance lacked that faculty, unfortunately for them both. But no, no. Make Kristine his wife? A girl with nothing to give him but her love, a girl in no respect his equal? And now that he had known Constance's love, there was nothing better life could offer; it was his curse that he could never forget the happiness her love had brought him. And to think that he had lost it . . . lost it—he moaned aloud—impossible!—it couldn't be true. . . .

Constance had long been in bed. Closing her eyes, she drove away the traces of her scene with Lorck. She thought about the moment when Meier had pulled her to his chest, felt his lips at the base of her throat. Again and again she relived it—and each time it was like being lifted by a wave that left her breathless and dizzy. At last she fell asleep and dreamed she was walking with Meier in a beautiful garden; their arms were around each other, and she could feel his kisses, his breath warm against her cheek.

When Lorck came to bed at three o'clock, she was sleeping soundly. He was quiet so as not to wake her.

The next day Constance behaved as if nothing had happened, and Lorck, regretting his violent words, tacitly accepted the reconciliation she offered him.

In the carriage on the way to the carnival, Lorck asked Constance if she would give him the first dance. When he learned she had promised it to Meier, he suppressed his disappointment and tried to look unconcerned.

Constance danced every dance. Lorck tried to keep an eye on her, but he couldn't keep track of her partners. He saw her whirl away with a Spanish grandee, a Neapolitan fisherman, and a copper-colored Indian. Then there were all the men wearing dominos. He knew Meier was hiding under one of them. Bored and irritated, Lorck longed for it to end. At last the unmasking took place and supper began. It was served on small tables in a number of grottos and arbors running down both sides of the ballroom; a curtain of Persian rugs separated them from the dance floor, which was decorated like the hall of an Assyrian castle. Lorck tried to get into the proper spirit by drinking a great deal of champagne, but it was no use. They ate with Meier and the Hansens. Marie was dressed like a Spanish fisherwoman. Laughing, flushed with pleasure and champagne, she engaged Lorck for the first dance after supper. Touching his glass to hers, he smiled and thanked her, secretly infuriated because he had planned to dance that one with Constance.

"Then I'll ask you, Constance, so we come out even," Hansen said, lifting his glass to toast her.

"Thank you, but I'm taken," she answered. "Here comes my partner." She pointed to a chimney sweep, who bowed in front of her and led her away.

"But don't you have a dance free?" Hansen called after her.

She looked at her dance card. "The next française," she answered.

He thanked her and waved as Constance disappeared into the crowd.

She was in high spirits, joyful that Meier would see the attention she received, and know she cared about no one but him.

But Meier was tormented by jealousy. It was torture for him to see Constance cheerful and smiling, dancing off in the arms of those men. He was helpless to do anything but trail around after her like a shadow.

The chimney sweep was one of the city's best known men-about-town. Constance had encountered him often during the previous winter. As they waltzed he held her so tightly against him that she could hardly breathe, and she neither heard nor responded to the soft words he whispered in her ear. Taking her silence for consent, he suddenly bent down and planted a hurried kiss on her shoulder.

"For shame," Constance cried, "how dare you! Stop, I won't go on."

He continued to dance. "Are you really so strict?" he whispered. "It's no good being prudish and delectable at the same time—the combination is impossible."

"Let me go, do you hear! I won't dance with you," she said, indignantly trying to free herself.

He led her to a sofa, bowed, and walked away.

At that moment, Meier appeared beside her.

"Oh thank heaven you're here," Constance said joyfully. "The nerve of that fellow—he was so forward you wouldn't believe it."

"You looked like you were enjoying his company well enough. Why did you stop dancing?"

She stared at him, astonished by his voice and manner.

"That's ridiculous," she answered. "Where can I get a glass of soda water?"

"I'll find your partner so he can fetch it for you."

"Really Harold!"

"A woman who lets strange men kiss her looks rather silly pretending to be furious."

Constance got up and walked away.

Meier followed her.

"Where are you going?"

"To find my husband and go home," she answered curtly, walking more quickly.

"Take my arm," he told her.

"No I will not."

"Are you angry, Constance?"

"I'm going home," she said, turning away.

"Constance, give me your arm, I have to talk to you." His tone was beseeching.

"So you can insult me again?" Her voice trembled on the edge of tears.

"Forgive me, I'm beside myself—mad; take my arm, do you hear!"

"No, I won't," she answered obstinately, continuing to walk.

"No? All right, then I'm leaving and you'll never see me again." He turned on his heel.

She ran after him and slipped her arm through his. He led her up to the balcony, which was divided into little terrace-like enclosures that were supposed to resemble hanging gardens. In the furthermost one they sat down on a couch. They were nearly alone; the dancing was going on down below, and the old ladies who were watching from above had chosen seats that offered them a better view.

"Don't be angry, Constance. I was utterly distracted," Meier began. "I'd been so miserable all evening, seeing you go off with these disgusting men. I can't bear it—if they even touch you, it's a defilement."

"Then I won't dance again until the last one with you," she answered, squeezing his hand gently.

"Thank you, darling," he whispered.

"If it upsets you, I don't get any pleasure from it, surely you know that," she went on.

"You are so sweet and good, Constance." He pressed his face against her shoulder.

"Because you're so dear to me, Harold," she said earnestly, snuggling closer to him.

Some one came in and they jumped apart. It was a waiter. Constance ordered soda water, which arrived shortly afterward.

They stayed there as one dance was applauded and another followed, heeding none of it.

"Quick, let's go down," Constance said, nervously clutching Meier's arm. "There's Lorck looking for me."

"Where?" he asked.

She pointed to the opposite balcony and they hurried down before Lorck caught sight of them.

The music began for the last number, which Constance and Meier danced together.

Just before they parted, Meier asked when he could see her again.

"Come as soon as you can, Harold," she whispered.

On the way home, Lorck wanted to know where Constance had been; he had searched everywhere for her.

She answered that she had been tired and wanted to sit quietly for a while.

"Where were you?" he asked.

"Up in the balcony."

"Everybody was talking about your behavior. You promised Hansen the française, and he was looking everywhere for you. Naturally I was the person who was least able to give him any information. What were you doing up there?"

"Drinking soda water."

"Who were you with?"

"Meier," she said defiantly.

He raised a fist to her. She turned away, squeezing herself tightly into the corner of the carriage.

"You whore," he swore through clenched teeth. Letting his hand drop, he threw himself violently back against the seat.

32

A MONTH HAD PASSED. The relationship between Constance and Meier had not progressed to a new stage. The day after the carnival, he had come to see her; she seemed confused and reserved, and dealt with the situation by chattering incessantly about one trivial thing after another. When Lorck came into the living room and, contrary to custom, sat down and made himself comfortable, Meier took his leave.

Things had been going on in the same way ever since. An unlucky star seemed to govern his visits. Either someone else was there when he arrived, or Constance was out, or Lorck was at home. A secret handclasp, a meaningful glance, an arm around her waist for a brief stolen moment, was all that passed between them.

Meier went around in a state of passion and suspense. Every day he was sure that something had to happen, and invariably, nothing did. He waited for a letter from her; she risked nothing by writing, of course; whereas he dared not take a chance.

There must be something she wanted to tell him—propose a meeting, try to reach an understanding. Now that she had let him hold her in his arms, had responded to his kiss, there was no longer any barrier between them. The love they shared gave them an irreproachable, boundless right. Why didn't she speak then? It was intolerable to go on without a clear idea of the form their relationship was going to assume. And he suffered at the thought that Constance could be so calm about the matter, could be as talkative and smiling as usual, could appear as if this were only of superficial interest to her. He found himself in a continual nervous uproar, jumping at the slightest unexpected noise, changing color suddenly, losing his appetite, passing sleepless nights.

It was one of the last days in April. Meier had finished his afternoon lessons and now was standing by the window of his living room, his thumbs hooked in the armholes of his vest.

There was a knock at the door. "Come in," he shouted without turning around.

A young blond girl, wearing a black spring jacket and a grey felt hat trimmed with blue velvet, walked timidly through the doorway. She leaned forward slightly, like someone nervously stepping over a ditch, and glanced rapidly around the room. Then she closed the door with a confident, pleased expression, as though some danger were now behind her.

"You can put the laundry on the bed," Meier said with his back still turned.

Holding a hand to her mouth to stifle her laughter, her features quivering with repressed mirth, she tiptoed over to him, slipped her hand under his arm, and with a lightening quick movement, ducked around him and laughingly planted a kiss on his mouth.

"What the . . .is that you, Emma? I was expecting the laundry woman." His tone was half-surprised, half-irritated.

She stopped laughing. "Have I come at a bad time?" she asked, giving him a timid, searching glance.

"To tell the truth, I'm just going out."

"But you don't really have to be in such a hurry, do you?" She put her face against his cheek entreatingly.

"I thought you were working these days."

"I have been. Oh I mean I'm supposed to be at Mrs. Lorck's, but I got off so I could come see you. I've been longing for you so terribly," she coaxed. "It's been almost a week since I was here. I can take off my coat, can't I?" She tilted her head and looked at him beseechingly.

"I really don't have much time." He pulled out his watch.

"Why aren't you glad I came? I think you're mean. Well, won't you give me a kiss, at least?" She embraced him eagerly, kissing him again and again.

"There, there . . . " he mumbled.

But when she pressed herself still closer, he put his arms

around her and returned her caresses.

"Did you take the key out of the front door?"

Smiling, she held it up to him.

An hour later Meier was standing in his shirtsleeves beside the window, combing his hair and moustache. Holding a mirror in his hand, he examined himself carefully: tilting his head backwards and to the side, inspecting his teeth, and finally making a face at himself. Then he trimmed his nails and opened both windows. They faced the west; the afternoon sun blazed in, and the air was heavy and oppressive. He sliced off the tip of a cigar and stood by the windows, lost in thought, staring at the laburnum and lilac bushes behind the low fence in the yard across the street. They were laden with buds that were just about to burst. He remembered vividly how naked the bushes had been the first time Emma had accompanied him up to his room—no, not the first time, that had been late one night—but the next, when she had arrived around four in the afternoon.

A few minutes later, he was strolling up Pilestredet. He was going to see Constance. Lorck ought to be out on his calls by now, and he was going to force her to have a real talk.

A streetcar came by; he thought for a moment about taking it, but decided he would rather walk. He needed time to put his thoughts in order, to prepare what he was going to say. But he was not successful; he couldn't imagine anything beyond the moment when he would be standing before her, her hand clasped in his; then, heart pounding, blood surging in his ears, he would have to start all over again.

The Lorcks had rented a country house for the summer out in Ladegårdsøen. Since the weather was so mild and beautiful, they planned to move in by the first of May. Constance was going out a little early to put up the curtains, to find out what the owner, a merchant travelling with his family abroad, had left in the way of furniture and kitchen utensils, and to give the gardener instructions about the yard.

Constance had spent the day putting together the things she and her housemaid Hanne would need to take with them. They had finished packing two large cases with tablecloths and bed linens, tucking wine bottles in among them, laying the freshly ironed curtains on top. Constance had gone to the bedroom to pack a small case of toilet articles. She and Hanne would stay several days and would leave the next morning on the nine o'clock train. All afternoon she had been expecting Meier to come, but she trembled at the thought and almost hoped he would not. Now that the afternoon had passed without bringing him, she grew impatient, unable to imagine why he stayed away. Had his feelings for her cooled? Oh no, since that night at the carnival she had felt his passion in every breath he drew, in every glance. That was when he had won her. She knew she was his, but still, ever since that evening her behavior toward him had been governed by this strange, stupid fear. The horror of being an unfaithful wife was so ingrained in her. Adulteress—whore. Oh, those words were unspeakable! There were better ways to describe this. "A woman only belongs to the man she loves," Mrs. Gyllembourg[22] had written. And even if. . . . Suppose Lorck were in love with a woman who wanted him as well. Would he think twice about it? Not for a minute. Not him, nor any of the other married men she knew. Why should women have all these scruples? Measure for measure—that was life's only valid principle.

But something else stuck in her throat. In these weeks since the carnival, Lorck had seemed oddly touching. The morning after the ball, when he had begged her to forget his ugly outburst in the coach, he had seemed heartbroken. When she replied that she hadn't given it a thought, he took her head between his hands, kissed her hair and said, "Constance, my own Constance, be careful not to hurt yourself."

Something in the sound of his voice still rang in her ears. And recently, she had often noticed him looking at her with an expression that pierced her to the heart whenever she thought of it. It was so tender, so filled with pain, so patient. When she met his eyes at those moments she felt stabbed with remorse.

But what was the good of remorse? She couldn't help it if she didn't love him anymore. What had happened could not be undone; what she had done she had not been able to help doing, not if her life had been at stake. Hadn't she struggled against it, slipped into it bit by bit? She had only yielded when something beyond her control had robbed her of her strength. It was pointless to brood and fret about it.

Hanne poked her head in the door.

"Mr. Meier is here asking for you, ma'am."

"I'm coming right away," Constance answered, turning around abruptly so the maid wouldn't see her blush. She closed her eyes, tilted her head back, and took a deep breath. Then she closed the valise with trembling fingers, straightened her hair absentmindedly and went in to him.

Meier was standing with his back to the door, apparently engrossed in a lithograph on the wall. He turned quickly and walked toward her with outstretched hands. Constance was struck by his look of misery. His eyes had the dull luster that accompanies mental exhaustion or long suffering; his lips were dry and his face looked flushed.

"Haven't you been well?" she asked sympathetically, giving him a tender look.

He took hold of both her wrists. "I'm never well away from you," he said softly, pulling her toward him.

His gaze was oddly complex—imploring, loving, helpless, confident, all at the same time. She wanted to cuddle him like a small child.

He had thought he would reproach her, force some clarification out of her, but the instant he saw her standing there before him, so gentle and good, his resolution was forgotten. "What a delight to find you home alone," he whispered. "Let's sit down."

He pulled her gently down on the sofa and slipped his arm around her waist. Constance was filled with a quiet rapture. Her head slipped down onto his shoulder. He pulled her around until she rested right against him, her face turned up toward his. He bent and kissed her.

By the time he left they had agreed that he would come to her country house the next evening, where they would be alone and undisturbed. Dizzy with happiness, Meier went home.

The next day brought dazzling sunshine and a mild southerly breeze. Streams and puddles, frozen during the night, had thawed in the warm sun; and everywhere there was even the gentlest slope, rivulets of water, large and small, came trickling down.

The morning had passed, and out at Løkken Constance and the maid had not finished hanging the curtains in the three rooms that faced the garden. Hanne had never seen her mistress so awkward and forgetful. They had taken the curtains down four times because the pattern was upside down or wrong side out. Long moments passed searching for things they needed, because if the mistress had anything in her hands for a second, she would lose it in some ridiculous place. Arranging the furniture had been just as bad; she had ordered the things for the dining room put in the sun-room, and the other way round, so Hanne and the scrubwoman had to do everything all over again. In the end the maid decided that they were just in the way, and she sent the scrubwoman down to clean the cellar, while she sat down in the kitchen to mend a torn seam in her dress.

The gardener came in and said he didn't know what to do about the garden. When he asked the mistress where he should set out the hyacinths, she said she would come right away, and then she never showed up. That's the way it had been all day. Hanne offered him a cup of coffee and a sandwich, which he ate seated at the kitchen table.

"Well, Heaven knows what's ailing the mistress today," Hanne mumbled, popping a lump of sugar in her mouth and pouring the steaming coffee into her saucer.

The gardener did not reply. He filled his pipe, lit it at the stove and looked at his watch.

"Might as well go over to the consul's house and plant the primroses. If the mistress wants me, I'll be close enough so you can shout."

Banging his muddy felt hat against his knee to dislodge the clumps of dirt, he put it on his head, thanked her for the coffee, and nodded good-bye.

Constance was sitting upstairs in a little panelled chamber

adjoining the large bedroom that opened onto a balcony over-looking the garden. She was perched on a chest, hunched forward on her elbows, her face in her hands. She had gotten up early, after an almost sleepless night, and dashed feverishly off to the station, arriving a quarter of an hour too early. The thought of the rendezvous with Meier nearly overpowered her. Assailed by conflicting feelings, she felt a gnawing anxiety, a sense of oppression in her breast that was sometimes so intense that she moaned aloud. At other times she was drunk with the thought that tonight she would have his arms around her, his lips against her mouth; then she would shudder as if she had seen an abyss yawning at her feet.

Now, sitting in the little room with the hours slipping by, her anxiety turned to dread that increased by the minute. How would she feel tomorrow morning? And when she saw Lorck, who suspected nothing, still believed in her, still longed for an affectionate word, a freely given caress.... She squeezed her eyes shut and turned her head aside. It was a dreadful injustice to him; he had loved her so steadfastly ever since she had been his wife; she was sure that even in his inmost thoughts he had never been untrue to her. If only she could believe he had deceived her, but there wasn't the slightest possibility of it. Just the same, she didn't love him. She couldn't do anything about that; her love belonged to someone else. But was she sure there was no possible way to avoid what she was about to do? She had to admit that she *could* stop it. She couldn't really tell herself that she would die if she let Meier go, and failing that, how could she justify giving herself to him? If Lorck suspected what she was about to do, he would come and kill her.... What a cruel humiliation she was inflicting on him. But it was too late to stop now. She had already betrayed him so profoundly in her mind—this wouldn't really make any difference one way or another.

It was three o'clock now. By ten Meier would be there. They had arranged that he would come to Løkken by the forest road, where she would meet him. When the lights went out in the kitchen they could go in through the veranda door.

"Tonight, tonight," she repeated, until her own voice

frightened her. She jumped up and paced back and forth; the distance she could walk was so short that the incessant turning made her dizzy. She sat down again on the trunk, pulled out her watch and began to study its face. She felt as if she were doomed. A sudden raging desire to break out came over her—to escape, to run, to dash like a wild animal from her pursuers. Wringing her hands she wailed, "too late, impossible—go where?" Suddenly she clapped a hand to her forehead, "Why is it impossible?" she said to herself. And like the first dim rays of dawn in a coal black sky, the idea began to glimmer in her consciousness that she could still save herself. Gripping her head in both hands, she bent forward as if she were staring intently and listening, and she talked to herself—whispering, then breaking off, an imploring note in her voice, like a child trying to regain her mother's good graces after a scolding. Straightening up with a jerk, she threw on her hat and coat and ran down the stairs.

At the door she met Hanne, who asked her if she was taking the train.

"Yes," she answered hurriedly—"I have to go to town again. Just do whatever you can."

"And spend the night out here alone? I daren't do that ma'am."

"Then come back when you're finished—that's perfectly all right."

"I will—there are so many tramps wandering around out here. But won't you have something to eat, or a cup of coffee, at least? The train won't be here for a quarter of an hour."

"Well give me something, but be quick—I'll have it in here."

Constance followed the maid into the kitchen. All of a sudden she felt hungry, and she stood there, eating the things Hanne took out of the food basket and placed in front of her. Finally she drank a large glass of red wine. When she heard the train whistle, she dashed off and took a seat in the compartment.

She would go talk to Lorck. By five o'clock his office hours would be finished; if she took a cab she would be there before he went out on his evening calls. She would tell him every-thing: she would throw herself in his arms, tell him that it was her turn now to yearn for him, that she would try to be as close to him as she had been in their first happy days together; she would beg him to forgive her if he could, to forget all the injuries she had done to him. She would lay her head on his chest and tell him it was her rightful, her only, resting place. So moved was she by the pictures she imagined, that her eyes filled with tears at the joy and relief she felt in her heart. Peace flooded her anguished soul.

It was four-thirty when she got to Kristiania, and at ten minutes before five she was walking up the steps of her house. Letting herself in, she went to her bedroom without seeing anyone. She tossed her outer clothes on the bed, washed her hands, and crept out of the room, as quiet as a thief. The dis-tance between Lorck's study and the bedroom was just a few steps. Originally the study had not opened on to the hall, but Lorck had installed a concealed door so that he would not have to go through the dining room to reach his office. The examining room was between the study and the waiting room, which in turn opened into the dining room.

Constance walked to the study door; the key was in the outer side. Lorck had gone in at four o'clock. He would be fin-ished soon, and then he could come this way to go to the bed-room to wash before going out. She would be sitting there in his study when he came out. How happy and surprised he would be. She could hear his voice saying "But Constance, are you back already?" With a beating heart she shoved open the door—it made no sound—and quietly walked in. The door to the examining room was standing ajar. She could hear that someone was with him—it must be the last patient of the day.

33

Lorck had treated five patients: two housemaids, a young woman with an abscessed ear, and two men—the last of whom was a stocky suntanned sailor with numerous tattoos on his hands. When Lorck had finished with him, he took out his watch and saw he still had five minutes left. As the sailor was leaving the room, Lorck called out, "Next, but then no more for today!"

A woman entered who seemed to have peculiar difficulty managing to close the door behind her. She hesitated, walked forward a few steps, and stood there uncertainly. She was a slender woman of medium height, with heavy dark hair, greyish almond-shaped eyes, a short broad nose, and a full, shapely mouth that would have been beautiful if the flesh around her lips had not appeared so taut and strained. Her clothing was modest and neat: a pleated black and white checked skirt, a black coat of finely woven cloth, and a hat of the same color trimmed with a stiff white feather. She was extremely pale; her breath came quickly, as if the situation were very painful to her.

"Please come closer," Lorck said, writing in his notebook.

She didn't move.

"Come, come," he went on, pointing toward an armchair next to his writing table. He laid a blotter over what he had written, and as he was smoothing it with his hand, turned to look at her.

He threw himself back in his chair with a jerk, and looked at her, wide-eyed.

"Kristine! Is it possible?"

She took a couple of steps, stopped and tried to speak, but

gave up. She took out her handkerchief and held it to her eyes.

"Are you here in town? I thought you moved to Drammen."

"I've come back," she stammered.

"And now you come here?" His tone was half wistful, half disapproving.

She shot him a glance. His hands were clasped on his stomach, his thumbs circling each other continuously.

"I wanted so much to talk to you."

An expression of perplexity and displeasure appeared on his face.

"Is there something I can do for you? You do understand, Kristine, that what's past is past."

She blushed furiously, then grew pale again.

"It's nothing like that—you mustn't think—I just wanted to ask you for a prescription."

"Are you ill?"

The tears she had been struggling against the whole time overcame her now.

"Yes," she wept.

"Poor thing, come and sit down," Lorck said sympathetically, getting up and pulling her gently to a chair. "Tell me what's the matter with you."

Kristine dried her eyes and stared at the floor as she spoke.

"I've been feeling so weak, and I have headaches—like that time I was anemic and took the iron pills, remember? But now I have such an awful pain in my chest."

"Have you had it long?"

"A couple of months. It's been really bad for the last two weeks."

Regarding her attentively, he took her pulse.

"And I sleep so badly at night—I'm more tired in the mornings than when I go to bed at night," she went on.

"Have you seen a doctor?"

"No," she said. "I've come to the door lots of times, but when I went to ring the bell, I didn't have the nerve." She lifted her eyes and looked at him with an expression that was indescribably touching. "I was so afraid you'd be angry," she added timidly.

"How could you think that," he said absentmindedly.

"But I wanted so terribly to see you one last time," the voice was again very close to tears, "just to hear your voice, and then I got so sick I had to have a doctor."

"How long have you been in the city?"

"Since just before Christmas."

"Why didn't you stay in Drammen?"

"Oh lots of reasons. I wasn't happy, and I couldn't always get work. Things can be hard for a stranger in a small town. And I didn't get along with my sister, well, her husband, actually. He wouldn't let me alone."

"Ah, so that was it. Poor thing . . . " Lorck said, shaking his head in sympathy. "And are things better now?"

"Yes, I have enough to do here, more than I can manage. If I wasn't sick—but I think it's consumption."

"What put an idea like that in your head, Kristine?"

"Because my two sisters died of it, and they started just like this. And then I've been grieving so terribly." Her last words were barely audible; she quickly wiped away the tears that were trickling down her cheeks.

"Hmm," Lorck said, with an involuntary sigh. "Poor girl. But just the same, I don't think there's any chance you have consumption."

"I really wouldn't be sorry if I did." Her tone was suddenly bolder. "On the contrary . . . I want to die."

Lorck regarded her intently. He found her basically unchanged, although she had seemed so at first glance. Perhaps she was a little bit thinner, but that suited her, actually. Undeniably she was just as sweet and attractive as she used to be. He could not resist the urge to pat her cheek.

"So you want to languish away with consumption, do you?" he said in a half-tender, half-teasing tone. Taking her by the chin, he shook her head gently back and forth. "No my dear, it's not that easy. Do you think patients with consumption have dimples like that?" He pointed to the tiny round indentation in her cheek that accompanied her reluctant smile. "Your old sweet dimple, Kristine," he said softly.

"My sisters had them, too," she answered dejectedly—"until just before they died."

"You don't have consumption any more than I do—but come on, we'll take a look. I'll have to examine you."

"Shall I unbutton my dress." she asked.

"Of course. I'll need the blouse off and the corset, too, if I'm going to find out anything."

She unhooked her broach and unbuttoned her dress. Lorck fiddled with his stethoscope and waited until she was ready.

Suddenly—he wasn't sure how it happened—the only thing he could think about was that Kristine, his old friend, his sweetheart, had come to see him; and before he could restrain himself, he was holding her in his arms, kissing her warm, naked bosom.

"Put it over there," he said taking off her hat.

She turned away from him with a deprecating gesture.

Quickly he walked over to the door of the examining room and locked it, then he came back and took her in his arms. "I want to hold you just the way I used to," he whispered.

Constance saw it all. She had gone into the study shortly after Kristine entered the examining room, and with her heart pounding, sat down on the edge of a chair.

Hearing a sudden peculiar sound, she got up, crept quietly across the carpet to the door, and peeked through the crack.

With a face as white and rigid as a sleepwalker's, she slipped out of the room a few minutes later, as soundlessly and unnoticed as she had come. Mechanically she put on her coat and hurried out of the house. The blood burned in her veins and she felt as if she were crying "fire," continually and with all her might—she couldn't imagine why nobody came running to put out the blaze. That faithless traitor, betraying her in her own home with half-naked women—and so calmly, so unrepentantly, so confidently—with a smile of delight on his lips. Oh that smile! That sneaking liar, that filthy beast, betraying her without struggle or thought—and not for any grand passion. Whereas she—oh she would get revenge—revenge—even if she had to purchase it with her own blood. Her heart was burning, scorching—it gnawed and stabbed in her breast.

How cooling, how soothing to get revenge. "Cooling, cooling, cooling," she repeated again and again. But he would have to know about it. Yes, certainly! Otherwise there was no point. She would tell him herself, laugh right in his shameless face. No, he'd find her in Meier's arms in the bedroom—some night when he came home late. She would be undressed; there wouldn't be any doubt. Let him see how he liked it. "Oh so soothing, soothing!" She said the word until her tongue felt dry and sick of it.

She started quickly down Karl Johansgate. Familiar faces passed her as if in a fog. She looked at them with glittering eyes, and if anyone spoke to her, bowed more deeply than usual, with a quick elastic movement. The people she greeted turned involuntarily and stared back at her.

She met Marie, who stopped and asked Constance to turn and walk with her a bit.

Without wanting to, driven by a nervous need to be agreeable, Constance started to walk with her. She spoke with animation, changing the subject rapidly, laughing uproariously when Marie told her about an amusing misadventure in a boutique. Suddenly she broke off.

"I must be out of my mind, walking along like this," she said. "I have to catch a train. Good-bye," and she patted Marie vigorously on the shoulder, nodded gaily and hurried away before Marie could offer to go with her.

Marie stood looking after her, unable to clarify the impression she had received. She had looked so extraordinarily handsome—it was really uncanny—there was something sparkling about her whole figure.

Constance hurried onward, nearly running. At Akersgaten, she paused to look at the clock on the corner building. Just six o'clock and the train didn't leave until six-thirty. Then she would be there before seven, and Meier wasn't coming until ten.

She walked more slowly now. She wanted some wine—strong sweet wine. Lots of wine in goblets, and cigarettes—no, cigars—strong fine ones.

She went into a cigar store and asked for the kind of cigars

Lorck usually kept in his cigar case. She got what she wanted and set off again. There was plenty of wine out there, and she had seen a corkscrew on a windowsill someplace.

She came down to the train station and paced restlessly back and forth on the platform. Then she remembered that she might meet someone she knew going in the same direction. So she sat down in a corner of the waiting room near the front door. She couldn't stay still. Bracing the tips of her toes on the floor, she jiggled her knees rapidly up and down, beating a tattoo with her heels, her fingers drumming.

Finally the train whistled and she was in the compartment.

Had it been this morning that she had travelled this same way? Impossible, it must have been a year ago. But just the same, it was today. "Yes, yes, of course," she said to herself with a defeated wave of the hand.

At Løkken, she met Hanne, with a basket over her arm and the key to the front door in her hand.

"But ma'am, didn't you go to town?" the maid asked, looking as if she couldn't believe her eyes.

"No, I didn't go after all. I took a long walk," Constance answered. "It's really better to stay here tonight so we can get an early start tomorrow."

Hanne appeared crestfallen, but quickly turned around, and without making a reply, went to unlock the door.

"Then should I get your room ready upstairs?" Hanne asked, as Constance was taking off her coat. "It's a good thing I lit the fire early today, so it's not cold up there."

Constance had drunk some tea, but not touched the sandwiches. As Hanne was taking out the tray, Constance said she wouldn't need her any longer; she could go to bed whenever she wanted.

Constance went upstairs to look at the bedroom. The bed was against the wall, covered with snowy white sheets and a crimson woolen spread. Directly across from it was a white dressing table with a large mirror. There was a wash basin and pitcher on a chair and water and a soap dish on the window sill. Hand towels hung on the back of a chair and a sheet served as a window shade. The only other furniture was a large white wardrobe and a wicker sofa. Her valise was on the floor, and a brass candlestick sat on a large trunk pulled up to the bed.

Constance prowled restlessly around the sun-room. She paused by the window for a moment, and took a puff of a cigar, then moving away, drank some wine from a mug and sat down in the rocking chair, then got up again.

She had blown out the lamp, and the moonlight floated in through the thin white curtains. Tossing the cigar on the floor, she ground out the butt, and pushed it into a corner. Then she went over to the window to look out. It was much too bright. The moon was directly in front of her, staring through the leafless trees and bushes. Down in the corner was the wooden arbor, its back to the light, casting an oblong shadow out in front of it on the grass. Everything was hushed and still. The monotonous barking of a distant dog was the only sound that could be heard. She drank more wine, lit a new cigar, took a few puffs and laid it on the window sill, sat down on the sofa, and then went back to see if the veranda was also filled with moonlight. She opened the door to see if it would creak, left it standing ajar, and finally looked at her watch. She had to light a match to be certain what it said. It was five of ten. She shuddered; pressing her hands tightly against her face, she bent her knees until she was almost crouching, then, straightening up, grabbed a large woolen cape she had laid at hand. Wrapping a large lace kerchief around her head, she crept out, running quickly to the spot they had agreed upon, about a hundred yards from the house. Here she struck off on the road to the left and suddenly found herself surrounded by towering fir trees. She leaned against a tree and waited. It was a while before she heard the train whistle. Her heart was pounding as if it were about to burst, and she felt a constant choking sensation in her throat.

She heard his steps before she saw him; she couldn't imagine how it could take so long for him to get there. Finally the light at the entrance of the woods was darkened by a figure hurrying toward her. She stood quietly until he was directly beside her; when she was sure it was him, she took a sudden step forward and touched his arm.

"Constance," he whispered, his voice flooded with tenderness. "My darling—you're mine—all mine . . . "

She threw herself violently against him. Their arms tight around each other, he covered her eyes and mouth with kisses.

"Thank God you've come, Harold," she said with her mouth at his ear. "I've been so afraid—so afraid."

Her anxiety had subsided now; a feeling of security and repose had come over her. Wonderful that the awful hours of waiting were over. It was such a relief to feel his arms around her. They went toward the house. The light in the kitchen was out. So Hanne had gone to bed; probably she was asleep already. Quietly and carefully, their arms intertwined, they walked through the garden and up the three low steps leading to the veranda. They didn't light a lamp but sat in the darkness until they went upstairs.

At four o'clock in the morning, Meier came out of the house through the veranda door. He glanced around furtively.

In the grey-gold morning light he looked pale and disheveled. He lit a cigar and stood listening for a moment. Then he threw a kiss up toward the still shaded balcony window and hurried out of the garden. He had nearly ten kilometers to walk and figured he would be home by six.

When he had gone a little way into the woods he stopped, opened his wallet and took out a photograph. "That damned picture," he muttered, striking a match and setting it afire.

"What an incredible moron!—carrying that with me," he said under his breath. He tossed the blazing picture away and ground out the fire with his foot.

"There, now you can't make any more trouble than you already have." He walked on with rapid steps, striking out with his hand occasionally, as if pushing away something disagreeable. The painful circumstance of their parting kept reappearing before him—Constance stooping down to pick up a picture that had fallen from his wallet to the floor—he could see her looking at the back of it, hear her voice as she read the words: "To Harold from Emma." Turning it over, she had blurted, "Good God, it's my seamstress Emma." Instantly she

283

had turned flaming red and given him a look that made him feel faint when he remembered it. And the way she looked at him when he kissed her good-bye!

34

CONSTANCE SLEPT DEEPLY for a couple of hours and woke when the sun was high in the sky. At first she had no clear idea of why she had such a feeling of oppression, but little by little it all stood sharply outlined before her. She closed her eyes tightly and buried her face in her pillow. She wanted to hide from it—get away, away—but it was no use. She had to go over it all, live through it again, bit by bit. She had gotten her revenge. But had it given her any relief? She was sickened by herself. She didn't have the courage of her convictions, that was clear enough. She was disgusted with her husband, with Meier, with life—but above all, with herself.

What should she do now? How should she behave? She sat up in bed to think about it. Then her glance fell on her reflection in the mirror. With a scream, she clapped her hands to her face and threw herself back on the pillows. The thought of meeting her husband was unbearable. She didn't want him to touch her; she didn't want to touch him—not for anything in the world. She didn't want to see him again. But where could she go? Demand a divorce? Start all that again—she couldn't be bothered with it. Meier flitted into her thoughts, then drifted away in the mist.

A consuming ennui took possession of her. Gone was hatred, revenge and pain. It had become so still inside her, so empty and dead. She realized she could not bear to live any longer. She said it to herself in a slow, calm voice. So there was just one thing left to do—to die. She lay there thinking about it carefully. Was she sure she was serious? That she really wanted, dared to do it? Yes, it was the only thing she could think of, the only way she could find rest.

But she had to act quickly—if she waited even an hour longer than necessary, she might not have the courage.

She got out of bed and put on her clothes, deliberately and carefully. Calmly she drank a cup of coffee and ate a couple of rusks. Glancing at the clock, she estimated that she would be home by twelve. Lorck would be out on his calls then, and the apartment would be empty. She gave the maid some instructions and told her to go to town when she was finished; then she walked down to the train.

In the compartment she sat huddled in a corner, her eyes closed. The conductor had to ask her twice for her ticket. Her thoughts revolved around one idea—to die without delay.

As on the previous day, she let herself into the house and reached her room unnoticed. She walked over to the desk and, as she stood there, wrote the following words to Lorck: "You shouldn't grieve for me. I was so tired of life. I couldn't stand it any longer. Constance."

Slipping the paper into an envelope, she sealed it, wrote Lorck's name on the outside, and laid it on a table in his examining room.

She went into the bedroom, locked the door, and took a bottle of morphine out of the cupboard; it had been there since the time Lorck had given her an injection for a toothache. There was a lot of it—enough, Lorck had joked, to kill three people.

Mechanically she loosened her heavy braids and put the hairpins on the dressing table. Just then her eye fell on a photograph that was hanging on the wall in a black, polished frame. It was her family in Molde. Her father and mother were in the middle with all the children grouped around them. Her mother was holding the littlest one in her arms, and she herself was standing behind her father's chair, her hand on his shoulder. Constance had been a little girl then, with a scooped neck bodice, little puff sleeves, and hair curling down her back. Her heart contracted into a knot in her breast—she grabbed the picture hastily and pressed a kiss on each of the faces, her own included. She realized that the child was someone quite alien to her. Then she remembered her father's words when they brought the proof of the picture home. He had been so pleased with all of them, but he had said about her: "Constance has the look of a person who views life skeptically." Her mother had laughed and said he was right.

Now she wasn't just skeptical about life, she was finished with it. If I'd been told more about the one thing that plays such a huge role in life—she thought, hanging the picture back on the wall—things would have gone better for me. She remembered something else her father had said shortly before her confirmation. "You are a terrible egotist, Constance," he had told her once disapprovingly, "and egotism is a mortal sin."

Yes it was true. She had been full of egotism. At that moment she saw it so clearly. It was the great sin of her life.

She unhooked her dress, loosened her corset, and lay down on the bed. Then she seized the bottle, closed her eyes, and emptied the contents in one gulp.

The evening of the incident with Kristine, Lorck had felt troubled. After returning from his calls he had gone into the study to find a book. Stepping into the room, he stopped and sniffed. He thought he noticed the fragrance of Constance, as he liked to call it. Involuntarily he glanced around. Yes, of course—there was her handkerchief on the sofa. He picked it up and looked at it—oh yes, it was hers. How had it gotten there? He had sat in there for a half an hour that morning. Had it been there then?

He felt strangely uneasy. In a moment he went over and rang the bell.

"Has the mistress been home today?" he asked the cook when she came in.

"No sir, the mistress hasn't been here since this morning. She and Hanne went out to Løkken."

"That's good," he said waving her away.

When she had gone, he crushed the handkerchief to his nostrils. Its scent brought Constance alive before him. He almost felt as if he held her in his arms. Finally he pressed his lips to the handkerchief and put it away.

He walked into the dining room where the supper table was

laid for him. During the meal he sat back in his chair several times, staring at the ceiling with a distracted, discontented air. Annoying, this thing with Kristine. How the hell had it happened! Something had come over him, and he'd forgotten himself for a moment. That was what was so irritating—he could have just as easily restrained himself. He clucked his tongue in disapproval and scratched his head; then he got himself a cigar, sat down in an armchair in the living room and tried to read. But the book kept falling out of his hands. He couldn't overcome the aversion he felt for himself. He had a sudden desire for something to drink and went in to investigate the contents of the buffet. Finding a decanter of port, he poured himself a large glass and drank it up. Smoking his cigar, he paced up and down the floor. Little by little he worked himself out of his depression. Really this was nothing to be concerned about. Constance would never know. So what harm could it do? He had not really hurt her or his relationship with her—he felt that from the bottom of his soul. This was something purely physical—something quite irrelevant—sheer nonsense, to put it plainly.

He had been moved by the sight of Kristine; she had seemed so miserable that he had felt the need to console and help her—and so what happened, happened. His kind heart was to blame. He wasn't an unfaithful husband—not in any way—he certainly would protest such an idea.

He went to bed in a mild, contented mood. Tomorrow night Constance was coming home and that was very good—he missed her already. Even if she wasn't as affectionate as he wished, everything seemed so empty without her. He was looking forward to their reunion—that proved he wasn't conscious of any sin; only a man whose mind was free of guilt could feel happiness, and he wasn't guilty if his conscience could excuse his actions.

The next day he returned from his calls around three o'clock. As was his custom, he went straight into the examining room to see if there were any messages. The first thing he saw was the letter from Constance. He felt an odd chill go through him. Quickly he opened it and read the few words.

The letters disappeared before his eyes, and he stumbled back, white as a corpse. Storming wildly through the rooms, he finally came to the closed door of the bedroom. He set his back against it, and after a couple of fruitless tries, made a supreme effort and managed to break it down.

She was lying on the bed. Her mouth hung open and her eyes were glazed. A bluish froth covered her lips and oozed down over her chin. One swollen hand dangled from the bed, and the empty bottle had rolled some distance across the floor.

He leaped to the bed and raised her lifeless body to his chest. He uttered a piteous cry; the body dropped from his grasp, and he fell across it.

Notes

1. The capital city of Norway, Kristiania was re-named Oslo in 1925.

2. The seaport of Molde is located on the western coast of Norway.

3. Ole Bull (1810-1880) was a world famous violinist and composer whose concert tours introduced Norwegian folk music to Europe and America.

4. The Danish writer B.S. Ingemann (1789-1862) wrote popular historical romances set in the medieval period.

5. In Norwegian, as in other European languages, two forms of pronouns are used in direct address. In most social interaction the impersonal "De" is used. The more intimate "du" is reserved for children, family members and intimate friends.

6. *Die Räuber* (1781) was the controversial first play of the German dramatist Johann Schiller (1759-1805).

7. "The Woman from Tjele" is probably an allusion to *Fru Marie Grubbe* (1876), a novel by the Danish writer J. P. Jacobsen.

8. The Storting is the legislative branch of the Norwegian government. During the 1870s and 80s, the period depicted in *Constance Ring*, the Storting became the focus of campaign for political change in Norway. Various segments of the population wanted greater independence from the Swedish monarch who ruled over the Swedish-Norwegian union. The union dated back to 1814, when Denmark was forced to cede Norway to Sweden at the end of the Napoleonic wars. Many Norwegians objected to entering a union with Sweden; eager to rule their own country, delegates from all over Norway met at

Eidsvoll in 1814 to draft a constitution. The constitution, signed on May 17, 1814, gave executive power to a king and his appointed ministers; legislative power went to a national assembly called the Storting.

Sweden did not favor Norwegian independence, and Norway, failing to win support from the European powers, had no choice but to enter a union with Sweden. Under the terms of the union, Norway was allowed to retain its constitution and the Storting.

From the beginning, there was tension between the Storting and the Swedish king. By the late 1870s opposition to the King and his government had crystallized into an unofficial political party, the Left (Venstre), under the leadership of Johan Sverdrup. Another party, the Right (Høyre), emerged in support of the king and his followers. Sverdrup's ultimate goal was the establishment of a parliamentary government, and toward that end he proposed a constitutional amendment requiring the king's ministers to sit in the assembly where they could be held accountable for their policies. The bill was passed over the king's veto in three successive sessions of the Storting, but he refused to order his ministers to comply. In 1884 the ministers were impeached by the Riksrett (body composed of members of one of the Storting's two houses, plus members of the High Court) and the king was forced to form a government with Sverdrup as Prime Minister. The dispute about the cabinet ministers led to the establishment of parliamentary government in Norway.

9. Bjørnstjerne Bjørnson (1832-1910) was a renowned political activist and writer. Along with Ibsen, Bjørnson was a founder of modern Norwegian drama, writing a series of controversial plays about contemporary society that fueled debate at home and abroad. In *The Editor* (*Redaktøren;* 1875), *A Bankruptcy* (*En Fallitt;* 1875) and *The King* (*Kongen;* 1877) Bjørnson used his dramas to urge greater morality in public and private life. One of his most influential plays, *The Gauntlet* (*En Hanske;* 1883), attacked the double standard, creating so much controversy that its first performance was held in Germany because no Norwegian theater would perform it. Actively involved in public issues, Bjørnson worked with Sverdrup and Jaabaek in their battles to increase the influence of the Left in governmen-

tal affairs. He fought for the enfranchisement of Norwegian farmers and supported the folk high school movement in rural Norway.

10. A lawyer and politician, Johan Sverdrup (1816–1892) forged an alliance in the Storting between farmers and a group of urban radicals. Sverdrup saw that the farmers were an important voting block and he worked to incorporate them into an opposition party, the Left. He served as Prime Minister for five years, and he was a member of the Storting from 1851 until his death.

11. Søren Jaabaek (1814-1894) founded a farmers collective (Bondevennerne) in 1865 that eventually became a national movement. The movement published a journal (*Folketidende*) that had a great impact in rural Norway. Jaabaek served in the Storting from 1845-1890, and worked with Sverdrup to achieve voting reforms in rural areas.

12. Probably a reference to Christopher Bruun (1839-1920), a controversial Norwegian clergyman who was a friend of Bjørnson and possibly the model for Ibsen's *Brand*. Bruun was one of the founders of the folk high school movement, which brought improved educational opportunities to rural areas.

13. *Kongen*, written by Bjørnstjerne Bjørnson in 1877, attacked the absolute power of the monarch. Conservatives regarded it as a personal attack on King Oscar. The play generated so much controversy that it was not performed in Norway until 1902.

14. "Then everything is finished."

15. The Storting is housed at 22 Karl Johansgate.

16. Founded in 1869, *Dagbladet* is still published today. The newspaper was regarded as the voice of the Left.

17. Best known for his satirical short stories, Alexander Kielland (1849-1906) was an important literary figure in Norway, ranked with Henrik Ibsen, Bjørnstjerne Bjørnson, and Jonas

Lie.

18. *Fromont jeune et Risler aîné* (1874) is a realistic novel by the French writer Alphonse Daudet.

19. Bjørnson's first social drama, *En Fallitt* (1875), depicted a financial speculator whose shady business dealings led him to financial ruin. *A Bankruptcy* was widely performed in Europe and America and brought Bjørnson international fame.

20. "Marshmen" were people who bought or leased worthless land (often marshland) in order to obtain voting rights. The practice, a form of voting fraud, enabled parties to swell their ranks.

21. A Norwegian newspaper founded in 1860, *Aftenposten* is still published today.

22. Thomasine Gyllembourg (1773-1856) was a popular Danish writer who wrote numerous stories, dramas and novels. In the process of getting a highly publicized divorce, she wrote a letter that asserted her right to enter a relationship with the man she loved. In 1845, she published anonymously a novel called *The Two Ages* (*To Tidsaldre*)—the first part of which, *The Revolutionary Age* (*Revolutionstiden*) deals with an illicit affair between a woman who has married unwisely and a family friend who has loved her for years.

Afterword

Constance Ring (1885) was published during a period of literary and social ferment in Scandinavia. Norwegian writers such as Henrik Ibsen, Bjørnstjerne Bjørnson, and Alexander Kielland had begun to examine contemporary social attitudes toward religion, marriage, and morality. In the years preceding the publication of *Constance Ring*, Ibsen wrote some of his most controversial plays: *The Pillars of Society* (1877), *A Doll's House* (1879), and *Ghosts* (1881). Like her male colleagues, Amalie Skram held up a mirror to the problems in Norwegian society. Her predecessor Camilla Collett had written about love and marriage from a feminist perspective, but no Norwegian woman before Amalie Skram had dared to attack the double standard, the hypocrisies of the church, and the social inequities of marriage and divorce.

In *Constance Ring*, Amalie Skram portrays a society in the throes of change. Her characters argue fiercely about politics, religion, and morality. The male characters represent a spectrum of political and moral viewpoints: The conservative businessman Edvard Ring is a staunch defender of King, church, marriage, and motherhood; Niels Lorck, a dedicated physician, is a free-thinker who regards a loveless marriage as prostitution; the young composer Harold Meier is a radical who wants to tear down the corrupt institutions of marriage, government and religion. Behind the protracted party conversations in chapters 4 and 5 is the so called "morality debate," which rocked Scandinavia in the 1880s following the publication of Bjørnson's play about the double standard, *The Gauntlet* (1883). In newspaper articles, stories, and plays, partisans on all sides debated the issues of sexual purity, free love, and prostitution.

Skram's novel is a blistering attack on the double standard.

A gulf lies between the men and women in *Constance Ring*. Middle-class young women raised in ignorance of sexual matters are married to older, more experienced men. Their purity is regarded as "natural." Equally "natural" are the affairs men are permitted to have with lower class women, both before and after marriage. In Skram's novel, political differences pale in comparison to the central fact of sexual oppression. Virtually every male figure in the novel—conservative or radical—engages in a sexual relationship with a woman of a lower class. Even the church condones the double standard. Reverend Huhn argues that a woman should forgive her errant husband, but an errant wife pollutes the home. The scene recalls Torvald's admonitions to Nora in *A Doll's House*.

Constance sees the exploitation of such arrangements. Middle-class women like Mrs. Sunde lose their youth and beauty bearing too many children. Lower class women like Kristine and Alette are seduced and abandoned by their middle-class lovers. Constance's own jealousy at being supplanted does not destroy the compassion she feels for these victims of masculine injustice. The pregnant housemaid, the beaten slum woman, the seduced and abandoned mistress are sisters to Constance. She sees through the accidental circumstances of birth and wealth to the common ground they share. As a married woman, she too exchanges sexual services for money.

Yet if the world of men is alien, so is the world of women. Constance's relationships with other women are problematic. She lives in a world where the victims of unequal marriage become its staunchest defenders. Among the exemplars of traditional femininity are Marie, Mrs. Sunde and Aunt Wleügel. Womanliness to Constance's mother means compliance and deception: she begs her daughter to obey her husband, to count the blessings of a wealthy and well-appointed household. She admonishes Constance for treating her husband coldly: a wife has no right to be repelled by her husband's caresses. Constance finds this female collusion intolerable. In intelligence and spirit, Constance is a new woman in the making. Dissatisfied with traditional female roles, she wants one standard of morality for men and women. She wants to end the exploitation of lower-class women. But if Constance can diagnose the diseases of society, she cannot create a life that cures them. Under pressure from friends and family, she gives up the idea of divorce. Like the other women in the novel, she colludes too.

Skram's novel is valuable for its portrayal of the changing social roles of men and women, but it is most powerful as it traces the effects of a divided society upon the mental landscape of its heroine. Constance is the battleground for opposing forces. She stands between the attackers and defenders of authority, drawn to both groups, repelled by both. Representatives from both groups court her. Plagued by simultaneous desires to approach and to avoid, she experiences the crippling form of conflict described by Kurt Levin. In her life there are no simple choices. Each of her alternatives has a powerful positive and negative element. As she approaches an object of desire, its negative qualities become more salient, overriding the original attraction. Constance's most characteristic action is to move forward, then retreat. In each of her relationships with men, she experiences some form of approach/avoidance conflict. Her marriage to Edvard Ring offers respectability and financial security, but Constance finds her husband sexually and morally repulsive. A second marriage to Lorck provides financial security, conjugal love, and for a time a "fully human life." The discovery that, like Ring, he has had an affair with a servant girl, transforms her love to anger and disgust. Harold Meier offers Constance the appeal of sexual passion, but betraying Lorck entails guilt and self reproach. At any moment these feelings coexist, leading to vacillation and confusion.

Throughout the novel, Skram emphasizes Constance's conflicts by the juxtaposition of interior and exterior spaces. The contrast between tightly closed rooms and the world of nature is a version of what Tony Tanner, in *Adultery in the Novel* calls "city" and "field." The city is a place of contracts and social obligations, the field a place of freedom and danger. Torn between city and field, Constance resembles the heroines of

Anna Karenina (1877), *The Awakening* (1899), and *Madame
Bovary* (1857). Constance Ring sits at the window of her husband's house and dreams about escape. Windows, as Victor
Brombert has observed, are boundaries between freedom and
convention. Inside is safety and boredom; outside is excitement and danger. Skram recognizes the risks that go with freedom. In *Constance Ring* the erotic content of the outdoor
games and excursions is only thinly disguised, as it is in the
novels of Jane Austen. Skram links the escape into nature with
mishap, shame, and eroticism. A mountain hike ends in a
twisted ankle, a game of tag in an illicit kiss, a walk in the garden with a declaration of love, a walk on the deck of a ship
with an passionate embrace. Skram's description of the climac-
tic storm that wrecks Constance's garden is filled with sexual
imagery, as Irene Engelstad has observed. Constance stands at
her window watching, while the storm foreshadows what an
escape into nature could bring—fronds intertwined, flowers
cut down by raging winds, water sluicing over the destruction.
Skram's use of imagery reflects the divisions in Constance's
consciousness—city and field in never-ending opposition.

The Madwoman in the Attic, Sandra Gilbert and Susan
Gubar's influential study of nineteenth-century women
writers, describes characteristic patterns of imagery in
nineteenth-century novels about domestic enclosure. In books
like *Middlemarch* (1871/72) and *Daniel Deronda* (1876), the
heroines' conflicts are mirrored in recurrent cycles of opposition: space and enclosure, light and darkness, movement and
paralysis, nature and artifice. The early chapters of *Constance
Ring* link the novel with the broad tradition of women's fiction. The Rings' apartment in Kristiania is filled with expensive objects: surfaces are covered, masked by the expensive
trappings of middle-class marriage. Plants grow brown at the
tips in these claustrophobic spaces and are quickly replaced by
new ones from a flower shop. The image of the house plant is
richly evocative, implying as it does the exchangeability of
women, the atmosphere that sickens, the decline from youthful vigor into disease. Outside the house a grapevine winds its
way skyward from the carefully groomed garden below. The

escape from careful cultivation and restraint is the central movement of Skram's novel.

The title of the novel suggests Skram's concern with enclosure. As Irene Engelstad has observed, Constance Ring is "konstant i ring"; the puns are bilingual—Skram's heroine is constantly ringed round by marital obligations. The wedding ring is a resonant symbol of Constance's discontent, its endless continuity a fitting representation of the golden trap in which she finds herself. The circle motif is persistent in *Constance Ring*, as it is in *Madame Bovary*. When Constance tries to escape from her marriage, "from every side, hidden wheels were set in motion to make her give up the thought of divorce." In the last chapters of the book the circles become more prominent as Constance runs from Kristiania to Løkken to see Meier; from Løkken to Kristiania to see Lorck; and back from Kristiania to Løkken and her final rendezvous with Meier. The literal circles trace a downward spiral that narrows her existence to a repudiated self and death.

Anne-Lisa Amadou has pointed to similarities in structure between *Constance Ring* and *Madame Bovary*. Both novels portray heroines in three disastrous relationships. Both depict a movement from marriage to adultery to death. For Constance, as for Emma Bovary, the present is always circumscribed. Constance moves beyond the boundaries of self toward an object of desire. Each choice widens her life for a time, but each expansion is followed by contracted expectations, narrowed views, obsessive concerns. Nowhere is this clearer than in the period after Ring's death, when suddenly liberated from the hateful chains of matrimony, Constance retreats into her house, her locked room, into paralysis, darkness, and attempted suicide. Constance's marriage to Lorck opens the world of sexuality to her but she quickly retreats from the realities of Lorck's past into a new expansion of expectation with Meier. Constance can not sustain love in the real world of imperfect and flawed human beings, nor can she pass through disillusionment to a mature acceptance of human weakness. All three relationships founder on Constance's discovery of a previous liaison with a servant girl. Three movements outward collapse back upon the self. Disgust is constantly threatening to overwhelm Constance; her disgust is never exceeded by her enthusiasms.

If the present can be viewed as a circle in which Constance makes repeated and abortive movements toward objects on the perimeter, there are at least two other circles, more expansive than the circle of the present moment, into which she escapes when her conflicts become intolerable. For Constance the past is a more commodious space than the present. In *Archetypal Patterns in Women's Fiction*, Annis Pratt has pointed to the regressiveness that characterizes so many female novels of development. The heroines do not grow up from childhood, they grow down—into situations of diminished mobility, opportunity, and freedom. Trapped in the claustrophobic spaces of matrimony, Constance dreams of her childhood home in Molde. She wants to be a child again, to live in a pre-sexual world that does not present the intolerable conflicts of the present. For Constance, the present is always the smallest circle. The expansive spaces of the past, the expansive spaces of her books are always her refuge.

Dreaming about the past is one way to escape mortification and disillusionment, reading is another. Above the circle of the present is a more expansive space, one that offers Constance escape into the plots and characters of her favorite books. Books are metaphoric windows, opening into other worlds of value, other possibilities for action. Like the heroine of Charlotte Lennox's *The Female Quixote* (1752), Constance reads to negate present boredom and the painful knowledge of her lack of freedom. In the course of the novel she reads works by Kielland, Daudet, Jacobsen, Gyllembourg, and—most importantly—Flaubert. Constance reads *Madame Bovary* and identifies her despair and disgust with Emma's. She sees her resemblance to Emma and denies it. Constance is a romancer—she wants life to be a place of true love, faithfulness, and justice. She does not want to be an immoral woman. But like Emma, Constance experiences the attractions and perils of quixotic escape.

As a heroine's texts suggest new possibilities for female behavior, they are empowering. In so far as they become coercive, they twist, restrict, and destroy. *Madame Bovary*, itself a quixotic text, becomes finally the book that guides Constance to destruction. Constance's involvement with *Madame Bovary* becomes the final sign of her acquiescence in patriarchal texts. Throughout her life she has turned toward men, sought their validation. At the end of her life she continues to let men define her. She leaves her beloved windows, apertures to expanded prospects, and retreats to a locked room in her husbands' home. Surrounded by the symbols of matrimony she picks up a family photograph, a frozen image of her childhood self. She remembers that her father once called her "an egotist." Constance's tragedy is that she accepts this judgment. She looks in the mirror and sees not the young girl who was optimistic, free to choose, longing for a fully human life, but instead an egotist, an adulterous woman. She sees Madame Bovary. Having first accepted her father's patriarchal text, she now accepts Flaubert's. Like Emma Bovary, she swallows poison.

It is ironic that a character who has lived so much in her imagination, dies finally of a lack of imagination. Beaten down by the repetition of cycles of confidence, betrayal, and alienation, she is unable to imagine any other life for herself. If men will always fail her, how can she go on? In this, Constance's marginality can be seen. She sees clearly the victimization of women by men in her society, sees the problems with marriage and religion, criticizes other women for their collusion. But like other suicidal heroines in nineteenth-century fiction (Anna Karenina, Effi Briest, and Edna Pontellier) her will is not as strong as her intellect. Fatally conflicted, she can see the problems of the old ways, but she cannot imagine new conventions to replace them. Constance's tragedy is that she gives up the "battle for her human dignity." She yields up her feminist principles and lets men define her.

Constance's suicide, taken with her feminist pronouncements, troubled initial reviewers of the novel, who looked for a single message and could not find one. Amalie Skram, like her heroine, sends contradictory messages. Skram's polemical aim is sometimes at odds with her sympathetic portrayal of a soul in torment. Constance is both victim and destroyer of men, rival and sister to other women, radical and conservative in her principles. Yet there is a unifying, liberating anger in *Constance Ring*. Though Constance in her time and place cannot keep from turning the anger inward, her creator finds a less destructive vent. In *Constance Ring*, anger is not hidden or displaced as it is in so many nineteenth-century novels about women and marriage; there is no madwoman in the attic. In the openness of her anger and the transparency of her protest, Amalie Skram is an important voice in the literature of women's empowerment.

Judith Messick
University of California,
Santa Barbara
1988

Works Cited

Amadou, Anne-Lisa. "Madame Bovary i *Constance Ring*." In *Fransk i Norge*. Oslo: Aschehoug, 1975.

Brombert, Victor. *The Novels of Flaubert: A Study of Themes and Techniques*. Princeton: Princeton University Press, 1966.

Engelstad, Irene. *sammenbrudd og gjennombrudd: Amalie Skram romaner om ekteskap og sinnssykdom*. Oslo: Pax Forlag, 1984.

Gilbert, Sandra and Susan Gubar. *The Madwoman in the Attic: The Woman Writer and the Nineteenth-Century Literary Imagination*. New Haven: Yale University Press, 1979.

Lewin, Kurt. *A Dynamic Theory of Personality*. New York: McGraw Hill, 1935.

Pratt, Annis. *Archetypal Patterns in Women's Fiction*. Bloomington: Indiana University Press, 1981.

Tanner, Tony. *Adultery in the Novel: Contract and Transgression*. Baltimore: The Johns Hopkins Press, 1979.

About the Translators

Judith Messick, Ph.D., teaches in the writing program at the University of California at Santa Barbara.

Katherine Hanson, Ph.D., is the editor of *An Everyday Story: Norwegian Women's Fiction,* and translated many of that anthology's stories.

International Women's Writing

WOMEN IN TRANSLATION
Explore the World of
International Women's Writing